Vulnerability, the Accused, and the Criminal Justice System

This book is concerned with the vulnerability of suspects and defendants in criminal proceedings and the extent to which the vulnerable accused can effectively participate in the criminal process. Commencing with an exploration of how vulnerability is defined and identified, the collection examines and analyses how vulnerability manifests and is addressed at the police station and in court, addressing both child and adult accused persons. Leading and emerging scholars, along with practitioners with experience working in the field, explore and unpack the human rights and procedural implications of suspect and defendant vulnerability and examine how their needs are supported or disregarded. Drawing upon different disciplinary approaches and a range of analyses – doctrinal, theoretical, and empirical – this book offers unique insights into the vulnerability and treatment of the criminal accused. In bringing together a diverse range of perspectives, the book offers key insights into the recognition of and responses to vulnerability among suspect and defendant populations in criminal justice systems across European jurisdictions. The book will be a valuable resource for academics, practitioners, and policymakers interested in how vulnerable suspects and defendants are protected throughout the criminal process, and those working in the areas of law, criminology, sociology, human rights, and psychology.

Roxanna Dehaghani is Senior Lecturer in Law, Cardiff School of Law and Politics, Cardiff University, UK.

Samantha Fairclough is Associate Professor in Law, Birmingham Law School, University of Birmingham, UK.

Lore Mergaerts is a Postdoctoral Researcher, Leuven Institute of Criminology, KU Leuven, Belgium and a Lecturer in Forensic and Legal Psychology, Erasmus School of Social and Behavioural Sciences, Erasmus University Rotterdam, the Netherlands.

Routledge Contemporary Issues in Criminal Justice and Procedure

Series Editor **Ed Johnston** is an Associate Professor of Criminal Justice and Procedure at the University of Northampton, UK.

Compensation for Wrongful Convictions
A Comparative Perspective
Edited by Wojciech Jasiński and Karolina Kremens

Efficiency and Bureaucratisation of Criminal Justice
Global Trends
Edited by Ed Johnston and Anna Pivaty

Murder, Wrongful Conviction and the Law
An International Comparative Analysis
Edited by Jon Robins

A History of Victims of Crime
How they Reclaimed their Rights
Stephen J. Strauss-Walsh

Vulnerability, the Accused, and the Criminal Justice System
Multi-jurisdictional Perspectives
Edited by Roxanna Dehaghani, Samantha Fairclough, and Lore Mergaerts

Covid-19 and Criminal Justice
Impact and Legacy in England and Wales
Edited by Ed Johnston

Witness Protection and Criminal Justice in Africa
Nigeria in International Perspective
Suzzie Onyeka Oyakhire

Autism and Criminal Justice
The Experience of Suspects, Defendants and Offenders in England and Wales
Edited by Tom Smith

Robotics, AI and Criminal Law
Crimes against Robots
Kamil Mamak

See more at https://www.routledge.com/Routledge-Research-in-Legal-History/book-series/CONTEMPCJP

Vulnerability, the Accused, and the Criminal Justice System

Multi-jurisdictional Perspectives

Edited by
**Roxanna Dehaghani, Samantha Fairclough,
and Lore Mergaerts**

Routledge
Taylor & Francis Group

LONDON AND NEW YORK

First published 2023
by Routledge
4 Park Square, Milton Park, Abingdon, Oxon OX14 4RN

and by Routledge
605 Third Avenue, New York, NY 10158

Routledge is an imprint of the Taylor & Francis Group, an informa business

British Library Cataloguing-in-Publication Data
A catalogue record for this book is available from the British Library

ISBN: 978-1-032-07056-8 (hbk)
ISBN: 978-1-032-07061-2 (pbk)
ISBN: 978-1-003-20516-6 (ebk)

DOI: 10.4324/9781003205166

Typeset in Galliard
by Taylor & Francis Books

Contents

Tables

Contributors

Stefan Aelbrecht, Content Staff Member, Kenniscentrum Kinderrechten vzw (KeKi) – Children's Rights Knowledge Centre

Stefan Aelbrecht joined KeKi in 2021 and is using his previous work experience (EU delegation to Soedan; Plan International Belgium) to help build the link between research, policy and practice. Stefan is also a volunteer researcher in the Interpreting Studies Research Group of KU Leuven. He previously worked there as a scientific collaborator for the Children in Legal Language Settings Project, a participatory research project with minors on interpreter-mediated encounters in criminal and asylum procedures.

Katalin Balogh, Lecturer, KU Leuven

Katalin Balogh is the coordinator of legal interpreting and translation (LIT) training at the Faculty of Arts, KU Leuven, Antwerp Campus. She is also a practising legal interpreter.

Miranda Bevan, Lecturer in Law, Goldsmiths, University of London

Miranda Bevan's research focuses on the experiences of children and young people when detained as suspects in police custody and, more widely, on the effective participation of children and vulnerable adults in criminal justice processes, both pre- and post-charge.

Alan Cusack, Senior Lecturer in Law, University of Limerick

Alan Cusack's research interests lie at the interface of criminal procedure and vulnerability, with a particular emphasis on the position of persons with intellectual disabilities. Alan's research has been widely published in national and international journals; and he has acted as an expert adviser to the Minister for Justice, the Garda Commissioner and the European Commission. In 2022 Alan was awarded a major national contract to deliver Ireland's first training scheme for registered intermediaries.

Roxanna Dehaghani, Senior Lecturer in Law, Cardiff University

Roxanna Dehaghani conducts research on the vulnerable accused, including vulnerable suspects, the appropriate adult safeguard and criminal defence, working closely with policy and practice. She has published widely across these areas, and her research has had a significant social and legal impact. She is currently an editorial board member of the *Howard Journal of Crime and Justice* and the *Journal of Adult Protection*, and co-investigator on a project examining the regulation of criminal justice detention.

Colum Dunne, Foundation Professor and Director of Research, School of Medicine, University of Limerick

Colum Dunne BSc (Hons), PhD, MBA, LLM, FRCPath is an inventor on multiple patents and has published extensively (250+ peer-reviewed articles, many of which focus on medico-legal aspects of vulnerable populations). Colum began his third-level education at University College Cork. Subsequent to postdoctoral positions, he joined multinational Glanbia Plc and served for five years as a director and member of the boards of the Glanbia Nutritionals group of companies. He is Foundation Professor and Director of Research at the University of Limerick School of Medicine. Colum served for two terms on the university's governing authority (university board).

Samantha Fairclough, Associate Professor in Law, University of Birmingham

Samantha Fairclough predominantly researches in the areas of vulnerability and criminal trials in England and Wales, with a particular focus on the treatment of vulnerable defendants. Her main interest is on the adaptations that are available for vulnerable defendants to give evidence in their defence at trial and their sufficiency. She has published widely on this issue, exploring it from various theoretical perspectives, as well as through empirical insights obtained from interviews with criminal practitioners.

Louise Forde, Lecturer in Law, Brunel University London

Louise Forde is a researcher in the area of international children's rights law and youth justice. She has published journal articles and book chapters on range of issues relating to the realisation of children's rights in youth justice systems, and has worked with advocacy groups and government stakeholders to promote the realisation of the rights of children in conflict with the law. She is a member of the editorial board of *Youth Justice: An International Journal*.

Holly Greenwood, Lecturer in Law, Cardiff University

Holly Greenwood helps to facilitate the Cardiff Law School Innocence Project and has linked research interests around miscarriages of justice in England and Wales, with a particular focus on the criminal appeal system and innocence projects.

Gautam Gulati, Adjunct Professor and Consultant Forensic Psychiatrist, University of Limerick

Gautam Gulati, a Consultant Forensic Psychiatrist, trained at Oxford and holds an Adjunct Professorial appointment at the University of Limerick. He holds fellowships with the Royal College of Physicians of Ireland, the Royal College of Psychiatrists (UK) and the Higher Education Academy (UK). His research interests lie at the interface of medicine and law. He has published extensively in international and national peer-reviewed journals. He has served a full term as Chair of the Faculty of Forensic Psychiatry at the College of Psychiatrists and has since founded the United Nations Convention on the Rights of Persons with Disabilities Sub-committee at the College.

Rebecca Helm, Associate Professor in Law, University of Exeter

Rebecca Helm is the Founder and Director of the Evidence-Based Justice Lab at the University of Exeter. She is a current UK Research and Innovation Future Leaders Fellow and is an expert in the field of psychology and law, using quantitative methodology to examine the legal system. Her research examines how legal procedures work in practice and how changing aspects of procedure can enhance the ability of the justice system to achieve normative goals.

Shane Kilcommins, Professor of Law, University of Limerick

Shane Kilcommins' areas of expertise are criminal law, evidence law, criminal procedure, penology and legal philosophy. He has published widely in these areas. He is a Fulbright scholar and has lent his expertise to the European Committee for the Prevention of and Inhuman or Degrading Treatment of Punishment, the Inspector of Prisons, the committee for the Victims Charter, Transparency International Ireland, *An Garda Síochána*'s Expert Review Group on Recruit Education and Entry Pathways and Learning and Development and more.

Ursula Kilkelly, Professor of Law, School of Law, University College Cork

Ursula Kilkelly researches international children's rights, examining ways in which these rights can be effectively enforced and implemented in law, policy and practice. Ursula has a particular interest in youth justice and detention and is co-editor in chief of *Youth Justice*.

Jantien Leenknecht, Independent Researcher, Research Foundation Flanders, KU Leuven, Institute for Social Law and Leuven Institute of Criminology

Jantien Leenknecht conducts research on different national youth justice systems and their relationship with EU criminal (procedural) law. She mainly focuses on age limits, the specialisation of youth justice actors and youth justice reactions in the jurisdictions of Austria, Belgium, the Netherlands and Northern Ireland.

Donna McNamara, Lecturer in Law, University of Newcastle, Australia

Donna McNamara specialises in human rights, disability law and criminal law. She has published widely in interdisciplinary journals and is the Co-chair of the Australian Disability Works-in-Progress series. Donna's work examines the rights of suspects with disabilities in contact with the pretrial criminal justice system.

Lore Mergaerts, Postdoctoral Researcher, Leuven Institute of Criminology, KU Leuven and Lecturer in Forensic and Legal Psychology, Erasmus University Rotterdam

Lore Mergaerts predominantly conducts research and publishes on suspect vulnerability in criminal proceedings and police questioning from a domestic Belgian and European perspective. Her main interests are the conceptualisation and identification of vulnerability, police questioning practices, and the implementation of procedural safeguards throughout criminal proceedings, also focusing on the interplay between law and psychology. Her research builds on theoretical analyses as well as comparative and empirical insights.

Joanne Morrison, PhD Student and Registered Intermediary, Tizard Centre, University of Kent

Joanne Morrison has a social work background and is currently a registered intermediary in Northern Ireland with vulnerable witnesses, complainants, suspects and defendants. Her PhD research focuses on communication challenges for adults with intellectual disabilities when giving evidence in court. Joanne is also a lay magistrate in family and youth courts and a part-time lecturer in intellectual disability for medical students at St George's University, London.

Daniel Newman, Reader in Law, Cardiff University

Daniel Newman conducts research on access to justice. His work looks at both criminal justice and social welfare law. He has a strong interest in the lawyer-client relationship. His work focuses on the impact of policy on justice – for example, exploring the effect of legal aid cuts.

Heidi Salaets, Associate Professor, KU Leuven

Heidi Salaets is the Head of the Interpreting Studies Research Group at the Faculty of Arts, KU Leuven, Antwerp Campus. Her current fields of research focus on LIT and specific expertise in LIT domains concerning language barriers, minors and other vulnerable groups, interception or 'wiretap' interpreting, human rights in prisons, languages of lesser diffusion, healthcare interpreting and community interpreting. Heidi mostly conducts transdisciplinary participatory action research.

John Taggart, Lecturer in Law, Queens University Belfast

John Taggart is a criminal barrister and has practised in both Northern Ireland and England and Wales. His research is sociolegal in nature and focuses on special measures within the criminal justice system and the treatment of vulnerable individuals. During the course of his PhD research examining the role of the intermediary special measure, John worked closely with the Ministry of Justice in England and Wales and the Department of Justice in Northern Ireland. He is currently conducting research on similar communication assistance provision in other jurisdictions.

Kim Turner, Senior Lecturer in Speech and Language Therapy, Manchester Metropolitan University

Kim Turner is a speech and language therapist and researcher. Her work focuses on identifying systems and processes in the criminal justice system which would benefit from adaptation to support equitable access for individuals with speech, language and communication needs.

Kasia Uzieblo, Associate Professor at Vrije Universiteit Brussels (VUB) and Senior Researcher at the Research Department of the Forensic Care Specialists, Utrecht

In her research, Kasia Uzieblo focuses on domestic and sexual violence, as well as on the usefulness of forensic psychological assessment tools and risk assessment. Kasia teaches forensic and criminological psychology at the VUB and is a trainer in risk assessment. She is the Founder and Coordinator of the Forensic Psychology Division of the Flemish Association of Clinical Psychologists. She also carries out psychological and risk assessments in forensic psychiatric and legal contexts.

Miet Vanderhallen, Associate Professor/Assistant Professor, Antwerp University and Maastricht University

Miet Vanderhallen conducts research on investigative interviewing, with an emphasis on interview models, young suspect interviews, legal assistance during police interviews and the evidential value of suspect statements. She is (co-) author of various (international) publications on these topics and is invited as a speaker on conferences. Miet has provided interview training at police academies and delivered training for lawyers on legal assistance at police stations. She also acts as an adviser and expert witness.

Claire Westwood, Lecturer in Speech and Language Therapy, Birmingham City University

Claire Westwood has set up speech and language therapy services in youth justice, violence reduction and adolescent mental health teams. She has presented this work within the United Kingdom and internationally. Claire has a particular interest in how supporting communication difficulties can effectively block the school-to-prison pipeline, as well as the intersection between sociolinguistics, disability studies and clinical language interventions.

Foreword

I congratulate the authors and the editors on this book, which highlights good practice, promotes cross-jurisdictional learning and draws much-needed attention to innovative developments. The fair treatment of suspects and defendants relies on the work of skilled professionals being supported by policies, procedures and resources which ameliorate the difficulties faced by vulnerable people. This book also highlights major obstacles that lie in the way of effective police investigations and fair trials.

Miscarriages of Justice

In Chapter 10, Fairclough and Greenwood issue this stark warning:

> Due to the inability of the criminal justice system to adequately support and mitigate against defendant vulnerability, miscarriages of justice are likely a routine occurrence. Furthermore, where a miscarriage of justice has occurred, it can be extremely difficulty to correct this in the criminal appeal process.

When there is a miscarriage of justice caused by lack of adjustments for the vulnerable suspect or defendant, the damage to individuals can be severe and permanent. The wrongly convicted person and their supporters can suffer emotionally, physically and financially. In addition, the reputation of the criminal justice system is dented and a guilty person evades justice. The reader of this book is privy to what research tells us about underlying problems that lead to such miscarriages of justice:

- The criminal justice system must make the necessary adjustments to support a vulnerable person to participate effectively. Yet there is no agreed definition of what it means to 'participate effectively' or what it means to be 'vulnerable'.
- A witness, suspect or defendant could be vulnerable and in need of special treatment to render the investigation and trial process fair. Yet a witness is more likely to have access to a framework of protections than a suspect or defendant. There is no reasonable justification for this difference in treatment.

- There are many reasons why a suspect or defendant might be vulnerable in the police investigation or trial process. They might be a child (under 18 years old) or an adult who does not have the capacity to participate effectively in the legal process. The instances of factors that lead to suspects and defendants being incapacitated – for example, due to speech, language and communication needs – are known to be high (Chapter 9). Yet there is no standard screening tool for the police and the courts to use to identify such vulnerability and the adjustments that ought to be made to support effective participation.
- Adequate funding for legal advice and representation is key; in this respect, the English criminal justice system was once seen as a benchmark to which other jurisdictions aspired. Yet the system is now viewed as 'broken' (Chapter 12), thanks in part to publicly funded representation being in severe decline.

The authors add to a substantial body of existing knowledge, but 'switched-on' policymakers, police and legal practitioners are unlikely to be surprised by the book's content. Problems have been brewing for years.

Spotlight on Criminal Justice in England and Wales

Anyone who works in the criminal justice system in England and Wales will be aware that the system is in desperate need of repair. By way of example, so dire is the situation that at the time of writing, further industrial action by the Criminal Bar of England and Wales is imminent; their 'all-out' strike is in protest at a system in crisis. But a vulnerable suspect and defendant lottery existed long before this crisis and is illustrated by two cases that I was involved in a few years ago. In each case the defendant went on trial at the Central Criminal Court ('the Old Bailey'). In each case the defendant had an autism spectrum condition. Only one defendant was diagnosed before their trial.

In the first case, not long after the defendant had been arrested and taken into custody for questioning about alleged terrorist activities, he was seen by a forensic medical examiner (FME). The FME noticed that he might have an autism spectrum condition and he was referred for specialist assessment. She was right. The transcripts of the police interviews and other evidence from his social media were among the evidence available to the jury; crucially, his communications could be read in the context of expert psychiatric and psychological evidence about the defendant's condition and how it affected his understanding and how he expressed himself. The defendant gave evidence in his defence from the witness box supported by a communication specialist (an intermediary) – a special adjustment directed by the trial judge. As I saw it, the defendant's solicitor and barrister were able to represent the defendant in a way that fully reflected his vulnerability. He was acquitted.

In the second case, the full extent of the other defendant's vulnerability, including his communication abilities and needs, was not apparent when he stood trial for murder. The prosecution relied on (among other things) what it saw as the accused's dishonest responses in interviews. The jury was aware that the defendant had an obsessive-compulsive disorder, but it was only after the trial that the defendant was diagnosed with an autism spectrum disorder; naturally, no psychiatric or psychological evidence had been available to the jury about this. He was convicted. Had his autism spectrum condition been known at trial, expert evidence might have assisted the jury and the defendant would probably have qualified for adjustments, including an intermediary. However, this is not enough to merit the case returning to the Court of Appeal, let alone to overturn his conviction.

Legal Reform

The brief discussion of the *Confait* case in Chapter 5 is a useful reminder that some miscarriages of the high-profile, politically embarrassing variety are catalysts for reviews of the law and legal reforms. The late Sir Louis Blom-Cooper QC, a barrister and a kind friend and mentor to me, represented the three boys (aged 14, 15 and 18) accused of murdering Maxwell Confait. Each defendant was vulnerable by virtue of age or limited mental capacity. Their convictions in 1972 (three for arson, one for manslaughter and two for murder) were quashed in 1975.

Some of Sir Louis' more recent reflections on the *Confait* case can be found in his 2015 book *Power of Persuasion – Essays by a Very Public Lawyer*. Sir Louis details how an inquiry was ordered into the circumstances leading to the wrongful convictions; the inquiry report of December 1977 'led up to the Royal Commission on Criminal Justice (the Phillips Commission) and the historic reform in the Police and Criminal Evidence Act 1984'. As we now know, the 'PACE' codes for police practice have achieved much to balance police powers and the rights of detainees and suspects. PACE undoubtedly changed the landscape for suspects for the better in England and Wales.

Yet, more than 40 years after the inquiry in *Power of Persuasion*, Sir Louis wrote this:

> The ultimate discovery of the true perpetrators of the unlawful killing of Confait, and the significant reforms of the criminal process in the legislation of 1984, should have restored public confidence in criminal justice. Alas, subsequent miscarriages of justice have not disappeared from the criminal courtrooms. Why is this? The inherent feature (I regard it as a weakness) of the Anglo-Saxon adversarial system of criminal justice is the absence of judicial control, or at least independent overseership, of the investigation of criminal events by police officers. Unlike other legal systems (which may have their own faults or deficits) the analysis of evidential material in the English system is not undertaken until the trial, often many months after the criminal events, which can lead to evidence being delayed or untested … it is incumbent upon reformers to conclude that the quality of our criminal justice might benefit from refurbishing in the context of criminality in Europe in the twenty first century.

Sir Louis was right about a key issue: the lack of 'independent overseership at police investigation'. Overseership is necessary because of the prevalence of vulnerability and the challenges of identifying vulnerability in the hurly-burly of the police station (research of Professor Gisli Gudjohnsen CBE was pioneering in this regard). In addition, some suspects will resist disclosing their vulnerability:

> The role of the police in ascertaining whether an individual has vulnerabilities and, separately, in obtaining evidence in relation to the charge could lead to individuals resisting the disclosure of such issues. It may be perceived by an individual that any issues that are voluntarily disclosed during an assessment into vulnerability could be used against them during any subsequent criminal proceedings.[1]

Reviewing and Reforming the System

The Law Society of Scotland's recent report also said this:

> Anyone who interacts with the criminal justice system may be vulnerable at any given time. Support for vulnerability is required consistently from the criminal justice system in order to achieve the interests of justice. Support requires to be tailored to the individual's requirements rather than the application of a one-size fits all approach.[2]

However, tailoring support to the needs of individuals is incompatible with criminal justice in crisis. Will it take a *Confait*-like miscarriage of justice to persuade politicians and policymakers to carry out a fundamental review of the criminal justice system in England and Wales? When that review does occur, this book will be part of the knowledge base for reform.

Professor Penny Cooper

1 Report – Vulnerable Accused Person, Law Society of Scotland, 2019.
2 Report – Vulnerable Accused Person, Law Society of Scotland, 2019.

Introduction

The Vulnerable Accused in the Criminal Justice System

Samantha Fairclough, Lore Mergaerts, and Roxanna Dehaghani

The last three decades have seen palpable concerns arise for the treatment of victims and witnesses in criminal justice systems around the world. Governments have steadily increased the provision of support and information to victims and witnesses involved in the criminal process in the wake of public and political concern, countless policy documents and legislative reforms. The European Court of Human Rights (ECtHR) has ruled that victims and witnesses have fair trial rights under Article 6 of the European Convention of Human Rights (ECHR),[1] providing strength to national campaigns for improved victims' rights. The Victims' Rights Directive has set minimum standards for European Union (EU) member states on the rights of victims and support owed to them in securing access to justice.[2] More recently, the new EU Strategy on Victims' Rights (2020–2025)[3] has been published, aiming to improve the support for and protection of victims and their rights even further. Combined, these initiatives have fundamentally changed the way in which such individuals experience criminal processes, addressing their treatment in police interviews; their pre-, during and post-trial care; and, importantly, their treatment throughout the process of giving evidence in trials where it is required. To use England and Wales as an example, this has been accompanied by several third-party agencies such as victim support, witness support and witness care units, which share the load of caring for these individuals. All of this support is intensified when a victim or witness is considered 'vulnerable' – in other words, when they are a child, or an individual with a mental health condition, a learning disability or disorder, or another form of social or cognitive impairment.

This is all, of course, commendable progress.[4] However, it is only much more recently that we have seen widespread recognition of the vulnerability of the

---

1 *Doorson v Netherlands* (1996) 22 EHRR 330.
2 Directive 2012/29/EU of the European Parliament and of the Council of 25 October 2012 establishing minimum standards on the rights, support and protection of victims of crime (replacing Council Framework Decision 2001/220/JHA).
3 Communication from the Commission to the European Parliament, the Council, the European Economic and Social Committee and the Committee of the Regions. EU Strategy on Victim's Rights (2020–2025), COM (2020) 258, final.
4 Though we must remember that the treatment of victims and witnesses in the criminal process still falls some way short of perfect in practice despite these efforts; see

DOI: 10.4324/9781003205166-1

accused – as both a suspect and/or defendant – within the criminal justice system and the need for an appropriate response. Significant progress has been made here of late, at both the European and domestic levels, but it is clear that more still needs to be done. This book brings together a collection of contributions that explore the extent to which vulnerable suspects and defendants are protected – in both law and practice – within criminal proceedings. The authors come from a range of academic and practice-based backgrounds, and bring their wealth of experience and research insights into law and practice to examine this important topic in different European jurisdictions.

By way of introduction to this collection, this chapter provides a whistlestop tour of some of the key issues of vulnerability that frequently plague suspects and defendants in the criminal justice system. This is accompanied by a snapshot examination of the prevalence of some of these types of vulnerability among suspect and defendant populations, showing that it is not merely a fringe problem, but one that is much more pervasive. We then outline some of the reasons for why we should be concerned about vulnerability in this arena among these populations. In other words, we highlight some of the potential consequences of the vulnerability of suspects and defendants on the proceedings (both process and outcome) if their vulnerability is left unaddressed. And, importantly, we further consider how overlooking such vulnerabilities can affect the individuals themselves. Combined, these insights demonstrate the importance of reforms which seek to address and cater for such vulnerability in law and practice.

Following on from this, the chapter then introduces the EU and ECtHR approaches and responses to vulnerability, showing the significant strides that have been taken at these levels to improve the protection of vulnerable suspects and defendants. While we should see these positive steps in the broader context of the significant increase in measures promoting enhanced police and judicial cooperation across Europe, and particularly within the EU (and thus as a counterbalance to these increased powers),[5] the overall progress made to protect accused persons remains laudable. The final section of this introduction provides a chapter outline and shows how the argumentation and insights provided therein are often more broadly applicable to other EU member states and beyond.

Vulnerability among Suspect and Defendant Populations

There are several ways in which those accused of a criminal offence are vulnerable within the criminal justice system. The most obvious – and most widely recognised – is vulnerability arising from childhood, and thus by extension the vulnerability of child suspects and defendants in the criminal process. Other sources of vulnerability include ill health, mental health issues, intellectual disability, physical

Samantha Fairclough and Imogen Jones, *The Victim in Court* in Sandra Walklate (ed) *The Handbook of Victims and Victimology* (Routledge 2017).

5 Jacqueline S Hodgson, 'Safeguarding Suspects' Rights in Europe: A Comparative Perspective' (2011) 14 *New Criminal Law Review* 611.

disability, addiction, language competency, educational levels, socio-economic status, race, religion – and the list goes on. Brown's classification of vulnerability into 'innate' and 'situational' vulnerability is a useful way to consider these different aspects.[6] According to Brown, innate vulnerabilities include factors that are inherent within a person, such as age, physical or sensory impairments, and issues of mental health. Situational vulnerability, on the other hand, relates to the circumstances in which an individual finds themselves because of, for example, their characteristics and/or their own or someone else's actions. Both types of vulnerability are relevant when considering suspects and defendants and their journeys through the criminal justice system. This is particularly so given that their position – as an individual accused of a criminal offence and held to account by the state – makes for a situation in which they are inherently vulnerable. Not only this, but it is the interplay between individual and situational factors rendering a person vulnerable that is important, moving us beyond a static view of the individual themselves that otherwise misses the relevant contextual factors.[7]

Fineman encourages us to think about vulnerability in a yet more inclusive way. She maintains that vulnerability is 'inherent in the human condition' and so is 'universal' – in other words, we are all vulnerable.[8] Differences in our 'embodiment' and 'embeddedness' still render individual experiences of our shared vulnerability unique, since it is affected by differences in embodiment (eg, vertical differences that occur over the life course, such as childhood and old age;[9] and horizontal differences – such as race, ability and gender – which can lead to social (dis)advantage) and embeddedness in social, economic and institutional relationships. People then, are not 'more or less vulnerable', but instead are differently resilient depending on the resources available to them to help them avoid and/or recover from setbacks.[10] Finally, Fineman places the onus on the state to provide 'assets' to individuals to build their resilience. In the context of individuals accused of criminal offences and appearing as suspects/defendants in the criminal process, therefore, it is for the state to ensure that all individuals suspected or accused of a crime – who are inherently vulnerable[11] – are provided with the support and safeguards they need to navigate the system as their most resilient selves.

---

6 See Kate Brown, *Vulnerability and Young People: Care and Social Control in Policy and Practice* (Policy Press 2015).

7 See Roxanna Dehaghani, 'Interrogating Vulnerability: Reframing the Vulnerable Suspect in Police Custody' (2021) 30(2) *Social and Legal Studies* 251; Lore Mergaerts and Roxanna Dehaghani, 'Protecting Vulnerable Suspects in Police Investigations in Europe: Lessons Learned from England and Wales and Belgium' (2020) *New Journal of European Criminal Law* 313, 324.

8 Martha Fineman, 'The Vulnerable Subject: Anchoring Equality in the Human Condition' (2008) 20 *Yale Journal of Law and Feminism* np.

9 Martha Fineman, 'Vulnerability and Social Justice' (2019) 53 *Valparaiso University Law Review* 341, 357.

10 Mitch Travis 'The Vulnerability of Heterosexuality: Consent, Gender Deception and Embodiment' (2019) 28(3) *Social and Legal Studies* 303, 320.

11 See, Roxanna Dehaghani, 'Interrogating Vulnerability: Reframing the Vulnerable Suspect in Police Custody' (2021) 30(2) *Social and Legal Studies* 251.

Prevalence of Vulnerability

When considering these issues around the vulnerability of suspects and defendants, it is useful to remember that this is not a small-scale issue. Many individuals accused of a crime will need special accommodations and adaptations in order to adequately understand the process and participate meaningfully in the procedures that follow. That said, even if vulnerability were only experienced by a small minority, the importance of adequately catering for these individuals would remain. What follows is a brief overview of some of the available research on the prevalence of vulnerability among suspect and defendant populations. We know that vulnerability often goes unidentified in the process.[12] This is for several reasons, including a lack of training among the police and legal professionals on vulnerability and how it manifests; austerity and funding cuts that limit individuals' contact time (and its quality) with the relevant professionals; and the inclination of some individuals to hide their vulnerability.[13] It is likely, therefore, that vulnerability is even more prevalent than some of these studies might indicate. It is also true that the Covid-19 pandemic and current economic crisis have, for many, exacerbated existing vulnerabilities, meaning that updated research would likely find yet more individuals whom we would classify as 'vulnerable' who are accused of criminal offences.

As Bevan (in Chapter 7 of this collection) highlights, there is a significant prevalence of dispositional vulnerabilities among children in conflict with the law in England and Wales. These vulnerabilities include communication disorders, developmental disorders and learning disabilities, and childhood adversities (eg, familial violence, bereavement, school exclusion and being 'looked after'). There is also significant prevalence of speech, language and communication needs (SLCNs) among adults in contact with the criminal justice system internationally, particularly

---

12 Andrew Sanders and others, *Victims with Learning Disabilities* (University of Oxford: Oxford Centre for Criminological Research 1997); Jessica Jacobson, *No-one Knows: Police Responses to Suspects Learning Disabilities and Difficulties – A Review of Policy and Practice* (Prison Reform Trust 2008) 27–28; Lord Bradley, *The Bradley Report* (Department of Health 2009) 20; Jessica Jacobson and Jenny Talbot, *Vulnerable Defendants and the Criminal Courts: A Review of Provision for Adults and Children* (Prison Reform Trust 2009), pp 5–6, 13–14; Ali Wigzell, Amy Kirby and Jessica Jacobson, *The Youth Proceedings Advocacy Review: Final Report* (Institute for Criminal Policy Research 2015) 46; Samantha Fairclough, '"It doesn't happen ... and I've never thought it was necessary for it to happen": Barriers to Vulnerable Defendants Giving Evidence by Live Link in Crown Court Trials' (2017) 21(3) *International Journal of Evidence and Proof* 209, 213; Iain McKinnon and Don Grubin, 'Health Screening in Police Custody' (2010) *Journal of Forensic and Legal Medicine* 209; Roxanna Dehaghani, *Vulnerability in Police Custody: Police Decision-making and the Appropriate Adult Safeguard* (Routledge, 2019).
13 Jenny Talbot, *Fair Access to Justice? Support for Vulnerable Defendants in the Criminal Courts* (Prison Reform Trust 2012) 17; Ali Wigzell, Amy Kirby and Jessica Jacobson, *The Youth Proceedings Advocacy Review: Final Report* (Institute for Criminal Policy Research 2015) 34.

when compared with the general population, as Turner and Westwood highlight in Chapter 9 of this collection.

For suspects in police custody, as highlighted in *There to Help 3*,[14] there is limited research on the number of adults who are considered vulnerable under the vulnerability provisions in Code C to the Police and Criminal Evidence Act 1984 in England and Wales. What is known is how prevalent mental disorder and (some forms of) mental vulnerability are in police custody. For example, McKinnon and Grubin found that, in relation to adults in police custody, 39% had a mental disorder (with 3% having a learning disability);[15] and 25.6% had psychosis, major depression or an intellectual (learning) disability, or lacked capacity to consent to their research questionnaire.[16] Young et al found, in their sample of 200 individuals in police custody aged 16 to 79, that 76.6% had a conduct disorder, 25.3% had attention deficit hyperactivity disorder (ADHD) and 6.7% had learning disabilities.[17] Earlier research by Gudjonsson et al found that 35% of adult suspects interviewed by the police had problems that could interfere with their functioning or coping ability in the police interview setting.[18]

Where defendants are concerned, the available evidence suggests that vulnerability may also be disproportionately common among those accused, and convicted, of criminal offences. For example, a Children's Commissioner Report highlights that the prevalence of neurodisability in young people who offend is often significantly higher than it is among young people in the general population.[19] Furthermore, Brooker et al found that the percentage

---

14 Chris Bath and Roxanna Dehaghani, *There to Help 3: The Identification of Vulnerable Adult Suspects and Application of the Appropriate Adult Safeguard in Police Investigations in 2018/19* (National Appropriate Adult Network: 2020) 14.

15 Iain McKinnon and Don Grubin, 'Health Screening of People in Police Custody – Evaluation of Current Police Screening Procedures in London, UK' (2013) 23(3) *European Journal of Public Health*, 399.

16 Iain McKinnon and Don Grubin, 'Evidence-Based Risk Assessment Screening in Police Custody: The HELPPC Study in London, UK' (2014) 8(2) *Policing* 174.

17 David Scott, Sinead McGilloway and Michael Donnelly, 'The Mental Health Needs of People with a Learning Disability Detained in Police Custody' (2006) 46(2) *Medicine Science and the Law* 111.

18 Gisli H Gudjonsson, Isobel CH Clare, Susan Rutter and John Pearse, *Persons at Risk during Interviews in Police Custody: The Identification of Vulnerabilities. Royal Commission on Criminal Justice Research Study No.12.* (HMSO: 1993).

19 For example, 5% to 7% of the general population suffer from communication disorders versus 60% to 90% of the offending population; and 0.6% to 1.2% of the general population suffer from autism, compared to 12% of the offending population. See Nathan Hughes and others, *Nobody Made the Connection: The Prevalence of Neurodisability in Young People Who Offend* (Children's Commissioner Report 2012) 23. See also Nathan Hughes, 'Understanding the Influence of Neurodevelopmental Disorders on Offending: Utilizing Developmental Psychology in Biosocial Criminology' (2015) 28(1) *A Critical Journal of Crime, Law and Society* 39.

of the probation population in Lincolnshire with a current mental illness is 39%.[20] In addition, a survey conducted in 2012 found that 36% of surveyed prisoners had a disability and/or mental health problem.[21]

Jacobson et al observed that 'defendants ... struggle on those occasions when they give evidence' due to the 'obvious educational and intellectual disparity between prosecution counsel and the defendant'.[22] Louck's review of the literature surrounding defendant vulnerability highlighted that many suspects/defendants/offenders suffer from learning disabilities and/or difficulties, although there is no consensus as to the exact numbers.[23] This may, in part, be due to the fact that the issues facing defendants can be multiple and complex. For example, Jacobson and Talbot identified that many individuals appearing before the courts 'do not have a single or clearly delineated form of intellectual or psychological difficulty' and instead that 'mental illness and learning disability (or learning difficulty) may co-exist'.[24] Furthermore, Lord Bradley noted that some have a 'dual diagnosis' where mental health problems combine with drug and/or alcohol problems.[25] Often, child defendants are also 'doubly vulnerable'[26] due to a combination of their young age and other mental, intellectual and emotional problems from which they may suffer.[27]

20 Brooker et al also found that almost 50% had past/lifetime mental illnesses; see Charlie Brooker and others, *An Investigation into the Prevalence of Mental Health Disorder and Patterns of Health Service Access in a Probation Area* (Lincoln: Criminal Justice and Health Research Group 2011) 39–41.

21 Charles Cunliffe and others, *Estimating the Prevalence of Disability Amongst Prisoners: Results from the Surveying Prisoner Crime Reduction* (SPCR) Survey (Ministry of Justice 2012) 141. For a summary of findings see Kathryn Thomson, 'Disability Among Prisoners' (2012) 59(3) *Probation Journal* 282.

22 Jessica Jacobson, Gillian Hunter and Amy Kirby, *Structured Mayhem: Personal Experiences of the Crown Court* (Criminal Justice Alliance 2015) 19.

23 See Nancy Loucks, *No One Knows: Offenders with Learning Difficulties and Learning Disabilities – a Review of Prevalence and Associated Needs* (Prison Reform Trust 2007). See also Jenny Talbot, *Fair Access to Justice? Support for Vulnerable Defendants in the Criminal Courts* (Prison Reform Trust 2012).

24 Jessica Jacobson and Jenny Talbot, *Vulnerable Defendants and the Criminal Courts: A Review of Provision for Adults and Children* (Prison Reform Trust 2009) 7.

25 Lord Bradley, *The Bradley Report: Review of People with Mental Health Problems or Learning Disabilities in the Criminal Justice System* (Department of Health 2009) 21. According to Offender Health Network Research, 78% of the sample with a severe enduring mental illness had a dual diagnosis; see Jenny Shaw and others, *A National Evaluation of Prison Mental Health In-Reach Services* (Offender Health Network Research 2009) 120.

26 Jessica Jacobson and Jenny Talbot, *Vulnerable Defendants and the Criminal Courts: A Review of Provision for Adults and Children* (Prison Reform Trust 2009) 37.

27 See also Ali Wigzell, Amy Kirby and Jessica Jacobson, *The Youth Proceedings Advocacy Review: Final Report* (Institute for Criminal Policy Research 2015) 4–5 for a summary of research findings on the prevalence of mental health issues/learning disabilities in children in custody.

Potential Impacts of Vulnerability

There are several concerns in relation to the potential impacts of vulnerability on suspects and defendants in the criminal justice system. This can be thought of in terms of both the impact on the ability of the system to effectively investigate crime and convict guilty individuals, and the impact on the individual as a subject involved in the process.

An accused person's vulnerability especially has received attention in criminological psychological research on false confessions.[28] Based on the results of this research domain over the past decades, an accused's vulnerability appears to be associated with three categories of risk factors for falsely confessing: individual factors, situational factors and innocence.[29] First, the concept of the 'vulnerable suspect' is explicitly used in relation to individual factors rendering a suspect prone to falsely confessing during police interviews. Kassin and colleagues, for instance, state that a suspect can be vulnerable 'by virtue of his or her youth, naiveté, intellectual deficiency or acute emotional state'.[30]Gudjonsson specifically refers to this category as 'psychological vulnerabilities' and defines these psychological vulnerabilities in the context of a police interview as 'psychological characteristics or mental states which render a suspect prone, in certain circumstances, to providing information which is inaccurate, unreliable (or invalid) or misleading'.[31] These individual factors constitute a wide-ranging category, including minors, certain personality traits (eg, suggestibility and compliance) and mental disorders (eg, an intellectual disability, ADHD and schizophrenia).[32]

---

28 See also Lore Mergaerts, 'Challenges in Defining and Identifying a Suspect's Vulnerability in Criminal Proceedings: What's in a Name and Who's to Blame?' in Penny Cooper and Linda Hunting (eds), *Access to Justice for Vulnerable People* (Wildy, Simmonds & Hill Publishing, 2018); Lore Mergaerts, 'Defence Lawyers' Views on and Identification of Suspect Vulnerability in Criminal Proceedings' *International Journal of the Legal Profession* (2021) 1, 3.

29 Saul M Kassin, 'On the Psychology of Confessions. Does Innocence put Innocents at Risk?' *American Psychologist* 60 (2005) 215–228; Saul M. Kassin, 'False Confessions: Causes, Consequences, and Implications for Reform' *Policy Insights from the Behavioral and Brain Sciences* 1 (2014) 114–116; Saul M. Kassin and Gisli H Gudjonsson, 'The Psychology of Confessions. A Review of the Literature and Issues' *Psychological Science in the Public Interest* 5 (2004) 51–56; Saul M Kassin, Steven A Drizin, Thomas Grisso, Gisli H Gudjonsson, Richard A Leo and Allison D Redlich, 'Police-Induced Confessions: Risk Factors and Recommendations' *Law and Human Behavior* 34 (2010) 16–23.

30 Saul M Kassin, Steven A Drizin, Thomas Grisso, Gisli H Gudjonsson, Richard A Leo and Allison D Redlich, 'Police-Induced Confessions: Risk Factors and Recommendations' *Law and Human Behavior* 34 (2010) 29.

31 Gisli H Gudjonsson, *The Psychology of Interrogations and Confessions. A Handbook* (John Wiley & Sons 2003), 316. See also Gisli H Gudjonsson, *The Psychology of False Confessions. Forty Years of Science and Practice* (John Wiley & Sons 2018), 124–134.

32 For a review, see Saul M Kassin and Gisli H Gudjonsson, 'The Psychology of Confessions. A Review of the Literature and Issues' *Psychological Science in the Public Interest* 5 (2004) 51–53 and Saul M Kassin, Steven A Drizin, Thomas Grisso, Gisli H

Second, the results of this research domain show that certain situational factors, inherent to the pre-trial investigation, can also render a suspect prone to falsely confessing during a police interview. These factors refer to isolation from family and friends, sleep deprivation and fatigue, lengthy interviews and certain (coercive) interview techniques.[33]

Lastly, the innocence in itself of the suspect also appears to be a risk factor for false confessions. Assuming that they have nothing to hide, innocent suspects often are willing to cooperate with the police and to waive their rights to access to a lawyer and to remain silent.[34] Moreover, innocent suspects may falsely confess – with or without pressure exerted by the police – because of a (false) belief that innocent persons are not convicted and that their innocence eventually will become apparent to the judicial authorities.[35] As such, increasing attention for vulnerability also relates to the occurrence of miscarriages of justice worldwide and efforts to prevent them.

With regard to defendants, vulnerability that manifests in communication difficulty is particularly problematic where a defendant cannot follow the proceedings and effectively participate in the case. While defendants are not compellable as witnesses, they have a right to testify in their defence if they so wish – and indeed in some cases their defence would be damaged if they did not do so. Assisting such vulnerable individuals, therefore, to give evidence to the best of their ability is important and a failure to do so has several potential negative consequences. The first is that some vulnerable defendants will give evidence unaided, but will do so badly. This risks them making a bad impression on the jury (where the trial involves a jury) or a bad impression on the judge(s) (in judge-only trials), which may affect the decision as to the defendant's culpability.[36] The second danger is

Gudjonsson, Richard A. Leo and Allison D. Redlich, 'Police-Induced Confessions: Risk Factors and Recommendations' *Law and Human Behavior* 34 (2010) 19–22.

33 See, for instance, Mark Blagrove, 'Effects of Length of Sleep Deprivation on Interrogative Suggestibility' *Journal of Experimental Psychology: Applied* 2 (1996) 48–59; Richard P Conti, 'The Psychology of False Confessions' *Journal of Credibility Assessment and Witness Psychology* 2 (1999) 14–36; Steven A Drizin and Richard A Leo, 'The Problem of False Confessions in the Post-DNA World' *North Carolina Law Review* 82 (2004) 891–1007; Saul M Kassin, Steven A Drizin, Thomas Grisso, Gisli H Gudjonsson, Richard A Leo and Allison D Redlich, 'Police-Induced Confessions: Risk Factors and Recommendations' *Law and Human Behavior* 34 (2010) 16–19; Christian A Meissner, 'Accusatorial and Information-Gathering Interrogation Methods and their Effects on True and False Confessions: a Meta-Analytic Review' *Journal of Experimental Criminology* 10 (2014) 459–486.

34 Maria Hartwig, Pär Anders Granhag and Leif A Strömwall, 'Guilty and Innocent Suspects' Strategies during Police Interrogations' *Psychology, Crime & Law* 13 (2007) 219–220; Saul M Kassin and Rebecca J Norwick, 'Why People Waive their *Miranda* Rights: The Power of Innocence' *Law and Human Behavior* 28 (2004) 216.

35 Saul M Kassin, 'On the Psychology of Confessions. Does Innocence put Innocents at Risk?' *American Psychologist* 60 (2005) 224. See also this publication for a full analysis of how innocence may induce suspects to falsely confess.

36 Penny Cooper and Clare Allely, 'You Can't Judge a Book by Its Cover: Evolving Professional Responsibilities, Liabilities and 'Judgecraft' When a Party has Asperger's Syndrome' (2017) 68(1) *Northern Ireland Legal Quarterly* 35.

that some will not give evidence because they do not feel sufficiently capable to do so unassisted. As a result, jurors and judges may be at liberty to draw adverse inferences from their silence,[37] which can legitimately contribute to a finding of guilt.[38] The third danger is that, in order to avoid both of these unfavourable outcomes, some vulnerable defendants will plead guilty.[39] This is most obviously problematic if the defendant is factually innocent, since the lack of support to them will mean they are convicted and punished for a crime they did not commit. But a guilty plea produced from a lack of support to a defendant is problematic irrespective of their guilt. A defendant – vulnerable or not, guilty or not – should have a real opportunity to have the state prove their guilt beyond reasonable doubt.[40]

These dangers need to be taken into account regardless of the system in play; but they are particularly problematic in adversarial jurisdictions. In contrast, in predominant inquisitorial systems, the procedure before the courts is, in principle, oral, public and contradictory, and therefore somewhat adversarial; but it should be noted that the emphasis lies in the pre-trial phase, which is carried out under the responsibility of the competent magistrate. Trial proceedings traditionally rely heavily upon the case file and the investigation that has been conducted during the pre-trial stage. As such, the accused overall has a more passive role compared to their role in adversarial systems.

Aside from these practical reasons for addressing vulnerability – which revolve around instrumental concerns for avoiding false confessions, avoiding poor quality testimony, and so on – we should also consider the issues around vulnerability in relation to the humaneness of the system. Honourable Justice Green stated that 'how … [we] treat those who are exposed and weak is a barometer of our moral worth as a society'.[41] Going further than this, Fairclough argues that leaving vulnerability unaddressed in the criminal justice system infringes the principle of humane treatment where it causes a heightened amount of suffering and stress compared to that which is necessary and proportionate to the aims of justice: to convict the guilt and acquit the innocent.[42] Individuals accused of criminal offences should be treated as:

---

37 In England and Wales, on the curtailment of the right to silence, see Criminal Justice and Public Order Act 1994, Section 35(3) subject to the safeguards set out in *R v Cowan* [1996] QB 373, affirmed by the House of Lords in *R v Becouarn* [2005] UKHL 55.

38 *Murray v DPP* [1994] 1 WLR 1.

39 And, in England and Wales for example, secure a sentence discount in the process as per the Criminal Justice Act 2003, Section 144.

40 See also Samantha Fairclough, '"It doesn't happen … and I've never thought it was necessary for it to happen": Barriers to Vulnerable Defendants Giving Evidence by Live Link in Crown Court Trials' (2017) 21(3) *International Journal of Evidence and Proof* 209, 213.

41 Quoted in Jacqueline Wheatcroft, 'Witness Assistance and Familiarisation in England and Wales: The Right to Challenge' (2017) 21(1/2) *International Journal of Evidence and Proof* 158, 158.

42 Samantha Fairclough, 'The Lost Leg of the Youth Justice and Criminal Evidence Act (1999): Special Measures and Humane Treatment' (2021) 41(4) *Oxford Journal of Legal Studies* 1066.

Thinking, feeling, human subjects of official concern and respect, who are entitled to be given the opportunity to play an active part in procedures with a direct and possibly catastrophic impact on their welfare, rather than as objects of state control to be manipulated for the greater good ...[43]

Legal Response(s) to Vulnerability

Before we move on to the outline of what is to come in each chapter that follows, we first provide an overview of the legal responses to vulnerability at the EU and ECtHR levels.[44] This legal framework is drawn upon, expanded upon and critiqued extensively throughout the collection, so it is sufficient to just provide the headlines here.

The ECtHR in *Salduz v Turkey* – and in subsequent case law[45] – stressed that during the investigative stage:

an accused often finds himself in a particularly vulnerable position ..., the effect of which is amplified by the fact that legislation on criminal procedure tends to become increasingly complex, notably with respect to the rules governing the gathering and use of evidence.[46]

The ECtHR also considers a number of relevant factors that may render an adult suspect 'particularly vulnerable', such as chronic alcoholism and/or acute alcohol intoxication; a physical disability or medical condition; belonging to a socially disadvantaged group; and a mental disorder (eg, ADHD).[47] With specific regard to defendants, there is an ever-growing body of case law concerned with the ability of vulnerable defendants to participate effectively in criminal proceedings, as per

---

43 Samantha Fairclough, 'The Lost Leg of the Youth Justice and Criminal Evidence Act (1999): Special Measures and Humane Treatment' (2021) 41(4) *Oxford Journal of Legal Studies* 1066.

44 See also Lore Mergaerts, 'Challenges in Defining and Identifying a Suspect's Vulnerability in Criminal Proceedings: What's in a Name and Who's to Blame?' in Penny Cooper and Linda Hunting (eds), *Access to Justice for Vulnerable People* (Wildy, Simmonds & Hill Publishing, 2018); Lore Mergaerts, 'Defence Lawyers' Views on and Identification of Suspect Vulnerability in Criminal Proceedings' *International Journal of the Legal Profession* (2021) 1, 1–2; Lore Mergaerts and Roxanna Dehaghani, 'Protecting Vulnerable Suspects in Police Investigations in Europe: Lessons Learned from England and Wales and Belgium' (2020) *New Journal of European Criminal Law* 313, 314–316.

45 See, for instance, also *Panovits v Cyprus* App no 4268/04 (ECtHR, 11 December 2008); *Shabelnik v Ukraine* App no 16404/03 (ECtHR, 19 February 2009); *Pishchalnikov v Russia* App no 7025/04 (ECtHR 24 September 2009); *Dayanan v Turkey* App no 7377/03 (13 October 2010).

46 *Salduz v Turkey* App no 36391/02 (ECtHR 27 November 2008).

47 *Plonka v Poland* App no 20310/02 (ECtHR 31 March 2009); *Bortnik v Ukraine* App no. 39582/04 (ECtHR 27 January 2011); *Orsus and others v Croatia* App no 15766/03 (ECtHR 16 March 2010); *Blohkin v Russia* App no 47152/06 (ECtHR 23 March 2016); *Borotyuk v Ukraine* App no 33579/04 (ECtHR 16 December 2010).

Article 6(1) of the ECHR.[48] In this regard, the ECtHR has explicitly stressed that an effective participation requires that:

> The accused has a broad understanding of the nature of the trial process and of what is at stake for him or her, including the significance of any penalty which may be imposed. The defendant should be able, inter alia, to explain to his own lawyer his version of events, point out any statements with which he disagrees and make them aware of any facts which should be put forward in his defence.[49]

The vulnerability of a suspect or defendant may therefore be relevant to the right to a fair trial under Article 6 of the ECHR if there has been an alleged or actual failure to make adjustments for a suspect or defendant's vulnerability. In the recent case of *Hasálikova v Slovakia*,[50] the ECtHR considered whether the applicant (A) – who had been convicted of murder – was a vulnerable person and whether she therefore required reasonable adjustments to understand and participate meaningfully in the criminal process. Information regarding A's (potential) vulnerability was put to the court: she had attended a 'special school', was entitled to disability benefits, attended a psychiatrist, and had an 'obvious' physical disability and an evident intellectual disability. An expert psychiatric assessment explained that A displayed infantile and simplistic thinking, and was 'very naïve, emotionally mature, and easily influenced'.[51] The majority stated that A was not vulnerable because she was not suffering from mental illness or disorder, could recognise the dangerousness of her actions, and had foresight of the consequences of those actions. They also took into consideration that A was an adult, was literate, had been assisted by a lawyer and had not indicated that she experienced difficulty understanding or expressing herself until a year into the criminal process. It has been argued elsewhere that the majority's interpretation of vulnerability is narrow and therefore problematic.[52] In their dissenting judgment, Judges Turković and Schembri Orland found that there had been a violation of A's fair trial rights, pointing to A's intellectual disability and how the consequences thereof would have made her vulnerable. To support their contention, they drew upon existing research on wrongful convictions and false confessions (eg, that explored above), in addition to the special consideration for vulnerable suspects from the Council of Europe and EU (as discussed below).

---

48 Including *SC v United Kingdom* App no 60958/00 (ECtHR 10 November 2004); *T v United Kingdom* App no 24724/94 (ECtHR 16 December 1999).
49 *Liebreich v Germany* App 30443/03 (ECtHR 8 January 2008).
50 *Hasálikova v Slovakia* App no 39654/15 (ECtHR 22 November 2021).
51 *Hasálikova* at para 2.
52 Roxanna Dehaghani, 'Not Vulnerable Enough? A Missed Opportunity to Bolster the Vulnerable Accused's Position in *Hasálikova v Slovakia*' (Strasbourg Observers, 23 November 2021). Available at: https://strasbourgobservers.com/2021/11/23/not-vulnerable-enough-a-missed-opportunity-to-bolster-the-vulnerable-accuseds-position-in-hasalikova-v-slovakia/ (last accessed 4 August 2022).

At an EU level, the vulnerability of accused persons has also been acknowledged through a non-exhaustive list of eight potentially vulnerable categories of suspects (and defendants) put forward in a green paper from the European Commission, including:

> (1) foreign nationals, (2) children, (3) persons suffering from a mental or emotional handicap, in the broadest sense, (4) the physically handicapped or ill, (5) mothers/fathers of young children, (6) persons who cannot read or write, (7) refugees and asylum seekers, (8) alcoholics and drug addicts.[53]

After a failed attempt to establish a Council Framework Decision in 2004 on this matter,[54] the European Council adopted a Resolution on a roadmap for strengthening procedural rights of suspected or accused persons in criminal proceedings, with the fifth measure – Measure E – specifically dedicated to special safeguards for suspected or accused persons who are vulnerable.[55] This measure defines 'vulnerability' as a difficulty in understanding or following 'the content or the meaning of the proceedings, for example because of their age, mental or physical condition'.[56]

Following on from this Roadmap, several Directives have been adopted to strengthen specific safeguards for all suspects and defendants involved in criminal proceedings, but these also include a provision that the special needs of vulnerable persons must be considered by member states when implementing them.[57] Furthermore, because minors are generally considered to be vulnerable, the European Commission also adopted a Directive to specifically protect minors containing procedural safeguards for children suspected or accused in criminal proceedings.[58]

---

53 Green Paper from the Commission on procedural safeguards for suspects and defendants in criminal proceedings throughout the European Union [2003] COM (2003) final, def, pp 32–34.

54 European Commission Proposal for a Council Framework Decision on Certain Procedural Rights in Criminal Proceedings throughout the European Union, April 28, 2004, COM (2004) 328 final.

55 OJ 2009, C 295/1.

56 See Annex, Measure E, Resolution Roadmap for Strengthening Procedural Rights.

57 Directive 2010/64/EU of the European Parliament and of the Council on the Right to Interpretation and Translation in Criminal Proceedings [2010] OJ L 280/1, recital 27; Directive 2012/13/EU of the European Parliament and of the Council on the Right to Information in Criminal Proceedings [2012] OJ L 142/1, recital 26, Article 1, Article 3.2; Directive 2013/48/EU of the European Parliament and of the Council on the Right of Access to a Lawyer in Criminal Proceedings and in European Arrest Warrant Proceedings, and on the Tight to have a Third Party Informed upon Deprivation of Liberty and to Communicate with Third Persons and with Consular Authorities while Deprived of Liberty [2013] OJ L 294/1, recital 51; Directive (EU) 2016/343 of the European Parliament and of the Council on the Strengthening of Certain Aspects of the Presumption of Innocence and of the Right to be Present at the Trial in Criminal Proceedings [2016] OJ L 65/1, recital 42.

58 Directive (EU) 2016/800 of European Parliament and the Council on Procedural Safeguards for Children Who are Suspects or Accused Persons in Criminal Proceedings [2016] OJ L 132/1.

In addition, the Commission adopted a non-binding Recommendation[59] to encourage member states to strengthen the procedural rights of so-called 'vulnerable persons' in criminal proceedings.[60] This aims to strengthen the right to liberty, the right to a fair trial and the rights of defence by offering appropriate assistance and support[61] to 'all suspects or accused persons who are not able to understand and to effectively participate in criminal proceedings due to age, their mental or physical condition or disabilities'.[62] However, it should be noted that this definition is not commonly accepted among member states of the EU; this is precisely the reason why the Commission opted for a (non-binding) recommendation.[63] The Recommendation especially puts forward the prompt identification of vulnerable persons. To assist the police and judicial authorities, they should be able to request the medical examination by an independent expert to identify any vulnerability. In addition, they should receive specific training; but the Recommendation does not contain any further requirements in relation to this training. The Recommendation furthermore stresses the adequate treatment of vulnerable persons by proposing specific rights, such as the right to information; the right of access to a lawyer and the inability to waive this right; the presence of an appropriate adult or legal representative; the audio-visual recording of any questioning; and systematic access to medical assistance while being held in custody, which should only be used as a last resort. The scope of these measures and how these should be implemented are, however, not specified within the Recommendation and are open to different interpretations.

Chapter Outline

What we can see, then, is that vulnerability has received attention in both the legal and academic domains. Both perspectives show some convergence, but the two often exist next to each other. As a consequence, and as will soon become apparent, vulnerability is often interpreted somewhat differently depending on the perspective taken, leading to inconsistencies in the approach taken to support suspects and defendants within and across criminal justice systems.

Against this background, this edited collection brings together a range of perspectives from academics and practitioners to examine and analyse the extent to which vulnerable suspects and defendants are protected within EU, ECHR and domestic frameworks. As such, the book is principally concerned with the

---

59 Recommendation of the Commission on Procedural Safeguards for Vulnerable Persons Suspected or Accused in Criminal Proceedings [2013] OJ C 378/8.
60 Recital 1.
61 Recommendation of the Commission on Procedural Safeguards for Vulnerable Persons Suspected or Accused in Criminal Proceedings [2013] OJ C 378/8, recital 18.
62 Recommendation of the Commission on Procedural Safeguards for Vulnerable Persons Suspected or Accused in Criminal Proceedings [2013] OJ C 378/8, recital 1.
63 European Commission Proposal for a Directive of the European Parliament and of the Council on Procedural Safeguards for Children Suspected or Accused in Criminal Proceedings, 27 November 2013, COM (2013) 822 final, 3.

vulnerability of suspects and defendants in criminal proceedings and the extent to which the vulnerable accused can effectively participate in the criminal process. To that end, it examines how safeguards manifest in law and how they work – or do not work – in practice. It brings together a range of contributions from a selection of jurisdictions across Europe, exploring different aspects of the criminal process, to critically interrogate the safeguarding and protection of vulnerable suspects and defendants throughout the criminal process.

Leading and emerging scholars, along with practitioners with experience working in the field, explore and unpack the human rights and procedural implications of suspect and defendant vulnerability and examine how their needs are supported or disregarded. Drawing upon different disciplinary approaches and a range of doctrinal, theoretical and empirical analyses, the chapters included in this edited collection offer unique insights into the vulnerability and treatment of the criminal accused. Among chapters on the situation in Ireland, Austria, Belgium, Scotland and the Netherlands, quite some chapters elaborate on the jurisdiction of England and Wales. This should not be entirely surprising, given that this jurisdiction – in relation to its protection for accused persons, and vulnerable people in particular – has been lauded as leading the way; and indeed many other European jurisdictions – and the EU itself – have looked towards England and Wales when considering how to implement these protections.[64] Yet the findings from the different chapters are of interest to those across Europe, particularly within the EU, and beyond Europe as well, owing to the focus on vulnerable suspects and defendants and some notable similarities in the legal provisions available to these populations in other continental and Anglo-Saxon countries.

The book contains 12 substantive chapters and is split into three parts. Part 1 explores how the European framework on vulnerability is implemented in different jurisdictions, with a particular focus on the guidance provided regarding the definition, identification and measures put forward to deal with vulnerability and its implementation in domestic law and practice. It is argued that the transposition is not always sufficient or evident, due to not only legal but also practical barriers.

In Chapter 1, McNamara addresses the rights of people with disabilities as suspects of crime, with a particular focus on the role and transposition of international human rights law, focusing on the UN Convention on the Rights of Persons with Disabilities (CRPD). Using Ireland as a case study, she demonstrates several barriers preventing people with disabilities from equally exercising their rights in criminal proceedings. The analysis in particular concentrates on barriers to the implementation of the duty to provide reasonable accommodations, the right of accessibility and the duty to provide training for all agents. McNamara, however, argues that the CRPD provides for a robust normative framework to enhance the rights of access to justice for all persons with disabilities getting involved in the criminal justice system.

---

64 Lore Mergaerts and Roxanna Dehaghani, 'Protecting Vulnerable Suspects in Police Investigations in Europe: Lessons Learned from England and Wales and Belgium' (2020) *New Journal of European Criminal* Law 313, 319.

Chapter 2 explores the impact of EU procedural rights on juvenile suspects and defendants. Leenknecht assesses this impact by analysing the child-specific safeguards in EU legal instruments and their transposition in the jurisdictions of Austria, Belgium and the Netherlands. The content and transposition of the right to interpretation and translation, the right to information, the right of access to a lawyer, the right to legal aid and the right to be present at trial are examined from a domestic and comparative perspective. The analysis demonstrates deficits in the content of the procedural rights and their implementation in domestic law. As such, Leenknecht argues that the full potential of the child-specific safeguards has not entirely been achieved, which may negatively impact the protection of the juvenile suspect's or defendant's procedural rights.

The last two chapters of Part 1 are concerned with the definition and identification of suspect vulnerability in criminal proceedings. Drawing on a comparison between Belgium and the Netherlands, in Chapter 3 Mergaerts elaborates on how vulnerability is addressed in law and practice, focusing on the responsibilities and training provided. As such, the chapter illustrates important shortcomings in how vulnerability is addressed in law and the guidance provided for practitioners with regard to its identification. Mergaerts argues that further steps need to be taken in law and practice to improve the early identification of suspect vulnerability and to warrant the (adequate) implementation of special provisions to address their vulnerability when becoming involved in criminal proceedings.

Part 1 is rounded off by Chapter 4, in which Vanderhallen and Uzieblo examine the issue of vulnerability from an expert witness perspective. The chapter provides unique insight into how vulnerability may manifest itself during police questioning based on the examination of a remarkable Belgian case. The authors build their analysis from their experience as expert witnesses in this case. As such, their chapter includes an overview of academic research providing insight into both individual and situational factors rendering a suspect prone to falsely confessing to a crime; but it also presents important lessons on the identification of vulnerability and the potential impact of vulnerability on the veracity of statements provided by vulnerable suspects. The authors highlight the importance of raising awareness of suspect vulnerability and its implications.

In Part 2, this book then examines and analyses how vulnerability manifests and is addressed at the police station and in court, focusing on both child and adult accused persons. In this part, the vulnerability of suspects is examined in detail with contributions from Ireland (where safeguards are nascent), England and Wales (where safeguards have existed since the implementation of the Police and Criminal Evidence Act 1984), and Belgium, with a particular focus on foreign-language vulnerability and the role of the interpreter.

In Chapter 5, Cusack et al examine the right to a fair trial – specifically physical access to a lawyer – placing particular emphasis on the position of vulnerable suspects. Detailing the manner in which the right of access to a lawyer is restricted in Ireland and thereafter exploring the non-interventionist approach emanating from recent ECtHR jurisprudence, Cusack et al explore the extent to which vulnerable suspects – particularly those with intellectual disabilities – are able to realise their fair trial rights, and question whether Ireland's pre-trial machinery sufficiently responds to the vulnerability of intellectually disabled suspects. After exploring the specific safeguards available for vulnerable suspects in Ireland, Cusack et al highlight the shortcomings within the Irish system and question the extent to which Strasbourg may tolerate Ireland's approach to safeguards during pre-trial proceedings in future cases. In doing so, they offer a compelling argument for reimagining pre-trial safeguards in Ireland.

Continuing the theme of Irish pre-trial safeguards, in Chapter 6 Forde and Kilkelly explore the right to legal advice and assistance for young suspects in Ireland. Beginning with an exploration of this right within European and international instruments, Forde and Kilkelly turn to the question of how these rights are realised in practice, outlining why legal assistance is crucial in the context of young suspects and then exploring how this right is realised in Ireland. Drawing upon original empirical research with children, parents and guardians, lawyers and members of *An Garda Síochána* (Ireland's police service), the chapter then examines children's experiences of their right to access legal advice and assistance, and offers suggestions for future areas of exploration.

In Chapter 7, drawing from original empirical research, Bevan casts light on the often-hidden world of police custody, focusing specifically on the protections available for child suspects in England and Wales. As with the previous two chapters, Bevan outlines why this particular category of suspects are vulnerable in pre-trial proceedings. Importantly, while children are vulnerable because of their young age, Bevan also highlights how other issues – such as communication disorders, developmental disorders and learning disabilities, and experiences of childhood adversities – may compound the general vulnerability of child suspects and may thus further interfere with their ability to realise their fair trial rights. Highlighting the tensions between the law in books and the law in action (from the child's perspective), Bevan demonstrates how children's procedural rights are being interfered with, urging for necessary reform to ensure children are adequately protected in law and in practice.

The final chapter in Part 2 – Chapter 8 – explores foreign language vulnerability and the need for an interpreter, drawing on original empirical research undertaken in criminal and asylum proceedings. In this chapter, Salaets et al demonstrate how foreign language vulnerability interacts with other vulnerabilities, highlighting the compounding nature of vulnerability. They begin by outlining the role of the interpreter according to European frameworks, after which they explain the challenges posed by interpretation before exploring the specific problems with interpreting in practice. The authors conclude with recommendations for law and practice.

The final section of this collection focuses on the treatment of vulnerable defendants in criminal trials. This sequentially builds on the need to ensure that vulnerable suspects are adequately protected and assisted throughout the investigation stage, as was the topic of Part 2, so that the accused enters the trial stage having properly understood the process until that point and having been the subject of fair questioning. The contributions here consider some of the support available to defendants at this stage both in law and in practice. What is clear is that some positive steps have been taken across jurisdictions to help vulnerable defendants to overcome their vulnerabilities in some way, or at least to make adjustments to cater for those vulnerabilities in this particular context. However, significantly more work needs to be done in terms of both the legal provision of support and adaptations and their implementation in practice. Furthermore, where vulnerability is identified (which is not always the case), inadequately funded criminal justice systems present serious barriers to securing support for said vulnerable defendants on trial.

In Chapter 9, Turner et al explore the role of the speech, language and communication therapist in the criminal justice system. Building on academic research and specific case examples, the chapter demonstrates the clear speech, language, and communication needs (SLCNs) of certain suspects and defendants and their potential negative impact within and outside of criminal justice systems. Being overrepresented in the criminal justice system, the authors argue for the importance of fostering their effective participation within the criminal justice system, demonstrating the added value and role of speech, language and communication therapists. However, the implementation of this support requires the identification of such needs, which appears to be challenging in practice, hampering the effective participation of suspects and defendants encountering speech, language and communication difficulties. As such, the authors argue for an improved and systematic identification, as well as standardised support measures.

In Chapter 10, Fairclough and Greenwood explore the provision of additional assistance, in the form of special measures, to defendants who are children and/or have mental health or intellectual disabilities or disorders. This chapter again focuses on England and Wales, though the measures discussed are available in similar forms across many common law jurisdictions (including Scotland, Northern Ireland, Australia and New Zealand). They show how the provision of special measures – such as live links, screens and intermediaries – to vulnerable defendants is insufficient, and argue that this risks undermining their ability to effectively participate in the proceedings and marks a violation of the principle equality of arms. They further argue that when vulnerable defendants are inadequately assisted in this way, they are the subject of miscarriages of justice; but that such injustices are essentially insulated from challenge under the current legal construction of wrongful (or unsafe) conviction. The authors conclude that more generous and effective provision of special measures is needed for vulnerable defendants, as well as a revamp of the appeals process to recognise the various challenges that defendants face throughout the process.

In Chapter 11, Taggart and Morrison continue this theme of exploring special measures provision for vulnerable defendants, focusing on intermediary provision. Their chapter draws on two datasets which secure insights from registered intermediaries working in England and Wales and Northern Ireland on their role in enabling defendants to effectively participate in the proceedings. It shows how intermediaries assist communication at the pre-trial stage, as well as during the trial, both generally and specifically at the point at which the accused gives evidence (if they choose to do so). The authors clearly signal the importance of the intermediary in assisting the court to ensure that vulnerable defendants participate effectively in their trials, by facilitating communication between and within the parties and before the jury.

The issue around funding occupies Dehaghani et al (Chapter 12). They examine how continuous cuts to criminal legal aid in England and Wales risk undermining the defendant's access to justice. They emphasise the importance of access to free legal representation to help guide defendants accused of a criminal offence and properly advocate on their behalf. The authors draw on insights from semi-structured interviews with solicitors and barristers practising in England and Wales on two aspects of cuts to legal aid. The first is the effect of the cuts on defendants themselves. In this regard, lawyers interviewed are critical of the effects of the 'means test' – part of the test that decides on eligibility for legal aid/the level of legal aid to which a defendant is entitled contingent on their household 'disposable income'. The chapter also considers the effect of cuts to lawyers' fees (or their stagnation), and the negative impact this has had on their motivation and capacity to effectively defend their clients. What is abundantly clear from this chapter is that all defendants involved in the criminal process are situationally vulnerable, and that this vulnerability is exacerbated when defence lawyers are not fairly renumerated and when access to legal representation is financially contingent.

Chapter 13 is the conclusion, in which we draw together some of the key themes that emerge across the contributions. Here we pay particular attention to the outstanding issues that remain in addressing vulnerability among suspect and defendant populations, and make some suggestions as to what could and should be done next both in terms of research, policy, and practice.

Part 1

The Implementation of the European Framework

1 Access to Justice for Persons with Disabilities as Suspects of Crime

The Transformative Power of Human Rights Laws

Donna McNamara

Introduction

The role of human rights in the context of the criminal justice system represents a highly contested and complex subject. On the one hand, the starting point of human rights law is the recognition of the inherent dignity of all persons,[1] which is 'the central value underpinning the entirety of international human rights law'.[2] The importance of ensuring respect for dignity must be considered when interpreting the human rights of suspects of crime, including the right to humane treatment in places of detention;[3] the prohibition on torture and cruel, inhuman or degrading treatment or punishment;[4] the presumption of innocence;[5] and the right to liberty and security.[6] On the other hand, despite the significant attention afforded to the notion of dignity in human rights law, the experience of being arrested by the police, searched, questioned, tried in court, sentenced and perhaps imprisoned may not evoke associations with respect for the rights and dignity of a person. This leads to questions about the effectiveness of normative principles as outlined in international human rights law and whether these principles can play a transformative role in reshaping domestic criminal justice reform.

In answering the above questions, I am principally concerned with the rights of people with disabilities as suspects of crime.[7] There is a large body of emerging research that seeks to explore and understand the relationship between persons with disabilities and the criminal justice system.[8] It is evident that persons with

---

1 Universal Declaration of Human Rights, GA Res 217A (Ii), UN Doc A/810 (1948) (UDHR).
2 Charles O'Mahony, 'There Is No Such Thing as a Right to Dignity' (2012) 10(2) *International Journal of Constitutional Law* 551, p 552.
3 Article 10 of the International Covenant on Civil and Political Rights (ICCPR).
4 ICCPR, Article 7.
5 ICCPR, Article 14(2).
6 ICCPR, Article 9.
7 For an evaluation of the right (to a fair trial) of vulnerable suspects generally, see Alan Cusack et al in Chapter 5 of this collection.
8 See, *inter alia*, Ruth McCausland and Eileen Baldry, 'I Feel like I Failed Him by Ringing the Police': Criminalising Disability in Australia' (2017) 19 *Punishment & Society* 230; Leanne Dowse, Eileen Baldry and Phillip Snoyman, 'Disabling

DOI: 10.4324/9781003205166-3

disabilities (specifically those with cognitive disabilities and psychosocial disabilities) are overrepresented throughout all stages of the justice system around the world;[9] are more vulnerable in the context of police interviews;[10] and may face a greater risk of incurring harsher prison sentences or even the death penalty.[11] Against this backdrop of increased criminological research, the last two decades have also seen a new focus on disability human rights law following the commencement of the United Nations (UN) Convention on the Rights of Persons with Disabilities (CRPD), the first human rights treaty of the twenty-first century.[12] Together with its Optional Protocol,[13] this new convention seeks to promote and protect the rights of all persons with disabilities and offers a benchmark against which we can assess national disability laws and policies.[14]

The CRPD has already influenced significant law and policy reform around the world and has raised awareness of the status of persons with disabilities as human rights holders. However, as I have argued elsewhere, there is still some uncertainty 'as to how (or if) the Convention will influence criminal justice and policing' in any substantive way.[15] On its face, there is only one provision of the CRPD which refers to the police and the justice system: Article 13. It is perhaps unsurprising, then, that there is little academic discourse on the potential application of the rights outlined in the CRPD to the justice system.[16] Questions abound as to how

Criminology: Conceptualising the Intersections of Critical Disability Studies and Critical Criminology for People with Mental Health and Cognitive Disabilities in the Criminal Justice System' (2017) 15(1) *Australian Journal of Human Rights* 29; and Linda Steele, *Disability, Criminal Justice and Law* (Routledge 2020).

9 Liat Ben-Moshe, Chris Chapman and Allison Carey (eds), *Disability Incarcerated: Imprisonment and Disability in the United States and Canada* (Palgrave Macmillan 2014).

10 Gisli Gudjonsson, 'Psychological Vulnerabilities During Police Interviews. Why Are They Important?' (2010) 15(2) *Legal and Criminological Psychology* 161–175.

11 Peter Bartlett, 'The United Nations Convention on the Rights of Persons with Disabilities and Mental Health Law' (2012) 75(5) *The Modern Law Review* 752, 776.

12 United Nations, Convention on the Rights of Persons with Disabilities 2006, GA Res 61/106 (hereinafter 'CRPD').

13 UN General Assembly, Optional Protocol to the Convention on the Rights of Persons with Disabilities 2006, GA Res 61/106, Annex II.

14 CRPD Article 1.

15 Donna McNamara, 'Policing in the Age of the Asylum: Early Legislative Interventions in the Lives of Persons with Disabilities' (2021) 41 *Disability Studies Quarterly*. Available at https://dsq-sds.org/article/view/6990 (accessed 24 September 2021); and Donna McNamara, 'Building a Collaborative Approach to Policing in an Age of Disability Human Rights Law' (2021) 28(1) *Journal of Psychiatric and Mental Health Nursing* 107.

16 Examples of existing scholarship include Tina Minkowitz, 'Rethinking Criminal Responsibility from a Critical Disability Perspective: The Abolition of Insanity/Incapacity Acquittals and Unfitness to Plead, and Beyond' (2014) 23 *Griffith Law Review* 434; Piers Gooding and Charles O'Mahony, 'Laws on Unfitness to Stand Trial and the UN Convention on the Rights of Persons with Disabilities: Comparing Reform in England, Wales, Northern Ireland and Australia' (2016) 44 *International Journal of Law, Crime and Justice* 122.

effective it will be as a vehicle for law and policy reform at a domestic level and whether it can influence meaningful change to enhance the rights of access to justice for all persons with disabilities navigating the justice system.

In this chapter, I explore the transformative role of human rights law and its potential application to the criminal justice system. I argue that, notwithstanding its limitations, the CRPD offers a useful framework for guiding criminal law and policy reform which could, in turn, enhance the right of access to justice for suspects with disabilities. The discussion begins by providing an overview of the right of access to justice as set out in Article 13 and its relationship with other rights, including the duty to provide reasonable accommodations (Article 5) and the right of accessibility (Article 9). It then proceeds to examine the duty to provide training for all agents of the justice system under Article 13(2). Finally, the discussion turns to consider the practical application of the CRPD and how it can enhance the right of access to justice for suspects with disabilities. To do this, I focus on Ireland as a case study to illuminate how its normative content can be translated into practice.[17]

The UN Convention on the Rights of Persons with Disabilities and Access to Justice

First, it is important to note that 'disability' is not defined in the text of the CRPD. Article 1 recognises that it includes 'those who have long-term physical, mental, intellectual or sensory impairments which in interaction with various barriers may hinder their full and effective participation in society on an equal basis with others'.[18] The Preamble also recognises that 'disability is an evolving concept' which 'results from the interaction between persons with impairments and attitudinal and environmental barriers that hinders their full and effective participation in society on an equal basis with others'.[19] The CRPD contains a mix of 50 separate articles relating to civil, political, economic, social and cultural rights. None of these are 'new rights';[20] the CRPD reimagines existing human rights in a new disability-specific manner, including the right to equality and non-discrimination (Article 5); the right to life (Article 10); the right to liberty and security of the person (Article 14); and the right to freedom from torture or cruel, inhuman or degrading treatment or punishment (Article 15). Many of the provisions include a positive obligation on states parties to take all necessary measures to ensure that persons with disabilities enjoy their rights 'on an equal basis with others'.[21] We must also be mindful of the

---

17 Ireland was one of the first countries to sign the CPRD in 2007 but was the last country in the European Union to formally ratify it in March 2018.
18 CRPD, Article 1.
19 CRPD, Preamble.
20 Rosemary Kayess and Phillip French, 'Out of Darkness into Light? Introducing the Convention on the Rights of Persons with Disabilities' (2008) 8 *Human Rights Law Review* 1.
21 The meaning of the term 'on an equal basis with others' was discussed in *General Comment No 6 on equality and non-discrimination*, 19th sess, UN Doc CRPD/C/

interrelationship between each right (as well as the guiding principles of the CRPD),[22] as together they 'will help to shape domestic disability law and policy … in a far more significant and multi-faceted manner than if they were read in isolation'.[23]

As noted above, Article 13 is the only right that expressly refers to the police and is arguably the most relevant provision for this discussion. This right elucidates the right of access to justice for all persons with disabilities:

> States Parties shall ensure effective access to justice for persons with disabilities on an equal basis with others, including through the provision of procedural and age-appropriate accommodations, in order to facilitate their effective role as direct and indirect participants, including as witnesses, in all legal proceedings, including at investigative and other preliminary stages.[24]

At its core, Article 13 includes the right to be treated equally; the right to have equal access to the courts; and the right to obtain timely remedies.[25] The concept of access to justice is widely recognised as being integral to the rule of law and transcends the fields of criminal, civil and administrative laws. It has long been recognised as a fundamental guarantee of human rights law, with Articles 6–11 of the Universal Declaration of Human Rights recognising principles of equality before the law and the presumption of innocence guarantee.[26] The right is also well established under the European Convention on Human Rights (ECHR), with the right to a fair trial stated under Article 6 and the right to an effective remedy listed under Article 13. States parties to the UN have also agreed to the Sustainable Development Goals 2030, which create further impetus to 'promote the rule of law at the national and international levels and ensure equal access to

---

GC/6, (6 April 2018) para [17]: 'The phrase "on an equal basis with others" is not only limited to the definition of disability-based discrimination but also permeates the whole Convention on the Rights of Persons with Disabilities. On the one hand, it means that persons with disabilities will not be granted more or fewer rights or benefits than the general population. On the other hand, it requires that States parties take concrete specific measures to achieve de facto equality for persons with disabilities to ensure that they can in fact enjoy all human rights and fundamental freedoms.'

22 The guiding principles are set out in Article 3 and include respect for inherent dignity, individual autonomy, non-discrimination, full and effective participation and inclusion in society; respect for difference, equality and accessibility; respect for the evolving capacities of children with disabilities; and respect for the right of children with disabilities to preserve their identities.

23 Charles O'Sullivan and Donna McNamara, 'The "Necessity" of Austerity and Its Relationship with the UN Convention on the Rights of Persons with Disabilities: A Case Study of Ireland and the United Kingdom' (2021) 21 *Human Rights Law Review* 157, 169

24 CRPD, Article 13(1).

25 See Esme Grant and Rhonda Neuhaus, 'Liberty and Justice for All: The Convention on the Rights of Persons with Disabilities' (2013) 19 *ILSA Journal of International & Comparative Law* 347.

26 See also ICCPR, Article 2(3) and Article 14.

justice for all'.[27] Despite such earlier protections outlining the right of access to justice, people with disabilities have traditionally experienced greater barriers to justice, which often included the complete denial of their legal standing and their due process guarantees.[28] In 2017, the Office of the United Nations High Commissioner for Human Rights (OHCHR) issued a report on access to justice for persons with disabilities in which it provided guidance for states parties in giving effect to this right.[29] The report noted that 'national legislation often contains provisions that deny equal treatment of persons with disabilities before courts and other jurisdictional bodies'.[30] It also observed that 'access to justice is most often denied as a result of lack of accessibility of and access to information, procedural accommodations, the right to claim justice and stand trial, respect for presumption of innocence and legal aid'.[31]

These examples illustrate the need for a disability-specific human rights convention which seeks to enhance the rights of access to justice in a disability-inclusive manner. Article 13(1) is therefore critical, as it recognises that persons with disabilities are entitled to procedural guarantees at all stages of the justice system and as outlined in previous human rights laws, such as the right to a fair trial and the presumption of innocence; but it also extends this right to ensure 'effective access to justice'. The term 'effective' implies that this is more than a general duty: it requires states parties to actively ensure that the systems and processes within the legal system are accessible and inclusive to enable persons with disabilities to participate on an equal basis with others.

Article 13 therefore offers a framework for inclusive justice and accommodations are key to this. In this way, there is a connection between Article 13 and

27 United Nations, *Transforming Our World: The 2030 Agenda for Sustainable Development*, Resolution adopted by the General Assembly on 25 September 2015, Article 16.3.

28 Office of the United Nations High Commissioner for Human Rights, 'Right to access to justice under article 13 of the Convention on the Rights of Persons with Disabilities' (annual report of the United Nations High Commissioner for Human Rights and reports of the Office of the High Commissioner and the Secretary-General, 26 February–23 March 2018, A/HRC/37/25) para [4].

29 Office of the United Nations High Commissioner for Human Rights, 'Right to access to justice under article 13 of the Convention on the Rights of Persons with Disabilities' (annual report of the United Nations High Commissioner for Human Rights and reports of the Office of the High Commissioner and the Secretary-General, 26 February–23 March 2018, A/HRC/37/25) para [4].

30 Office of the United Nations High Commissioner for Human Rights, 'Right to access to justice under article 13 of the Convention on the Rights of Persons with Disabilities' (annual report of the United Nations High Commissioner for Human Rights and reports of the Office of the High Commissioner and the Secretary-General, 26 February–23 March 2018, A/HRC/37/25) para [4].

31 Office of the United Nations High Commissioner for Human Rights, 'Right to access to justice under article 13 of the Convention on the Rights of Persons with Disabilities' (annual report of the United Nations High Commissioner for Human Rights and reports of the Office of the High Commissioner and the Secretary-General, 26 February–23 March 2018, A/HRC/37/25), para [19].

Article 5, which sets out the duty to provide 'reasonable' accommodations for persons with disabilities as part of the principle of non-discrimination – an interpretive principle which underpins the interpretation of each of the other rights contained in the Convention.[32] Article 5(3) provides that: 'In order to promote equality and eliminate discrimination, States Parties shall take all appropriate steps to ensure that reasonable accommodation is provided.'[33] The requirement to provide 'procedural and age-appropriate accommodations' pursuant to Article 13 is therefore distinguished from the general duty to provide 'reasonable accommodations' under Article 5, as was confirmed by the UN Committee on the Rights of Persons with Disabilities ('CRPD Committee'), the monitoring body for the implementation of the CRPD:

> The rights and obligations with respect to equality and non-discrimination outlined in article 5 raise particular considerations with respect to article 13, which, among others, call for the provision of procedural and age-appropriate accommodations. These accommodations are distinguishable from reasonable accommodation in that procedural accommodations are not limited by disproportionality. An illustration of a procedural accommodation is the recognition of diverse communication methods of persons with disabilities standing in courts and tribunals. Age-appropriate accommodations may consist of disseminating information about available mechanisms to bring complaints forward and access to justice using age-appropriate and plain language.[34]

As such, the duty to provide appropriate accommodations under Article 13 'cannot be mitigated by arguments about unreasonableness and the extent of the burden they would place on the duty-bearer'.[35] Moreover, Flynn has rightly observed that the providers of any accommodations within the justice system will inevitably be the state itself.[36] This means that all states parties are under an obligation to provide all procedural and age-appropriate accommodations as necessary to ensure the full realisation of Article 13. This extends to ensuring that accessible information is given to people at all stages of the criminal process, such as providing the charge sheet in braille or affording access to a sign language interpreter during questioning.[37] A failure to provide such accommodations may amount to a

32 CRPD, Article 5; and see Donna McNamara, 'Building a Collaborative Approach to Policing in an Age of Disability Human Rights Law' (2021) 28(1) *Journal of Psychiatric and Mental Health Nursing* 107.

33 CRPD, Article 5.

34 *General Comment No 6 on equality and non-discrimination*, 19th sess, UN Doc CRPD/C/GC/6, (6 April 2018) para [51].

35 Eilionoir Flynn and Anna Lawson, 'Disability and Access to Justice in the European Union: Implication of the United Nations Convention on the Rights of Persons with Disabilities' (2013) 4 *European Yearbook of Disability Law* 7, 25.

36 Eilionoir Flynn, *Disabled Justice? Access to Justice and the UN Convention on the Rights of Persons with Disabilities* (Routledge, 2016) 36.

37 *Draft General Comment on equality and non-discrimination* (CRPD/C/GC/6, 26 April 2018) para [52].

violation of the right to a fair trial the effective exclusion of an individual suspect from their proceeding; and ultimately places them at a higher risk of being found guilty and subject to unfair sentences.[38]

The duty to provide accommodations in respect of Article 13 was explored by the CRPD Committee in *Noble v Australia*.[39] The applicant, Mr Noble – an Aboriginal man with an intellectual disability – was found unfit to stand trial in relation to alleged sexual assaults in 2001 and was subsequently incarcerated for almost a decade. In acknowledging the 'irreparable psychological effects that indefinite detention may have on a detained person',[40] the committee found that the applicant's right to a fair trial was suspended and that the state party failed to provide any appropriate supports to support Mr Noble to exercise his legal capacity.[41] It was noted that Article 13(1) provides a duty to ensure effective access to justice on an equal basis with others, which includes the provision of procedural and age-appropriate accommodations; and that the absence of any such supports amounted to a breach of the applicant's right to a fair trial. To date, this is one of the only rulings on the right of access to justice and the duty to provide accommodations within the context of the justice system. It is therefore significant – not only because it offered the CRPD Committee the rare opportunity to consider a state party's obligations pursuant to Article 13, but also because it reaffirmed the importance of providing accommodations to suspects of crime.

Finally, in considering the meaning of 'access', Article 9 is noteworthy as it details the duty on behalf of states parties to identify and eliminate obstacles and barriers to accessibility for all persons with disabilities.[42] Examples of barriers within the justice system are plentiful and include inaccessible buildings such as police stations, courtrooms and prisons; communication barriers (including the failure to provide easy read documents and the failure to accommodate sign language users); and attitudinal barriers, such as the existence of entrenched stigma and stereotypes, particularly towards people with neurodiversity and psychosocial disabilities. The imperative to consider accessibility in the context of Article 13 was

38 Office of the United Nations High Commissioner for Human Rights, 'Right to access to justice under article 13 of the Convention on the Rights of Persons with Disabilities' (annual report of the United Nations High Commissioner for Human Rights and reports of the Office of the High Commissioner and the Secretary-General, 26 February–23 March 2018, A/HRC/37/25), para [31].

39 Committee on the Rights of Persons with Disabilities Decision: Communication No 7/2012, 16th session, UN Doc CRPD/C/16/D/7/2012 (15 August–2 September 2016) ('*Noble v Australia*'). See also Fiona Mcgaughey, Tamara Tulich and Harry Blagg, 'UN Decision on Marlon Noble Case: Imprisonment of an Aboriginal Man with Intellectual Disability Found Unfit to Stand Trial in Western Australia' (2017) 42 (1) *Alternative Law Journal* 67.

40 *Noble v Australia* supra (39), para [8.9].

41 *Noble v Australia* supra (39), para [8.4]. The committee pointed to Article 12(3), which provides that states parties are required to provide access to supports to enable individuals to exercise their right to legal capacity.

42 CRPD, Article 9.

emphasised by the CRPD Committee in its General Comment on Article 9.[43] It noted that:

> There can be no effective access to justice if the buildings in which law-enforcement agencies and the judiciary are located are not physically accessible, or if the services, information and communication they provide are not accessible to persons with disabilities.[44]

Accordingly, it is necessary for all states parties to identify barriers to accessibility within the justice system (from the pre-trial stage to imprisonment), and for all such barriers to be removed to ensure that persons with disabilities can assert their rights on an equal basis with non-disabled suspects. In 2020, the International Principles and Guidelines on Access to Justice for Persons with Disabilities ('2020 Guidelines') were released and offer further assistance to states parties as to the relevant principles and strategies to ensure compliance with the CRPD.[45] Among its recommendations, the Special Rapporteur outlined that facilities and services must be universally accessible; and that all persons have capacity and have the right to procedural accommodations (including procedural guarantees).[46] The final principle outlines the importance of training for all those working in the justice system and this is outlined further in the following section.

The Duty to Provide Training: Article 13(2)

Ensuring physical access to the justice system is the first step towards realising the right of access to justice under the CRPD. Beyond that, the next step is the duty to raise awareness and provide training for all agents of the criminal justice system. Article 13(2) outlines this duty: 'In order to help to ensure effective access to justice for persons with disabilities, States Parties shall promote appropriate training for those working in the field of administration of justice, including police and prison staff.'[47]

---

43 General comment No 2 (2014) *Article 9: Accessibility* (CRPD/C/GC/2, 2014) para [37].

44 General comment No 2 (2014) *Article 9: Accessibility* (CRPD/C/GC/2, 2014) para [37].

45 Special Rapporteur on the Rights of Persons with Disabilities, *International Principles and Guidelines on Access to Justice for Persons with Disabilities* (15 August 2019). Available at https://www.ohchr.org/EN/Issues/Disability/SRDisabilities/Pages/GoodPracticesEffectiveAccessJusticePersonsDisabilities.aspx (accessed 24 September 2021).

46 Special Rapporteur on the Rights of Persons with Disabilities, *International Principles and Guidelines on Access to Justice for Persons with Disabilities* (15 August 2019). Available at https://www.ohchr.org/EN/Issues/Disability/SRDisabilities/Pages/GoodPracticesEffectiveAccessJusticePersonsDisabilities.aspx (accessed 24 September 2021).

47 CRPD, Article 13(2).

By recognising the need to implement appropriate training, Article 13(2) goes beyond the normative imperatives outlined in other human rights conventions to consider how the right of access to justice can be realised in practice. The is one of the best examples of the transformative powers of the CRPD: it recognises the need to build better awareness of the rights of persons with disabilities among key decision makers, which in turn can help improve compliance levels on the ground. As Grant and Neuhaus explain: 'Article 13 also confirms that establishing a policy is simply not enough, but that trainings are a key component to accomplishing access to justice.'[48] Although the CRPD Committee has not yet defined the exact nature of training and what it should involve, it has regularly called upon states parties to build awareness regarding the barriers to justice experienced by persons with disabilities and their rights as outlined in the CRPD.[49] Article 8 further recognises the need for states to promote awareness-raising programmes regarding persons with disabilities and their inherent rights; and to promote recognition of their 'skills, merits and abilities of persons with disabilities'.[50]

The duty to provide training under Article 13(2) offers a significant opportunity to give meaning to disability rights in practice. It offers the potential to overcome false stereotypes and stigmas which are often entrenched within criminal justice systems and are commonly held among police officers.[51] As I have argued previously, regular police training which is grounded in a human rights-based approach, is perhaps one of the most effective means of overcoming stigma and negative attitudes which seek to discriminate against persons with disabilities.[52] This view accords with the views of the OHCHR, which noted in its 2017 report that: 'Attitudinal barriers affect access to justice ... as they may negatively influence the way in which laws, legal policies, procedures and practices are implemented.'[53] Such barriers are said to 'stem from lack of awareness of the rights of, and appropriate practices for, persons with disabilities in the justice system on the

---

48 Esme Grant and Rhonda Neuhaus, 'Liberty and Justice for All: The Convention on the Rights of Persons with Disabilities' (2013) 19 *ILSA Journal of International & Comparative Law* 347, 353.

49 Donna McNamara, 'Building a Collaborative Approach to Policing in an Age of Disability Human Rights Law' (2021) 28(1) *Journal of Psychiatric and Mental Health Nursing* 107.

50 CRPD, Article 8.

51 Donna McNamara, 'Policing in the Age of the Asylum: Early Legislative Interventions in the Lives of Persons with Disabilities' (2021) 41 *Disability Studies Quarterly*. Available at https://dsq-sds.org/article/view/6990 (accessed 24 September 2021).

52 Donna McNamara, 'Policing in the Age of the Asylum: Early Legislative Interventions in the Lives of Persons with Disabilities' (2021) 41 *Disability Studies Quarterly*. Available at https://dsq-sds.org/article/view/6990 (accessed 24 September 2021).

53 Office of the United Nations High Commissioner for Human Rights, 'Right to access to justice under article 13 of the Convention on the Rights of Persons with Disabilities' (annual report of the United Nations High Commissioner for Human Rights and reports of the Office of the High Commissioner and the Secretary-General, 26 February–23 March 2018, A/HRC/37/25), para [59].

part of police officers'.[54] Mandatory (and properly funded) training is therefore recommended in order to combat prejudices and stereotypes held against persons with disabilities.[55]

Principle 10 of the 2020 Guidelines provides that states must remove barriers to justice by providing disability rights training to all those working in the justice system to eliminate prejudice and promote recognition of rights.[56] In developing such training, the guidelines note that people with disabilities and their representative organisations should have an active involvement at all stages, including in monitoring and evaluating content.[57] This is in line with the 'Nothing About Us Without Us' motto which was adopted by the disability rights movement and reflects the extensive involvement of persons with disabilities in the drafting of the CRPD itself.[58] In keeping with this participatory spirit, which is embedded within the rights contained in the CRPD, all disability rights training should be designed by persons with disabilities themselves, particularly those who may have experience with the police and the justice system. The guidelines also note that training for police officers should emphasise 'good practices in interactions with persons with disabilities, including response, behaviour and appropriate accommodations', and should address some of the following topics:

- the barriers to justice for people with disabilities and the removal of those barriers;
- the rights as outlined in the CRPD, including the acknowledgement of the right to recognition as persons before the law, the recognition of legal capacity and a focus on overcoming stereotypes and ableism;

54 Office of the United Nations High Commissioner for Human Rights, 'Right to access to justice under article 13 of the Convention on the Rights of Persons with Disabilities' (annual report of the United Nations High Commissioner for Human Rights and reports of the Office of the High Commissioner and the Secretary-General, 26 February–23 March 2018, A/HRC/37/25), para [59].

55 Office of the United Nations High Commissioner for Human Rights, 'Right to access to justice under article 13 of the Convention on the Rights of Persons with Disabilities' (annual report of the United Nations High Commissioner for Human Rights and reports of the Office of the High Commissioner and the Secretary-General, 26 February–23 March 2018, A/HRC/37/25), para [59].

56 Special Rapporteur on the Rights of Persons with Disabilities, International Principles and Guidelines on Access to Justice for Persons with Disabilities (15 August 2019). Available at: https://www.ohchr.org/EN/Issues/Disability/SRDisabilities/Pages/ GoodPracticesEffectiveAccessJusticePersonsDisabilities.aspx (accessed 24 September 2021), Principle 10.

57 Special Rapporteur on the Rights of Persons with Disabilities, International Principles and Guidelines on Access to Justice for Persons with Disabilities (15 August 2019). Available at: https://www.ohchr.org/EN/Issues/Disability/SRDisabilities/Pages/ GoodPracticesEffectiveAccessJusticePersonsDisabilities.aspx (accessed 24 September 2021), Principle 10.

58 For more see Arlene Kanter, *The Development of Disability Rights Under International Law From Charity to Human Rights* (Routledge, 2017) 40: the extensive involvement of persons with disabilities and their representative organisations 'represents the first time in which the UN invited the people directly affected by the proposed treaty to participate directly' in its drafting.

- communication skills, de-escalation skills and prevention of the use of force;
- procedural and reasonable accommodations; and
- the recognition of intersecting forms of discrimination on disability and other grounds, including sex, gender, indigenous status, race, sexual orientation and poverty.

These guidelines offer the most beneficial and practical lens through which states parties can begin to interpret Article 13. They offer insight as to how normative rules of international human rights law can potentially play a transformative role in achieving greater protections for people in navigating the complexities of the justice system.

The Transformative Power of Human Rights Law

For the CRPD to take on a transformative role in Ireland, its principles must be embedded into national law. As Rioux and Carbert have acknowledged: 'Human rights instruments are not only guidelines for states, but they also create obligations that require governments to reform their policies and practices to realize human rights for all citizens.'[59] To this end, it is argued that mere ratification is not enough to effect meaningful change. Article 4(1)(a) of the CRPD requires all states parties to 'adopt all appropriate legislative, administrative and other measures for the implementation of the rights recognized in the present Convention'.[60] This implies that states parties enjoy a margin of discretion in terms of how they interpret this obligation: legal measures include direct incorporation into national law (eg, at a legislative or constitutional level); whereas non-legal measures may include taking creative approaches to give the CRPD effect at the national level, such as the introduction of policy guidelines and frameworks.[61] A full discussion on the variety of incorporation methods is outside the scope of this chapter; however, it is argued that direct incorporation of the full text of the CRPD is the preferred method to ensure its transformative effect in Ireland. As a dualist state, the Irish Constitution recognises that international instruments such as the CRPD do not become part of national law unless they have been expressly incorporated by or under statute.[62] This means that the rights contained in the CRPD are not directly enforceable until the *Oireachtas* (the Irish Parliament) has incorporated it into law.[63] In the absence of direct incorporation, the CPRD will

---

59 Marcia Rioux and Anne Carbert, 'Human Rights and Disability: The International Context' (2003) 10(2) *Journal on Developmental Disabilities* 1, 3.
60 CRPD, Article 4.
61 See Ursula Kilkelly, 'The UN Convention on the Rights of the Child: Incremental and Transformative Approaches to Legal Implementation' (2019) 23(3) *The International Journal of Human Rights* 323, 323.
62 *Bunreacht na hÉireann*, Article 29.6: 'no international agreement shall be part of the domestic law of the State save as may be determined by the Oireachtas.'
63 For example, the ECHR has been transposed into national law by way of the European Convention on Human Rights Act 2003, which requires the Irish courts to interpret legislation in line with the ECHR insofar as it is possible (Section 2).

possess only persuasive authority, which means that while it can be used to assist the courts in their interpretation of domestic laws,[64] it lacks the force and weight of a fully incorporated treaty.

To date, Ireland has given effect to certain rights contained within the CRPD through a range of legislation (ie, legal measures),[65] as well as introducing non-binding policies and strategies (ie, non-legal measures).[66] In the Roadmap to Ratification, which the Irish government issued in advance of ratifying the CRPD, a number of existing statutes were referenced as being in need of reform or repeal.[67] Within that document, there was very limited consideration of criminal laws and policies,[68] which is significant for the purposes of this discussion. No attention was paid to the rights of persons with disabilities in contact with the police; nor was any consideration given to the interpretation of Article 13 and the procedural accommodations of persons with disabilities as suspects of crime. This is a disappointing shortcoming as there are numerous systemic barriers within the justice system that need to be addressed to ensure the right of access to justice for persons with disabilities, including the lack of a guaranteed right of access to a solicitor during police questioning[69] – a right which is fundamental to securing the right to a fair trial. Other accommodations could also be incorporated to enhance the right of effective access to justice. For example, Ireland lacks an appropriate adult system – a service which exists in other jurisdictions to facilitate 'effective communication' between vulnerable suspects and the police.[70] In England and Wales, for example, an appropriate adult can offer support to an individual suspect during their police interview and can help them to understand the complicated processes of the criminal pre-trial system. This safeguard, while not without its shortcomings, is an example of the kind of accommodation which

---

64 Primary sources of Irish law will be held to take precedence over international laws. In *In Re Ó Laighléis* [1960] IR 93, the Supreme Court held that it could not give effect to the ECHR because it was not part of domestic law at that time.

65 Assisted Decision-Making (Capacity) Act 2015.

66 For example, see the National Disability Inclusion Strategy (2017–2021) and the Comprehensive Employment Strategy for People with Disabilities (2015–2024).

67 The Juries Act 1976, the Electoral Act 1992, the Companies Act 2014, the Equal Status Acts and the Mental Health Act 2001.

68 The main criminal provisions which were tabled for amendment were Section 4 of the Criminal Law (Insanity) Act 2006 and Article 5 of the Criminal Law (Sexual Offences) Act 1993.

69 There is a right to be 'informed' of the right of access to a solicitor under the Criminal Justice Act 1984; however, there is no express right to have a solicitor present in the interrogation room. See *DPP v Gormley and DPP v White* [2014] IESC 17; Vicky Conway and Yvonne Marie Daly, 'From Legal Advice to Legal Assistance: Recognising the Changing Role of the Solicitor in the Garda Station' (2019) 1 *Irish Judicial Studies Journal* 103.

70 See Roxanna Dehaghani, *Vulnerability in Police Custody: Police Decision-Making and the Appropriate Adult Safeguard* (Routledge 2019) and Roxanna Dehaghani, 'He's Just Not That Vulnerable: Exploring the Implementation of the Appropriate Adult Safeguard in Police Custody' (2016) 55 *The Howard Journal of Crime and Justice* 396.

could be implemented to enhance greater access to justice and should be considered as an example of best practice for Ireland following its ratification of the CRPD.

Conclusion

There is no doubt that the CRPD has created new momentum in the field of disability human rights. Admittedly, though, it is only 13 years old, which makes it difficult to fully assess its full impact and implementation to date. Nevertheless, since its commencement in 2008, it has been ratified by almost every country in the world and was the first human rights treaty to be ratified by the European Union.[71] While it is still early days to assess its effective implementation in practice, it has been 'hailed as a great landmark in the struggle to reframe the needs and concerns of persons with disability in terms of human rights'. 'Hyperbole' aside,[72] I am optimistic about the commencement of the CRPD and hopeful that this momentum will trickle down to state criminal law and policy reforms. The impetus for such reform is clear, as there are a multitude of barriers within the Irish criminal justice process which actively discriminate against persons with disabilities and in turn prevent them from exercising their rights on an equal basis with others. The CRPD provides a blueprint to identify and address such barriers, thereby offering a robust normative framework for criminal justice reform.

To achieve its potential, we should view the CRPD as a vehicle for improving the lives of persons with disabilities across all sectors of society. Article 13 is key to this, as it offers an avenue for increasing awareness levels across major decision makers and professions. Perhaps then the duty to provide training for agents working in the justice system under Article 13(2) is the essential ingredient to ensure the success of the CRPD as a whole. Moving beyond the duty to combat attitudinal barriers through the use of training, the full text of the CRPD should be incorporated into Irish law as a matter of priority. This aligns with the CRPD Committee's recent observation in respect of Australia – specifically, its recommendation that Australia bring all its laws (including state, territory and federal criminal laws and policies) into compliance with the CPRD to ensure due process guarantees for all persons with disabilities.[73] Formal incorporation of the CRPD into national law is therefore the preferred route to ensure a transformative shift in the protection of the rights of suspects with disabilities in Ireland.

---

71 European Commission, 'EU Ratifies UN Convention on Disability Rights' Press Release, Brussels, 5 January 2011. Available at: https://ec.europa.eu/commission/p resscorner/detail/en/IP_11_4> (accessed 19 September 2021).

72 Rosemary Kayess and Phillip French, 'Out of Darkness into Light? Introducing the Convention on the Rights of Persons with Disabilities' (2008) 8 *Human Rights Law Review* 1, 4: 'Perhaps it is not unusual for new human rights treaties to be drenched in hyperbole and hopefulness.'

73 Concluding observations on the combined second and third periodic reports of Australia (CRPD/C/AUS/CO/2–3, 15 October 2019) para [26c].

2 The Impact of the Procedural Rights Directives on Juvenile Suspects and Defendants

Jantien Leenknecht

Introduction

Increased attention has been paid to vulnerable suspects at the EU level in recent years, including in the area of procedural rights.[1] The EU Roadmap for strengthening procedural rights of suspects or defendants in criminal proceedings ('Procedural Rights Roadmap') requires, under Measure E, that special attention be paid to suspects or defendants who cannot understand or follow the content or the meaning of the proceedings due, for example, to their age, mental or physical condition.[2] Despite vulnerability thus being a multifaceted concept,[3] children are the only group of suspects and defendants that EU member states unanimously consider to be vulnerable. As a consequence, they are granted extra safeguards compared to adults when faced with judicial proceedings.[4] Those extra safeguards are laid down in Directive 2016/800 on procedural safeguards for juvenile suspects or defendants ('Children Directive'), which was adopted following the Procedural Rights Roadmap. This is the first instrument at an EU level containing binding provisions that explicitly and exclusively concern children involved in criminal proceedings.

The Procedural Rights Roadmap also resulted in five other directives that apply to all suspects and defendants (ie, adults and children). Each of them discusses a specific procedural right:

- Directive 2010/64 on the right to interpretation and translation ('Interpretation and Translation Directive');

1 Lore Mergaerts and Roxanna Dehaghani, 'Protecting Vulnerable Suspects in Police Investigations in Europe: Lessons Learned from England and Wales and Belgium' (2020) 11 *New Journal of European Criminal Law* 313, 315.
2 Resolution of the Council on a Roadmap for strengthening procedural rights of suspected or accused persons in criminal proceedings (2009) OJ C 295/1.
3 Lore Mergaerts, *Kwetsbare Verdachten in de Strafprocedure: De Conceptualisering van Kwetsbaarheid en de Rol van de Advocaat Bij de Vaststelling ervan Tijdens Het Strafrechtelijk Vooronderzoek* (Boom juridisch Antwerpen, 2022), 179–203.
4 United Nations Convention on the Rights of the Child, Article 40(3); Children Directive, recital 9; Steven Cras, 'The Directive on Procedural Safeguards for Children Who Are Suspects or Accused Persons in Criminal Proceedings' (2016) *Eucrim* 109, 111.

DOI: 10.4324/9781003205166-4

- Directive 2012/13 on the right to information ('Information Directive');
- Directive 2013/48 on the right to access to a lawyer ('A2L Directive');
- Directive 2016/343 on the presumption of innocence and the right to be present at trial ('Presumption of Innocence Directive'); and
- Directive 2016/1919 on the right to legal aid ('Legal Aid Directive').

All emphasise the importance of taking into account the vulnerability of suspects and defendants, and require that particular attention be paid to their special needs in the implementation of the directives.[5] However, none – except the A2L Directive to a limited extent – contains specific provisions that explain how EU member states should take the particular vulnerability of juvenile suspects and defendants into account.[6] The lack of child-specific provisions in those five directives is not necessarily problematic, as long as the Children Directive elaborates on those procedural rights and the member states subsequently correctly transpose those safeguards. In this chapter, it is argued that the Children Directive in particular and the Procedural Rights Directives more generally have not always reached their full potential in terms of content on the one hand and national implementation on the other.

As far as the content is concerned, this chapter focuses on:

- the right to interpretation and translation;[7]
- the right to information;
- the right to access to and assistance from a lawyer;[8]
- the right to presence at trial; and
- the right to legal aid.[9]

The five Procedural Rights Directives covering these procedural rights specifically do not explain how they should be interpreted in relation to minors. One would therefore assume that the Children Directive grants special procedural safeguards to children when compared to the safeguards provided for adults. While this is certainly the case for some of those procedural rights, the safeguards for other rights are less elaborate, giving minors the same type of protection as adults. This is not always desirable given the vulnerability of juvenile suspects and defendants. As far as the national implementation of the provisions for the protection of juvenile suspects and defendants is concerned, the transposition of the aforementioned five rights is analysed in three member states. The impact of potential child-specific safeguards hinges on their transposition into national law, which can reduce the efficacy of procedural protection at the EU level by

---

5 Interpretation and Translation Directive, recital 27; Information Directive, Article 3 (2); A2L Directive, recital 51 and Article 13; Legal Aid Directive, recital 18 and Article 9.
6 The terms 'child', 'minor' and 'juvenile' are used interchangeably.
7 More generally, see Heidi Salaets et al, Chapter 8 of this collection.
8 More generally, see Alan Cusack et al, Chapter 5 of this collection.
9 More generally, see Roxanna Dehaghani et al, Chapter 12 of this collection.

member states.[10] The three member states reviewed in this chapter are Austria, Belgium and the Netherlands. These jurisdictions have been selected due to the diverse ways in which they respond to offences committed by minors: Austria represents the justice model; Belgium has developed a welfare and restorative justice tradition; while the Netherlands is a typical example of the sanction model.[11]

Austria and Belgium have separate acts that contain procedural provisions for juvenile offenders: the Youth Court Act (*Jugendgerichtsgesetz* (JGG)) and the Youth Protection Act (*Jeugdbeschermingswet* (JBW)), respectively. The Netherlands, on the other hand, does not have separate legislation addressing juvenile offenders and instead has integrated specific provisions regarding youth justice proceedings in the general Code of Criminal Procedure.[12] While Austria and the Netherlands refer to their youth justice system as 'juvenile criminal law' ('*Jugendstrafrecht*' and '*Jeugdstrafrecht*', respectively), Belgium has a tradition of 'youth protection law'. This is an essential observation, as the Procedural Rights Directives apply only to criminal proceedings and not to 'proceedings which are specially designed for children and which could lead to protective, corrective or educative measures'.[13] This limitation would exclude the Belgian youth protection system from the scope of the instruments resulting from the Procedural Rights Roadmap, even though it also contains punitive reactions to juvenile suspects and offenders. Unlike the European Court of Human Rights, the Court of Justice has not yet recognised the punitive nature of youth justice proceedings as a decisive criterion to grant procedural rights to children.[14]

10 The only exception is the limited extent to which the provisions of the Procedural Rights Directive have a so-called direct effect. If a provision is unconditional and sufficiently clear and precise, individuals can – even if the transposition deadline of a directive has expired – evoke and claim the right directly before their national courts. Case 41–74 *Van Duyn* (1974) ECR 1337; Valsamis Mitsilegas, 'The European Union and the Rights of Individuals in Criminal Proceedings' in Darryl Brown, Jenia Iontcheva Turner and Bettina Weisser (eds), *The Oxford Handbook of Criminal Process* (OUP 2019) (114) 130.

11 The different youth justice models are explained in the following research: Eef Goedseels, *Jeugdrechtmodellen in theorie en praktijk: Een empirisch onderzoek naar het discours en de praktijk van Belgische jeugdrechters* (KU Leuven 2015). The selection of the national youth justice systems is explained in the following research: Jantien Leenknecht, *An EU Cooperation in Youth Justice Matters: Mission Impossible? An Analysis of the EU Competence in Criminal Matters and the Diversity of Youth Justice Systems* (KU Leuven 2022).

12 Anton M van Kalmthout and Zarif Bahtiyar, 'The Netherlands' in Frieder Dünkel and others (eds), *Juvenile Justice Systems in Europe: Current Situation and Reform Developments*, vol 2 (Forum Verlag Godesberg 2011) 912; Jantien Leenknecht and others, 'Age Limits in Youth Justice: A Comparative and Conceptual Analysis' (2020) *Erasmus Law Review* 2.

13 Children Directive, recital 17.

14 Jantien Leenknecht and Wendy De Bondt, 'Jeugddelinquentierecht over de grenzen heen' in Johan Put and Jantien Leenknecht (eds) *Het Vlaamse Jeugddelinquentierecht* (Larcier 2019) 233.

Child-Specific Procedural Safeguards and Their Transposition

Right to Interpretation and Translation

Directive 2010/64 contains no provisions that elaborate on the right to inter-pretation and translation for juvenile suspects and defendants; but neither does the Children Directive. As a result, the general provisions of the Interpretation and Translation Directive apply without any adaptation to the age of the suspect or defendant.[15] With regard to the right to interpretation, member states must pro-vide the services of an interpreter free of charge to suspects or defendants who do not speak or understand the language of criminal proceedings during the criminal proceedings. This right also extends to police questioning and court hearings.[16] With regard to the right to translation, suspects or defendants who do not understand the language of the criminal proceedings should receive, within a rea-sonable period of time, a written translation of all documents which are essential to ensure that they can exercise their right of defence and to safeguard the fairness of the proceedings.[17]

All three countries have now transposed the Interpretation and Translation Directive,[18] but none of the three member states have introduced specific pro-visions for minors. The findings from the European Union Agency for Funda-mental Rights (FRA) similarly state that member states provide no detailed rules or guidelines on how to accommodate the particular needs of children and per-sons with disabilities with regard to the rights to interpretation and translation.[19] The Netherlands does stipulate that the notification of rights shall be made in a language that the juvenile suspect or defendant understands if they do not speak an adequate level of Dutch.[20] However, this is a repetition of a general rule; it is not an additional child-specific protection. In Belgium, by contrast, the legis-lature expressly rejected the proposal to include a reference to the right to interpretation and translation in the Youth Protection Act, as safeguards in

---

15 The directive does require appropriate assistance for persons with hearing or speech impediments: Interpretation and Translation Directive, Article 2(3). European Union Agency for Fundamental Rights, 'Rights of Suspected and Accused Persons across the EU: Translation, Interpretation and Information' (2016) 98.

16 Interpretation and Translation Directive, Articles 2(1) and 4.

17 Interpretation and Translation Directive, Article 3(1).

18 *Bundesgesetz, mit dem die Strafprozessordnung 1975, das Strafregistergesetz 1968 und das Sicherheitspolizeigesetz geändert werden* (Strafprozessrechtsänderungsgesetz 2013) (AT); *Wet van 28 oktober 2016 houdende verdere omzetting van de Richtlijn 2010/64/ EU van het Europees Parlement en de Raad van 20 oktober 2010 betreffende het recht op vertolking en vertaling in strafprocedures* (BE); *Wet van 28 februari 2013 tot imple-mentatie van richtlijn nr. 2010/64/EU van het Europees Parlement en de Raad van 20 oktober 2010 betreffende het recht op vertolking en vertaling in strafprocedures* (NL).

19 European Union Agency for Fundamental Rights, 'Rights of Suspected and Accused Persons across the EU: Translation, Interpretation and Information' (2016) 98, 100.

20 Dutch Code of Criminal Procedure (*Wetboek van Strafvordering*, Sv), Article 488aa (5).

criminal proceedings were not considered applicable to the national youth 'protection' proceedings.[21]

Right to Information

Child-Specific Safeguards

Both the Information Directive and the Children Directive stipulate that the information provided for in the respective directive must be given, orally or in writing, in simple and accessible language.[22] This does not necessarily refer to the interpretation or translation of those rights, but to non-technical language that can easily be understood by a layperson or someone who cannot understand the content or meaning of the information (eg, because of their youth or their mental or physical condition).[23] This is in line with the international recommendation that professionals working with children should be trained in communication skills and in using child-friendly language.[24]

The Children Directive also provides for further complementary safeguards to account for the specific needs and vulnerabilities of children.[25] First, the juvenile suspect or defendant should be informed about the general aspects of the conduct of the proceedings.[26] Those aspects consist of a brief explanation about the role of the authorities involved and the subsequent procedural steps in the proceedings, and only insofar as this is possible in the light of the interest of the criminal proceedings.[27] That limitation is intended to avoid holding up the procedure too much and anticipating situations that may not necessarily occur.[28]

In addition, suspects or defendants who are arrested or detained are generally provided promptly with a written letter of rights.[29] Where minors are concerned, this letter must include a reference to, and clear information on, the rights included in the Children Directive.[30] Otherwise, no attention has been paid to how information should be given to juvenile suspects and defendants.[31]

---

21 *Projet de loi complétant la transposition de la Directive 2010/64/UE relative au droit à l'interprétation et à la traduction dans le cadre des procédures pénales et de la Directive 2012/29/UE établissant des normes minimales concernant les droits, le soutien et la protection des victimes de la criminalité et remplaçant la décision-cadre 2001/220/JAI du Conseil, Doc.Parl. Chambre* 2015–16, nr 54–2029/001, 31.

22 Information Directive, Article 3(2); Children Directive, Article 4(2).

23 Information Directive, recital 26 and 38.

24 Guidelines of the Committee of Ministers of the Council of Europe on Child-Friendly Justice (2010) 23 and 65.

25 Children Directive, recital 18.

26 Children Directive, Article 4(1).

27 Children Directive, recital 19.

28 Steven Cras, 'The Directive on Procedural Safeguards for Children Who Are Suspects or Accused Persons in Criminal Proceedings' (2016) *Eucrim* 109, 113.

29 Information Directive, Article 4 (1).

30 Children Directive, recital 21 and Article 4(3).

31 Dorris De Vocht and others, 'Procedural Safeguards for Juvenile Suspects in Interrogations: A Look at the Commission's Proposal in Light of an EU Comparative Study' (2014) 5 *New Journal of European Criminal Law* 480, 492.

Finally, the same information that the juvenile suspect or defendant has a right to receive must also be provided, as soon as possible, to the individual with parental responsibility for that minor – typically the parent.[32] The A2L Directive also requires that the parents be notified of the minor's deprivation of liberty and the reasons pertaining thereto. If member states temporarily derogate from that right, a child welfare or protection authority must be informed of the deprivation of liberty of the child without undue delay.[33] The notification of parents is recommended at an international level, as they play an important role in providing moral and psychological support and adequate guidance to the juvenile suspect or defendant.[34] Moreover, parents can be held civilly liable for the behaviour of the child, and thus bear financial responsibility for their child, so the information is also in their interests.[35] Parents can be replaced by another 'appropriate adult' if sharing information with the parents would be contrary to the child's best interests or physically impossible, or could substantially jeopardise the criminal proceedings.[36] As the notion of 'appropriate adult' also concerns a specific role in England and Wales, it is referred to as 'suitable adult' in the following discussion, in order to avoid confusion.

National Transposition

In Austria, the general Code of Criminal Procedure (*Strafprozessordnung* (StPO)) provides that legal information should be given in a language that the defendant understands and in an understandable manner, whereby special personal needs are taken into account.[37] In addition, the same instructions provided to the juvenile suspect or defendant must also be brought to the attention of the legal representative as soon as possible.[38] The provisions do not, however, refer to the need to secure a suitable adult when conflicts of interest arise with those who hold parental responsibility.

The Belgian legislation does not stipulate that rights should be notified in simple and accessible language. However, Article 48*bis*, § 1 of the Youth Protection Act does require that the holder(s) of parental responsibility be informed

---

32 Children Directive, recital 22, Articles 3(2) and 5(1); guardians and appointed legal representatives can also be holders of parental responsibility.
33 A2L Directive, recital 55 and Article 5(2) and (4).
34 Guidelines of the Committee of Ministers of the Council of Europe on Child-Friendly Justice (2010) 20–21; Committee on the Rights of the Child, 'General comment No. 24 on children's rights in the child justice system' (2019) para 57.
35 Commission, 'Commission Staff Working Document – Impact Assessment accompanying the document Proposal for a Directive of the European Parliament and of the Council on procedural safeguards for children suspected or accused in criminal proceedings' SWD (2013) 480 final, 21.
36 A2L Directive, Article 5(2); Children Directive, Article 5(2). A conflict of interest might, for instance, occur when the holder of parental responsibility is allegedly involved in the case themselves.
37 StPO, § 50 (2).
38 JGG, § 38 (1a).

when their child is deprived of their liberty. This provision existed before the Procedural Rights Roadmap was issued and is in line with the A2L Directive. It is, however, too restrictive in comparison with the general right to information under the Children Directive, as the Children Directive also requires the provision of information in other cases than the minor's deprivation of liberty.

In the Netherlands, Article 488aa (5) of the Sv stipulates that the notification of rights for juvenile suspects shall be made in simple and accessible language. In addition, police stations make documents available for children which set out the legal position of juvenile suspects and contain the information required by the Children Directive. However, this is not legally required and there are concerns about the accessibility of the police leaflet for minors.[39] The obligation to notify the parents or guardian is limited to cases where the child is deprived of liberty.[40] This is in line with the A2L Directive, but not with the Children Directive (which provides for a more general obligation). It is possible to replace the person with parental responsibility with a 'confidant' in case the notification of the former would be contrary to the child's interests or the person with parental responsibility is unknown or cannot be reached.[41]

Right to Access to a Lawyer and Assistance from a Lawyer

Child-Specific Safeguards

Article 3 of the A2L Directive provides the opportunity to have a lawyer and is a prerequisite for any guarantees concerning assistance from a lawyer, as laid down in Article 6 of the Children Directive.[42] The right to assistance from a lawyer thus applies only if the minor has a right of access to a lawyer according to Article 3 of the A2L Directive.[43] The provisions on access to and assistance from a lawyer are nevertheless almost identical, with the understanding that the scope of Article 3 of the A2L Directive includes both minors and adults, whereas Article 6 of the Children Directive covers only juvenile suspects and defendants. In addition, the Children Directive allows member states to derogate from the obligation to provide for legal assistance if the circumstances of the case justify that immediate legal assistance is not proportionate. That exception is known as the 'proportionality clause' and can be based on the seriousness of the alleged criminal offence, the

---

39 Defence for Children, *Procedural Rights of Juveniles Suspected or Accused in the European Union: Nationaal Onderzoeksrapport Nederland* (2016) 51.

40 Sv, Article 488b.

41 Sv, Article 488b(2).

42 Steven Cras, 'The Directive on Procedural Safeguards for Children who Are Suspects or Accused Persons in Criminal Proceedings', *Eucrim* iss 2016/2, (109) 113; Valsamis Mitsilegas, 'The European Union and the Rights of Individuals in Criminal Proceedings' in Darryl Brown, Jenia Iontcheva Turner and Bettina Weisser (eds), *The Oxford Handbook of Criminal Process* (Oxford University Press, 2019), (114), 126.

43 Children Directive, recital 26; Steven Cras, 'The Directive on Procedural Safeguards for Children Who Are Suspects or Accused Persons in Criminal Proceedings' (2016) *Eucrim* 109, 115.

complexity of the case and the possible measures.[44] The counterbalance, however, is that a minor should in any case receive legal assistance when they are brought before a judge in order to decide on detention.[45] The competent authorities should moreover postpone any interrogations or other investigative or evidence-gathering acts for a reasonable period when a minor's lawyer is not (yet) present.[46]

Another important aspect of both the A2L Directive and the Children Directive for juvenile suspects and defendants concerns the possibility to waive their right of access to and assistance from a lawyer. The A2L Directive explicitly provides for a waiver of rights in this respect, provided that two conditions are fulfilled;[47] and that the specific conditions – such as age and mental and physical condition – of the suspect or defendant are taken into account.[48]

In the Children Directive, by contrast, there is no specific waiver of the right to assistance from a lawyer, but it is not explicitly forbidden either. The European Commission's proposal of the Children Directive did contain a waiver prohibition for children as an additional safeguard,[49] but that was removed in the final version of the directive. However, there are indications that a juvenile suspect or defendant still cannot waive their right to legal assistance. First, there is no provision allowing a waiver similar to the A2L Directive.[50] As legal assistance is the starting point, including the obligation for member states to arrange a lawyer if the minor has not appointed one themselves,[51] one may expect for all exceptions to those principles to be expressly specified.[52] In addition, the Children Directive indicates that the right of access to a lawyer should be applied in accordance with the A2L Directive, unless it would make it impossible for the child to be assisted by a lawyer under the Children Directive.[53] As transposing the waiver possibility from the A2L Directive would result in the deprivation of legal assistance, it should not

---

44 Children Directive, Article 6(6). This exception is particularly relevant with regard to diversionary measures that are often present in youth justice systems to avoid formal criminal proceedings or a conviction in less serious cases; 122.

45 Children Directive, Article 6(6), second paragraph.

46 Children Directive, Article 6(7).

47 The waiver must be given voluntarily and unequivocally; and the suspect or accused person must have been provided, orally or in writing, with clear and sufficient information in simple and understandable language about the content of the right concerned and the possible consequences of waiving it.

48 A2L Directive, recitals 39 and 55 and Article 9(1) and (3).

49 Commission, 'Proposal for a Directive of the European Parliament and of the Council on procedural safeguards for children suspected or accused in criminal proceedings' COM (2013) 822 final, para 27.

50 Defence for Children, *Manual for EU Member States: How to Ensure the Rights of Children in Conflict with the Law? Focus on the Role of the Lawyer at the Different Stages of Juvenile Justice Proceedings* (2018) 65.

51 Children Directive, recital 25 and Article 6(7); Steven Cras, 'The Directive on Procedural Safeguards for Children Who Are Suspects or Accused Persons in Criminal Proceedings' (2016) *Eucrim* 109, 114.

52 Defence for Children, *Le Rôle de l'avocat Du Mineur Dans Les Procédures Protectionnelles et Pénales En Belgique* (2017) 19.

53 Children Directive, recital 26.

apply to the Children Directive.[54] Finally, the European Commission's recommendation on procedural safeguards for vulnerable suspects and defendants states that if a vulnerable person is unable to understand and follow the proceedings, the right to access to a lawyer should not be waived.[55] Nevertheless, an explicit prohibition of waiver by minors in the Children Directive would have been clearer.

National Transposition

In Austria, § 39 (1) of the JGG states that a juvenile suspect or defendant must be assisted by a lawyer for the entire duration of the criminal proceedings. A minor cannot waive legal assistance after being appointed a lawyer *ex officio* because they do not have a lawyer of their own.[56] However, this prohibition applies only in case of arrest or invitation for questioning, so that a juvenile suspect or defendant seems to be allowed to waive legal assistance in other situations.

According to Belgian law, a minor can never waive the right to be assisted by a lawyer during interrogation or when appearing before the judge.[57] A juvenile suspect or defendant therefore always has access to and assistance from a lawyer. A circular letter from the Public Prosecutor's Office nevertheless provides for two exceptions that allow the interrogation of the juvenile suspect to take place in the absence of a lawyer:

- if the lawyer does not show up at the agreed time or within two hours of being summoned; or
- if the lawyer, with the minor's consent, decides that assistance is not necessary.[58]

In the Netherlands, Article 489(2) of the Sv explicitly declares that the waiver possibilities that exist in criminal procedural law are inapplicable to juvenile

---

54 Contra: Stephanie Rap and Daniella Zlotnik, 'The Right to Legal and Other Appropriate Assistance for Child Suspects and Accused' (2018) 26 *European Journal of Crime, Criminal Law and Criminal Justice* 110, 121–22.

55 Commission, Recommendation on procedural safeguards for vulnerable persons suspected or accused in criminal proceedings (2013) OJ L 378/8, recital 11.

56 JGG, § 39 (3) *juncto;* StPO, § 59 (4).

57 Code of Criminal Procedure (BE), Article 47*bis,* § 3; Pre-trial Detention Act, Articles 2*bis,* § 3 and 24*bis*/1; Openbaar Ministerie, *Addendum 2 aan de omzendbrief COL 8/ 2011 betreffende de organisatie van het recht op toegang tot een advocaat – situatie van de minderjarigen en de personen die ervan verdacht worden voor de leeftijd van 18 jaar een als misdrijf omschreven feit gepleegd te hebben* 4–5 and 13; Dorris De Vocht and others, 'Procedural Safeguards for Juvenile Suspects in Interrogations: A Look at the Commission's Proposal in Light of an EU Comparative Study' (2014) 5 *New Journal of European Criminal Law* 480, 497–98; Bart De Smet, 'De Salduz bis-Wet. Een nieuwe waaier van procedurele rechten', *Rechtskundig Weekblad* 2016–17, 722; Johan Put, *Handboek Jeugdbeschermingsrecht* (die Keure 2021) nr 1064.

58 Openbaar Ministerie, *Addendum 2 aan de omzendbrief COL 8/2011 betreffende de organisatie van het recht op toegang tot een advocaat – situatie van de minderjarigen en de personen die ervan verdacht worden voor de leeftijd van 18 jaar een als misdrijf omschreven feit gepleegd te hebben* 6–7.

suspects.[59] In principle, therefore, minors can always consult a lawyer for half an hour before police hearings and receive legal assistance during questioning.[60] As in Belgium, the Netherlands nevertheless allows for the questioning to start without a lawyer if the lawyer does not arrive within two hours of notification[61] or in case of minor offences.[62] In addition, the right to legal assistance applies only to arrested suspects, so that suspects – including minors – are expected to arrange a lawyer themselves when they are simply invited for interrogation (rather than arrested).[63] However, the Amsterdam court recently ruled that, according to Article 6 of the Children Directive, legal aid should also be provided when the juvenile suspect is not arrested.[64]

Right to Be Present at Trial

Both the Presumption of Innocence Directive and the Children Directive grant suspects and defendants the right to be present at their trial;[65] but the Children Directive does provide some additional safeguards for juvenile suspects and defendants in this regard. It requires that member states take all necessary measures to enable children to participate effectively in the trial, including by giving them the opportunity to be heard and to express their views.[66] The child is furthermore granted the right to be accompanied by the holder of parental responsibility during the proceedings.[67] It is in principle the minor's parent(s) or guardian(s) who accompany them during court hearings, as well as during other stages of the proceedings, such as interrogation by the police.[68] In the latter case, the accompaniment should be in the minor's best interests and cannot prejudice the criminal proceedings. The same arrangements for the appointment of another suitable adult apply as under the right to information.

In Austria, there is no child-specific right to be heard; but § 6 of the StPO clearly stipulates that the defendant has the right to participate in the entire proceedings, the right to be present during the main hearing and the right to an appropriate fair hearing.[69] With regard to the accompaniment of the child at trial, there is a *lex specialis* found in § 42 (2) of the JGG, which allows the legal

---

59 Defence for Children, *The Role of the Youth Lawyer in the Juvenile Justice System in the Netherlands* (2017) 31.
60 Marije Jeltes, *De rechtspositie van aangehouden minderjarige verdachten in de eerste fase van het strafrechtelijk onderzoek* (Boom Strafblad, 2020) 2.6.
61 Sv, Article 28b(4).
62 Sv, Article 28ab.
63 Defence for Children, *The Role of the Youth Lawyer in the Juvenile Justice System in the Netherlands* (2017) 18.
64 Court Amsterdam (NL) 9 November 2021, nr 21/809, ECLI:NL:RBAMS:2021:6411.
65 Presumption of Innocence Directive, Article 8(1) and Children Directive, Article 16(1).
66 Children Directive, Article 16(1).
67 Children Directive, Article 15.
68 Children Directive, Article 15(1) and (4).
69 The right to be present at the main hearing is nevertheless laid down in JGG, § 32a (1) 7°.

representative and guardian of the juvenile defendant to attend the main hearing. No reference is made to the presence of another suitable adult in case of a conflict of interest with the parent(s).

The Juvenile Delinquency Decree of the Belgian Flemish Community legally enshrines the right to be heard at trial by the youth court (judge).[70] It is moreover included as a fundamental principle that the special needs of juvenile suspects and defendants require attentive listening, advice and assistance.[71] Parents(s) or guardian(s) are not automatically present at trial, but they are informed that they can be present if they wish and the youth court judge can summon them at any time.[72] As with Austria, there is no reference made to the presence of another suitable adult where there is a conflict of interest with the parent(s).

The Dutch Code of Criminal Procedure contains a general provision where the president of the court questions the defendant at trial,[73] but juvenile defendants are only specifically heard in two situations: where extensions are being made to pre-trial detention; and where the public prosecutor is planning to impose a community service exceeding 32 hours or a fine exceeding €200.[74] As far as the accompaniment of the juvenile defendant is concerned, the Children Directive was correctly transposed: Article 496 of the Sv even obliges the parent(s) or guardian (s) to be present at trial. A 'confidant' can be designated in the three situations mentioned in the Children Directive.[75]

Right to Legal Aid

Child-Specific Safeguards

The final Procedural Rights Directive concerns the right to legal aid, which is inevitably linked to the right to access to a lawyer. In order to benefit from the Legal Aid Directive, suspects and defendants should therefore be subject to the A2L Directive, but should also be in one of the following situations:

- deprived of liberty;
- mandatorily assisted by a lawyer in accordance with national or EU legislation; or
- attending an investigative or evidence-gathering act.[76]

Children fall within the second category, since the Children Directive, as a piece of EU legislation, requires juvenile suspects and defendants to be assisted by a lawyer.[77]

---

70 Juvenile Delinquency Decree (JDD), Article 15, § 1.
71 JDD, Article 3, § 3, 1°.
72 Youth Protection Act, Article 51 and JDD, Article 15, § 3.
73 Sv, Article 286.
74 Sv, Articles 491(2) and 493(4).
75 Sv, Article 496(2).
76 Legal Aid Directive, Article 2(1).
77 Steven Cras, 'The Directive on the Right to Legal Aid in Criminal and EAW Proceedings' (2017) *Eucrim* 35, 40.

The right to legal aid implies payment for the assistance of a lawyer by the member state when the suspect or defendant lacks sufficient resources and when the interests of justice so require.[78] Determining whether legal aid is to be granted can thus be based on a means test and/or a merits test, which gives member states a considerable margin of discretion.[79] The means test considers, for example, the financial and family situation, legal expenses and the national living standard; while the merits test is based on the seriousness of the offence, the complexity of the case and the severity of the sanction.

Although the Legal Aid Directive stresses that any particular needs of vulnerable suspects or defendants should be taken into account,[80] it does not provide more specific provisions concerning children involved in criminal proceedings. The explanatory memorandum calls for not making a request by vulnerable persons a substantive condition in order for them to be granted legal aid, but explicitly leaves the remainder of legal aid arrangements up to the member states.[81]

The Children Directive, by contrast, does have a provision concerning legal aid that is directed towards juvenile suspects and defendants. This provision contains an obligation for member states to provide legal aid where this is 'necessary to guarantee the effective exercise of the right to be assisted by a lawyer'.[82] However, the conditions are not further elaborated, as it was assumed at the time of the adoption of the Children Directive that all aspects of legal aid would be covered by a separate instrument.[83] The recitals of the Children Directives nevertheless refer to the EU Charter of Fundamental Rights and the European Convention on Human Rights (ECHR),[84] which both state that legal aid should be provided to those who lack sufficient resources insofar as such aid is necessary to ensure effective access to justice.[85] The A2L Directive similarly requires that national legislation concerning legal aid is in accordance with the charter and the ECHR.[86] A

---

78 Legal Aid Directive, Articles 3 and 4(1).
79 Steven Cras, 'The Directive on the Right to Legal Aid in Criminal and EAW Proceedings' (2017) *Eucrim* 35, 40, 40 and 42.
80 Legal Aid Directive, recital 18 and Article 9.
81 Legal Aid Directive, recital 18.
82 Children Directive, recital 25 and Article 18.
83 Commission, 'Proposal for a Directive of the European Parliament and of the Council on procedural safeguards for children suspected or accused in criminal proceedings' COM (2013) 822 final, para 63; Dorris De Vocht and others, 'Procedural Safeguards for Juvenile Suspects in Interrogations: A Look at the Commission's Proposal in Light of an EU Comparative Study' (2014) 5 *New Journal of European Criminal Law* 480, 499; Stephanie Rap and Daniella Zlotnik, 'The Right to Legal and Other Appropriate Assistance for Child Suspects and Accused' (2018) 26 *European Journal of Crime, Criminal Law and Criminal Justice* 110, 124.
84 Children Directive, recital 26.
85 ECHR, Article 6(3)(c); EU Charter of Fundamental Rights, Article 47. Those conditions are copied almost identically in Article 4 of the Legal Aid Directive, as the latter was influenced to a large extent by the charter and the ECHR; Steven Cras, 'The Directive on the Right to Legal Aid in Criminal and EAW Proceedings' (2017) *Eucrim* 35, 44.
86 A2L Directive, Article 11.

referral to the Legal Aid Directive was impossible as the latter was not yet adopted.

Altogether, no general obligatory legal aid for juvenile suspects and defendants can be derived from the reading of the three directives (the A2L Directive, the Legal Aid Directive and the Children Directive). Yet free legal assistance is a pre-condition for a juvenile suspect or defendant to be assisted independently and freely in criminal proceedings.[87] Minors are generally not yet self-sufficient, so legal aid is undoubtedly of greatest importance for that target group. As such, if their right to legal aid is to be restricted, at least one of the instruments should clarify the limitations that apply. While each instrument emphasises the importance of taking into account the specific needs of vulnerable people, they appear to avoid developing provisions that would ensure that specific needs are met.

National Transposition

In Austria, § 39 (2) of the JGG adopts the principle that a juvenile defendant shall bear the lawyer's fees, with two exceptions. First, minors can obtain legal aid under the same conditions as adults.[88] The defendant should more specifically be unable to bear the full costs of the defence – at least not without affecting their maintenance costs – and legal aid should be necessary in the light of an adequate defence.[89] Austria therefore combines a means and merits test, of which the passing leads to the *ex officio* appointment of a *pro bono* lawyer by the competent bar association. This should easily be the case in most proceedings involving juvenile suspects. The second exception to the payment of the lawyer's costs is where the payment would make the progress of the juvenile defendant more difficult. However, the juvenile suspect is not informed of this possibility of legal aid.[90]

In Belgium, juvenile suspects and defendants receive legal advice, assistance and representation entirely free of charge upon presentation of their identity card.[91] More specifically, minors are automatically designated a lawyer through the system of second-line assistance when they do not have (the money to afford) a lawyer of their own.[92] The means test that applies to adults is therefore not applicable to minors in Belgium.

---

87 Dorris De Vocht and others, 'Procedural Safeguards for Juvenile Suspects in Inter-rogations: A Look at the Commission's Proposal in Light of an EU Comparative Study' (2014) 5 *New Journal of European Criminal Law* 480, 500.

88 JGG, § 39(2) 1988 *juncto* Article 2(16) *Strafrechtliches EU-Anpassungsgesetz* 21 March 2020; Council of Europe, 'Evaluation of the Judicial Systems (2016–2018 Cycle): Austria' (2018) 10.

89 StPO, § 61(2); DLA Piper, 'The Role of the Youth Lawyer in the Juvenile Justice System in Austria' (2017) 26.

90 DLA Piper, 'The Role of the Youth Lawyer in the Juvenile Justice System in Austria' (2017) 26–27.

91 Royal Decree 8 December 2003, Article 1, § 4 laying down the conditions for full or partial free second-line legal assistance and legal aid; Eric Van Der Mussele, 'Jeug-dadvocatuur' in Orde van Vlaamse Balies, *Handboek voor de advocaat-stagiair 2014–2015: Jeugdrecht*, Wolters Kluwer, 2014, (151) 196.

92 Youth Protection Act, Article 54*bis*; Judicial Code, Articles 508/1 ff.

In the Netherlands, there is also a mandatory assignment of legal counsel free of charge to juvenile suspects and defendants where they have not appointed their own lawyer.[93] The right to legal aid applies throughout the entire proceedings, but only from the moment that a juvenile suspect is arrested or officially prosecuted, or if the public prosecutor wants to impose a diversion measure where the duration or amount reaches a certain threshold.[94] As a consequence, juvenile suspects are obliged to pay the lawyer's honorary themselves when they are simply invited for interrogation (rather than arrested for these purposes), or when the diversion measure at prosecutor level does not exceed 20 hours or €115.[95] The Netherlands therefore has a merits test approach to legal aid for minors.

Comparative Remarks

As far as the right to interpretation and translation is concerned, no additional safeguards for juvenile suspects and defendants could be identified in the Procedural Rights Directives or in national legislation. However, the lack of such additional safeguards in relation to the right of interpretation and translation is somewhat compensated by the requirement in the Information Directive and the Children Directive to share information in simple and accessible language. This requirement is generally transposed by member states, although it typically concerns a general provision that also applies to adults. National legislatures do not tend to introduce more detailed rules on how to accommodate the needs of vulnerable suspects and defendants, but include a reference to those needs at best. This is in line with the FRA's findings and the European Commission report on the implementation of the Information Directive.[96] Best practices such as using letters of rights that are specifically adapted for children are nevertheless strongly welcomed.[97] With regard to the notification of rights to the parent(s) or guardian (s), none of the analysed countries have fully transposed that obligation of the Children Directive: in the Netherlands, it is limited according to the situations in which it is required; while in Austria and Belgium, it is possible to assign another 'suitable adult' where necessary. As far as the right to legal assistance is concerned, all three analysed member states revisited their legislation after the introduction of

---

93 Sv, Article 489(1); JAC Bartels, *Jeugdstrafrecht* (Kluwer 2011) 189.
94 Sv, Articles 489(1) and 491(1).
95 Defence for Children, *The Role of the Youth Lawyer in the Juvenile Justice System in the Netherlands* (2017) 18.
96 Commission, *Report on the implementation of Directive 2012/13/EU of the European Parliament and of the Council of 22 May 2012 on the right to information in criminal proceedings* COM (2018) 858 final; European Union Agency for Fundamental Rights, *Rights of Suspected and Accused Persons across the EU: Translation, Interpretation and Information* (2016) 100.
97 Commission, *Report on the implementation of Directive 2012/13/EU of the European Parliament and of the Council of 22 May 2012 on the right to information in criminal proceedings* COM (2018) 858 final; European Union Agency for Fundamental Rights, *Rights of Suspected and Accused Persons across the EU: Translation, Interpretation and Information* (2016) 100.

the Procedural Rights Roadmap. In addition, all three member states seem to be going further than the Children Directive, as they all prohibit juvenile suspects and defendants from waiving the assistance of a lawyer. While juvenile suspects and defendants should thus in principle always be assisted by a lawyer, Belgium and the Netherlands do make use of the proportionality clause of the Children Directive. They moreover attach a time limit to the right to legal assistance during questioning. Two hours after the lawyer has been summoned, questioning automatically takes place in Belgium regardless of whether the lawyer has arrived. In the Netherlands, it is the assistant of the public prosecutor who decides whether the interrogation will start without a lawyer. As the Children Directive allows such decisions to be taken only on a case-by-case basis,[98] the Netherlands seems to be more in line with the EU standard.

Furthermore, the right to be heard is often part of the general course of the proceedings and is not necessarily repeated towards proceedings involving a juvenile suspect or defendant, except in Belgium. The presence of the parent(s) or guardian(s) at trial, by contrast, is at least a possibility in all three member states. However, there is not always an alternative developed in case of a conflict of interest with those holders of parental responsibility, which is contrary to the EU standard.

Legal aid in principle automatically applies to juvenile suspects and defendants in Belgium and the Netherlands (save for two exceptions in the Netherlands). In Austria, the right to legal aid depends on a test including an assessment of the means of the minor in question and the necessity of free legal aid in respect of their defence. However, those conditions appear to be rather easily fulfilled in relation to a minor, so it may be concluded that in all three analysed member states, the threshold to obtain legal aid is lower for children when compared with adults.

Conclusion

This chapter assessed the impact of the instruments emanating from the Procedural Rights Roadmap in general, and of the Children Directive in particular, on juvenile suspects and defendants. Two aspects were examined: the presence of child-specific safeguards in the Children Directive compared with the rights in the five other Procedural Rights Directives, in addition to their transposition in Austria, Belgium and the Netherlands. The analysis demonstrates that the full potential of the Children Directive in particular, and the Procedural Rights Directives more generally, has not always been achieved in terms of content and national implementation.

Whereas the Children Directive elaborates the rights to information, legal assistance and presence at trial for minors, it does not provide for additional safeguards regarding the rights to interpretation, translation and legal aid. For those rights, better coordination between the instruments would have been appropriate,

---

98 Children Directive, Article 6(8), final paragraph.

and would have made the references to children's rights and special needs in the Procedural Rights Directives more than merely symbolic. In addition, some matters deserve greater clarification in the Children Directive, such as the way in which information is communicated to minors; whether minors are forbidden to waive their right to legal assistance; and the conditions which apply to grant legal aid to minors.

The transposition analysis of the procedural safeguards also led to some interesting findings. National implementation was revealed to be deficient with regard to the notification of rights to the holder(s) of parental responsibility and the right to be heard. Although these practices are also international recommendations with which the analysed member states should have already been compliant, non-compliance with EU legislation triggers the monitoring mechanism at the EU level and urges member states to take responsibility. Concerning other procedural rights, the national legislation applicable to juvenile suspects and defendants has been effectively amended in accordance with the Procedural Rights Roadmaps. Examples include the notification of rights to the minor, the right to legal assistance and the right to be accompanied by the holder of parental responsibility. Finally, at some points where the Procedural Rights Directives fell short, the national legislation already provided a higher level of protection for juvenile suspects and defendants, such as a prohibition on waiving legal assistance and a lower threshold to be granted legal aid. These examples illustrate that the Procedural Rights Directives have established common *minimum* standards that sometimes prioritise national concerns over the protection of the juvenile suspect or defendant. This is confirmed by the scope of the Children Directive, which applies only to youth justice proceedings that are nationally labelled as 'criminal'. A juvenile suspect or defendant should nevertheless receive an equivalent level of protection in all cases in which they are exposed to some form of punishment, irrespective of whether the formal nature of the proceedings is criminal or educative and/or protective.

3 Assessing Vulnerability Prior to and During Police Questioning

Responsibilities and Training in Belgium and the Netherlands

Lore Mergaerts

Introduction

A significant number of suspects questioned by the police can be considered vulnerable.[1] Their vulnerability may stem from a variety of individual factors (eg, juvenility or mental disorders) and situational factors (eg, detention in custody or police and judicial treatment during questioning).[2] Depending on the perspective taken, the vulnerability of suspects is interpreted either narrowly – focusing only on the individual factors – or rather broadly, also taking into account situational factors.[3]

1 See, for instance, Laura Farrugia, 'Identifying Vulnerability in Police Custody: Making Sense of Information Provided to Custody Officers (2021) *Journal of Forensic Legal Medicine*; Gisli H Gudjonsson, Isabel CH Clare, Sue Rutter and John Pearse, *Persons at Risk During Interviews in Police Custody: The Identification of Vulnerabilities. Royal Commission on Criminal Justice* (HMSO, 1993) 27; Victoria Herrington and Karl Roberts, 'Addressing Psychological Vulnerability in the Police Suspect Interview' (2012) *Policing* 177; Richard H Lamb, Linda E Weinberger and Bruce H Gross, 'Mentally Ill Persons in the Criminal Justice System: Some Perspectives' (2004) *Psychiatry Quarterly* 107; Chiara Samele, Iain McKinnon, Penelope Brown, Samir Srivastana, Aleksandra Arnold, Nicholas Hallett and Andrew Forrester, 'The Prevalence of Mental Illness and Unmet Needs of Police Custody Detainees' (2021) *Criminal Behaviour and Mental Health* 1.
2 Compare Recommendation of the Commission on Procedural Safeguards for Vulnerable Persons Suspected or Accused in Criminal Proceedings [2013] OJ C 378/8, recital 1 and Gisli Gudjonsson, 'The Science-Based Pathways to Understanding False Confessions and Wrongful Convictions' (2021) *Frontiers in Psychology*; Saul Kassin and Gisli Gudjonsson, 'The Psychology of Confessions. A Review of the Literature and Issues' (2004) *Psychological Science in the Public Interest* 33; Saul Kassin, Steven A Drizin, Thomas Grisso, Gisli H Gudjonsson, Richard A Leo and Allison D Redlich, 'Police-Induced Confessions: Risk Factors and Recommendations' (2010) *Law and Human Behavior* 3.
3 See the introduction of this collection. See also Lore Mergaerts, Dirk Van Daele and Geert Vervaeke, 'Challenges in Defining and Identifying a Suspect's Vulnerability in Criminal Proceedings: What's in a Name and Who's to Blame?' in Penny Cooper and Linda Hunting (eds), *Access to Justice for Vulnerable People* (Wildy, Simmonds and Hill Publishing 2018).

DOI: 10.4324/9781003205166-5

Unfortunately, vulnerability is often not recognised in a timely manner because the identification of vulnerability is challenging and insufficient in practice.[4] Consequently, vulnerable suspects often do not receive the necessary and appropriate support that they require. The adequate implementation of special provisions to address vulnerability, however, requires that such vulnerability be identified early on.

In this regard, the European Commission has emphasised the need for a prompt identification of vulnerability. The Recommendation of 27 November 2013 on procedural safeguards for vulnerable suspects and accused persons in criminal proceedings provides that member states should ensure that the police and judicial authorities have recourse to an independent expert to identify vulnerability and to determine the degree of their vulnerability and their specific needs.[5] In addition, the recommendation stresses that police officers, law enforcement and judicial authorities dealing with vulnerable people should receive specific training.[6] Member states, however, appear to differ with regard to the implementation of these provisions, the responsibilities for identifying and addressing vulnerability, and the training provided for the authorities involved.[7]

Against this background, this chapter discusses and compares Belgium and the Netherlands. The rationale for comparing the two jurisdictions can be substantiated as follows. First, Belgium and the Netherlands are neighbouring countries with comparable criminal justice systems. Both jurisdictions are predominantly inquisitorial, but with some adversarial characteristics.[8] Second, both jurisdictions have undergone extensive legislative changes with regard to police questioning following the European Court of Human Rights (ECtHR) case law and EU Directive 2013/28/EU on access to a lawyer prior to and during police questioning. As a result of these

---

4 See, for instance, Roxanna Dehaghani, *Vulnerability in Police Custody. Police Decision-Making and the Appropriate Adult Safeguard* (Routledge 2019) 107–16; Koen Geijsen, *Persons at Risk During Interrogations in Police Custody. Different Perspectives on Vulnerable Suspects* (Ipskamp Printing 2018); Fair Trials, *Defence Rights in the EU* (Fair Trials International 2012) 25; Iain McKinnon and Don Grubin, 'Health Screening in Police Custody' (2010) *Journal of Forensic and Legal Medicine* 209. See also Council of Bars and Law Societies of Europe, *Commission Recommendation on Procedural Safeguards for Vulnerable Persons Suspected or Accused in Criminal Proceedings* (Brussels 2014) 1–2.

5 Recommendation of the Commission on Procedural Safeguards for Vulnerable Persons Suspected or Accused in Criminal Proceedings [2013] OJ C 378/8, Article 4. See also Miet Vanderhallen and Kasia Uzieblo, Chapter 4 of this collection, for such an expert witness perspective.

6 Recommendation of the Commission on Procedural Safeguards for Vulnerable Persons Suspected or Accused in Criminal Proceedings [2013] OJ C 378/8, Article 17.

7 Lore Mergaerts, 'European Safeguards for Vulnerable Suspects and Defendants: Good Intentions, But with Limited Effect in National Proceedings' (*Defending Vulnerability Blog*, 30 September 2020). Available at: https://defendingvulnerability.wordpress.com/2020/09/30/european-safeguards-for-vulnerable-suspects-and-defendants-good-intentions-but-with-limited-effect-in-national-proceedings/ (accessed 9 March 2022).

8 Chrisje Brants, 'Wrongful Convictions and Inquisitorial Process: The Case of the Netherlands' (2011) *University of Cincinnati Law Review* 1069; Raf Verstraeten, *Handboek Strafvordering* (Maklu 2012).

developments, greater attention has been paid to vulnerability.[9] Whereas the ECtHR explicitly stressed the importance of access to a lawyer prior to and during police questioning to address vulnerability, EU Directive 2013/48/EU requires that the special needs of vulnerable suspects be taken into account when transposing the directive.[10] The legislative changes made in Belgium and the Netherlands to comply with this European framework imply the introduction of the right of access to a lawyer prior to and during police questioning in general, and the inability to waive this right for vulnerable suspects in particular.[11] However, despite the common European legal framework, the similar impetus to address vulnerability prior to and during police questioning and the comparable legal systems, the approach taken to define, identify and address vulnerability nevertheless differs in Belgium and the Netherlands.

Third, the influence of legal psychological research on law enforcement practice appears greater in the Netherlands than in Belgium.[12] One probable explanation for this varied impact stems from the fact that reforms often arise in light of miscarriages of justice, and that official recognition of these cases varies greatly between the two jurisdictions. This is largely because in Belgium, despite the existence of a procedure to review court decisions, it is criticised and little used, due to issues with its accessibility.[13] The result is that in Belgium, there are no documented or officially recognised miscarriage of justice cases from which to learn and thus improve practices concerning vulnerable suspects.[14] This is unfortunate given that in Belgium,

---

9 See the introduction of this collection.

10 See *Salduz v Turkey* App no 36391/02 (ECtHR 27 November 2008) and subsequent case law; Directive 2013/48/EU of the European Parliament and of the Council on the Right of Access to a Lawyer in Criminal Proceedings and in European Arrest Warrant Proceedings and on the Right to have a Third Party Informed upon Deprivation of Liberty and to Communicate with Third Persons and with Consular Authorities while Deprived of Liberty [2013] OJ L 294/1, Article 13.

11 *Infra*, 2.

12 Marieke Dubelaar, 'De Rechtspsychologie en het Strafrecht' in Peter J Van Koppen, Jan W De Keijser, Robert Horselenberg and Marko Jelicic (eds), *Routes van het Recht. Over de Rechtspsychologie* (Boom juridisch 2017); Robert Horselenberg, Jan W De Keijser, Marko Jelicic and Peter J Van Koppen, 'Over de Rechtspsychologie' in Peter J Van Koppen, Jan W De Keijser, Robert Horselenberg and Marko Jelicic (eds), *Routes van het Recht. Over de Rechtspsychologie* (Boom juridisch 2017) 25, 30; Ricardo Nieuwkamp and Lore Mergaerts, 'Psychologie en Recht: een Geslaagd Huwelijk? Over de Moeizame Doorwerking van de Rechtspsychologie in de Belgische Strafprocedure' in Robert Horselenberg, Vere van Koppen and Jan De Keijser (eds), *Bakens in de Rechtspsychologie. Liber Amicorum voor Peter Van Koppen* (Boom criminologie 2021).

13 Cyrille Fijnaut and Katrien Verhesschen, 'Minder Juristen, Meer Andere Deskundigen bij de Herziening van de Herziening in Nederland en België?' (2018) *Expertise & Recht* 268; Philip Traest and Jan Roelandt, 'De Herziening van de Herziening Anno 2019' (2019) *Nullum Crimen* 481; Katrien Verhesschen and Cyrille Fijnaut, 'Chosen Blindness or a Revelation of the Truth? A New Procedure for Revision in Belgium' (2021) *Erasmus Law Review* 13.

14 Peter J Van Koppen and Robert Horselenberg, 'Waarom er in België en Nederland Geen Rechterlijke Dwalingen Gebeuren' (2018) *Expertise & Recht* 276. As to the

statements provided by suspects during police questioning play a central role in legal decision making on guilt or innocence. In this regard, vulnerability can be problematic – especially given that inaccurate or even false statements provided by vulnerable suspects are one of the best-known factors in miscarriage of justice cases.[15]

In light of the foregoing, the remainder of this chapter provides a brief overview of the legal provisions addressing vulnerability in Belgian and Dutch law, focusing on the definition of 'vulnerability', the responsibilities for identifying vulnerability and the training provided on dealing with vulnerability in both jurisdictions. The chapter concludes with a critical comparison of the approaches taken in both jurisdictions, and suggestions on how to bridge the remaining gaps in the identification and protection of vulnerable suspects.

How Vulnerability is Addressed in Law

Belgium

Belgian law provides no definition of 'vulnerability'.[16] The Belgian Code of Criminal Procedure merely states that the language used by the police to inform a person about their rights should be adapted to the person's 'age or potential vulnerability which hampers their ability to understand these rights'.[17] Furthermore, the assistance of an interpreter is required for persons who are 'vulnerable' because of language barriers or a speech or hearing disability.[18] These provisions apply to all individuals questioned by the police, including victims, witnesses and suspects.

In relation to suspects, a Circular of the Board of Procurators General[19] provides further (limited) guidance, stipulating that the police should also apply the regulations for minors when interviewing adult suspects who are 'weak or vulnerable, for example because of a mental weakness'.[20] This implies that vulnerable

---

Netherlands, see Johannes A Blaauw, *De Puttense Moordzaak. De Volledige Geschiedenis van Nederlands Grootste Gerechtelijke Dwaling* (De Fontein 2009); Posthumus, *Evaluatieonderzoek in de Schiedammer Parkmoord* (2005); Peter J Van Koppen, *De Schiedammer Parkmoord: een Rechtspsychologische Reconstructie* (Ars Aequi 2003).

15 See, for instance, Saul Kassin, Steven A Drizin, Thomas Grisso, Gisli H Gudjonsson, Richard A Leo and Allison D Redlich, 'Police-Induced Confessions: Risk Factors and Recommendations' (2010) *Law and Human Behavior*.

16 For a more detailed analysis of the Belgian provisions, see Lore Mergaerts and Roxanna Dehaghani, 'Protecting Vulnerable Suspects in Police Investigations in Europe: Lessons Learned from England and Wales and Belgium' (2020) *New Journal of European Criminal Law* 313, 324–26. See also Lore Mergaerts, 'Defence Lawyers' Views on and Identification of Vulnerability in Criminal Proceedings' (2021) *International Journal of the Legal Profession* 1.

17 Belgian Code of Criminal Procedure, Article 47*bis*, § 6, 2.

18 Belgian Code of Criminal Procedure, Article 47*bis*, § 6, 4. See also Heidi Salaets et al, Chapter 8 of this collection, on the problem of language barriers and the right to an interpreter.

19 This board consists of representatives from the public prosecutorial agency and may take binding decisions – laid out in circulars – to secure a coherent criminal policy.

20 Circular no COL 8/2011, 18 October 2018, 67 and 133–34.

adult suspects, just like minors, cannot waive their right of access to a lawyer prior to and during police questioning.[21]

The Netherlands

The Dutch Code of Criminal Procedure has long included provisions aimed at protecting mentally ill suspects and defendants, albeit without explicitly referring to the concept of vulnerability.[22] These provisions address suspects and defendants with a severe mental illness that hampers their ability to participate in the proceedings (ie, those who lack capacity). As such, their scope can be assumed to be narrower than specific provisions that address individual and/situational factors which may hinder a suspect from participating in the proceedings. It also appears that these provisions are rarely used in practice.[23] Therefore, this chapter does not address these provisions, but concentrates on the provisions that explicitly reference vulnerability.

Following the implementation of EU Directive 2013/48/EU on access to a lawyer, Article 28b of the Dutch Code of Criminal Procedure requires that vulnerable suspects be given access to a lawyer prior to police questioning.[24] However, this provision does not contain a definition of 'vulnerability'. Rather, the exploratory memorandum indicates that the legislature considered juvenile suspects and suspects with a mental disorder or an intellectual disability as vulnerable for the purposes of this provision.[25] Further, prior to adoption, there were proposals to amend Article 28b to include the following definition of 'vulnerability:' 'A vulnerable suspect refers to a juvenile suspect, an intellectually disabled suspect or a suspect deprived of his liberty who is not capable of understanding the consequences of his decisions due to his mental state'.[26] This amendment was not retained, resulting in no definition being included in the Dutch Code of Criminal Procedure.[27]

---

21 Belgian Code of Criminal Procedure, Article 47*bis*; Belgian Pretrial Detention Act, Article 2*bis*.

22 See in particular Dutch Code of Criminal Procedure, Articles 16 and 509a. See also Eline Gremmen, *De Kwetsbare Psychisch Gestoorde Verdachte in het Strafproces. Regelgeving, Praktijk en Europese Standaarden* (Wolf Legal Publishers 2018) 41.

23 Eline Gremmen, *De Kwetsbare Psychisch Gestoorde Verdachte in het Strafproces. Regelgeving, Praktijk en Europese Standaarden* (Wolf Legal Publishers 2018) 152; Michiel Van der Wolf, 'Waarborgen voor Kwetsbare, Psychisch Gestoorde Verdachten: Europa Vraagt om Versterking van de Rechtspositie' in Pieter A.M. Verrest and Sanne Struijk (eds), *De Invloed van de Europese Unie op het Strafrecht* (Boom juridisch 2016) 73, 80.

24 Dutch Code of Criminal Procedure, Article 28b, para 1 (amended by the Act of 17 November 2016, amendment into force since 1 March 2017).

25 *Kamerstukken* II 2014/15, 34157, no 3, 40.

26 *Kamerstukken* II 2014/15, 34157, no 10, 1.

27 See also Dorris De Vocht and Miet Vanderhallen, 'Kwetsbaar Maar Wel Bekwaam? De Kwetsbare Verdachte Vanuit het Perspectief van de Nederlandse Zittingsrechter' in Marc Bockstaele, Fréderic Declercq, Robin Kranendonk, Koen Geijsen and Auke Van Dijk (eds), *Verhoor van Kwetsbare Volwassenen* (Gompel & Svacina 2021) 93, 97.

However, until recently, the *Aanwijzing auditief en audiovisueel verhoor* – a binding instrument for the Dutch Public Prosecution Service addressing the audio and visual recording of police questioning – did contain a definition of 'vulnerability', referring to juveniles under the age of 16 and individuals with a (manifest) [28] intellectual disability or functional cognitive disorder. In this regard, it is important to point out that police interviews are not automatically audio recorded if the suspect is not vulnerable. The audio and/or visual recording of police questioning is also not enshrined in the Dutch Code of Criminal Procedure; but according to the *Aanwijzing*, all police interviews with vulnerable suspects should be audio and visually recorded. The assistant public prosecutor[29] can exercise discretion by audio or visually recording the police interview in other cases.[30]

Yet, there have been recent changes in the instructions provided for the Dutch police and prosecution to address vulnerability. In 2021, the *Aanwijzing* was replaced by an '*Instructie*', which is non-binding on third parties. Consequently, the audio and visual recording of police interviews with vulnerable suspects is no longer enforceable. This instruction also no longer contains a definition of 'vulnerability', but only refers to a 'manifest vulnerability during police questioning'. Moreover, it explicitly states that it is up to the legislature to provide a definition of 'vulnerability'.[31] The *Instructie*, however, stresses that all minors under the age of 18 are considered 'manifestly vulnerable during police questioning'.[32] In addition, if there is any doubt about whether the suspect is vulnerable, the suspect should be treated as such, requiring the police interview to be audio and visually recorded. Finally, the *Instructie* refers to guidance provided to assess vulnerability in practice, consisting of a non-exhaustive list of indicators of manifest vulnerability during police questioning. However, the *Instructie* fails to refer to or contain a reference on this list, and thus the indicators of vulnerability remain unclear.[33]

This recent shift towards what can be considered an open definition of 'vulnerability' instead of a categorical approach needs further consideration. Such an open approach is beneficial because it no longer only addresses the suspect's individual characteristics and circumstances, but also acknowledges situational factors (eg, being stressed, suffering from being held in custody, fatigue and the police questioning style). However, the open approach can be problematic because it implies

---

28 'Manifest' here refers to a clear/apparent/obvious disability or disorder.

29 In Dutch, '*Hulpofficier van Justitie*', referring to the person authorised to assist the public prosecutor to investigate criminal offences.

30 This will depend upon who is being interviewed, the nature of the case and peculiarities during the police interview itself. What is to be understood by these peculiarities is not specified within the *Aanwijzing*. See *Aanwijzing Auditief en Audiovisueel Registreren van Verhoren van Aangevers, Getuigen en Verdachten* 2018.

31 *Memo Instructie Auditieve en Audiovisuele Registratie van Verhoren van Aangevers, Getuigen en Verdachten* 2021, 2.

32 *Memo Instructie Auditieve en Audiovisuele Registratie van Verhoren van Aangevers, Getuigen en Verdachten* 2021, 2.

33 *Memo Instructie Auditieve en Audiovisuele Registratie van verhoren van Aangevers, Getuigen en Verdachten* 2021, 3.

less practical guidance for police officers, which in turn may lead to greater unclarity and confusion. Providing clear categories of who may be considered vulnerable has the distinct advantage of a clearer demarcation of to whom special provisions do and do not apply. This is particularly important in the absence of further guidance in law or of training programmes.[34]

Responsibility for Identifying Vulnerability

Belgium

In Belgium, the primary responsibility for identifying and adequately addressing vulnerability rests with the police. This is not explicitly enshrined in law, but their responsibility can be delineated from the Belgian provisions on vulnerability.[35] In addition, Flemish defence lawyers have increasing responsibilities for identifying vulnerability. In this regard, the Salduz Code of Conduct for defence lawyers, promulgated by the Flemish Bar Association,[36] stipulates that defence lawyers are expected to assess whether their client is physically and/or mentally capable of withstanding police questioning during the confidential consultation with their client. If a lawyer doubts their client's capabilities in this regard, they must first report this to the police officers involved and, if necessary, insist on medical assistance to be called in/or and the postponement of the police interview.[37] As such, identifying vulnerability is a shared responsibility between the police and the defence lawyer.

The Netherlands

In the Netherlands, the primary responsibility for identifying and addressing vulnerability also rests with the police. Since 1 March 2017, when the legislative changes on access to a lawyer prior to and during police questioning came into force, the police have assessed whether a suspect can be considered vulnerable.[38] However, it is the assistant public prosecutor who shoulders ultimate responsibility for identifying and addressing vulnerability. When the assistant prosecutor reviews

---

34 *Infra*, 4.
35 *Supra*, 2.1.
36 Belgium has two jurisdictions in respect of the organisation of the legal profession (one for the Flemish part of Belgium and one for the French part), which also applies to other Belgian agencies. Belgium actually contains three jurisdictions, as it also has a German part. This chapter, however, only elaborates on the Flemish Bar Association to avoid too much complexity and because this chapter builds on research conducted in the Flemish part of Belgium (as the author is Flemish).
37 Flemish Bar Association, *Salduz Code of Conduct Revised Edition* (2017) 3.2; Lore Mergaerts and Roxanna Dehaghani, 'Protecting Vulnerable Suspects in Police Investigations in Europe: Lessons Learned from England and Wales and Belgium' (2020) *New Journal of European Criminal Law* 313, 329.
38 Sam Van den Akker and Alrik De Haas, 'Oog voor de "Kwetsbare Verdachte" In en Rondom het Verhoor' (2021) *Fiscaal Up to Date* 27.

the continuation of a vulnerable suspect's detention in custody, they must also take the necessary steps to arrange the assistance of a defence lawyer.[39] In addition, the assistant public prosecutor is responsible for assessing any 'manifest vulnerability' requiring the police questioning to be audio and/or visually recorded.[40] In practice, however, contact between the suspect and the assistant public prosecutor will be rather brief, rendering it difficult to assess any potential vulnerability.[41] Consequently, the assistant public prosecutor must mainly rely on information provided by the police officers involved, which underlines their primary role once again.

Furthermore, Dutch defence lawyers assisting a client during police questioning are also authorised to draw the police officer's attention to the suspect's physical or mental condition whenever their condition would render the continuation of the police interview unfair.[42]

Training Provided for Practitioners to Identify and Address Vulnerability

Belgium

There is minimal guidance in Belgium to identify and address vulnerability.[43] Vulnerability receives little attention in training provided for the police and judicial authorities. This lack of training and (clear) guidance is a pressing issue, especially for police officers conducting interviews with suspects. There is no universal, national training programme applicable to all Belgian police academies[44] because training is mainly organised on a regional level. Consequently, training provided to practitioners differs between the police academies across Belgium, resulting in significant variation and fragmentation across police forces.[45]

---

39 Dutch Code of Criminal Procedure, Article 28b, para 1.
40 *Memo Instructie Auditieve en Audiovisuele Registratie van Verhoren van Aangevers, Getuigen en Verdachten* 2021, 2–3.
41 See also Jaantje Kramer, 'Geef Elke Kwetsbare Verdachte een Advocaat bij het Politieverhoor. Het Recht op Rechtsbijstand vanuit het Perspectief van de Kwetsbare Verdachte' (2022) 3(2) *Boom Strafblad* 66, 68–71.
42 *Besluit Inrichting en Orde Politieverhoor* 2017, Article 6 c.
43 See also Michaël Meysman, 'Quo Vadis with Vulnerable Defendants in the EU?' (2014) 4(2) *European Criminal Law Review* 179, 188–190; Lore Mergaerts and Roxanna Dehaghani, 'Protecting Vulnerable Suspects in Police Investigations in Europe: Lessons Learned from England and Wales and Belgium' (2020) *New Journal of European Criminal Law* 313, 329.
44 Each region (province) in Belgium has its own police academy; see https://www.jobpol.be/bij-de-politie-staan-mensen-centraal (accessed 28 April 2022).
45 For a profound analysis of suspect interview training in Belgium, see Miet Vanderhallen, Alexandra De Jong and Geert Vervaeke, 'Interviewing Suspects in Belgium' in Dave Walsh, Gavin E Oxburgh, Allison D Redlich and Trond Myklebust (eds), *International Developments and Practices in Investigative Interviewing and Interrogation. Volume 2: Suspects* (Routledge 2016).

In the past 10 years, training on police questioning has increasingly emphasised the legal framework with regard to access to a lawyer prior to and during police questioning. This has occurred due to fundamental changes to the legal regulation of police questioning following the case law of the ECtHR on access to a lawyer during the pre-trial investigation and EU Directive 2013/48/EU on the right of access to a lawyer in criminal proceedings.[46] However, current training does not specifically address the identification of vulnerability prior to and during police questioning. Where any such attention is given, it is restricted to providing basic knowledge of psychological factors rendering a suspect vulnerable and the legal provisions to be considered. Because the training does not cover indicators to aid the identification of vulnerability, practitioners struggle to adequately address vulnerability in practice.

External initiatives by private organisations have filled some of the gaps in formal training programmes. Examples include a recently developed police questioning training programme organised by the Belgian Centre for Policing and Security[47] – a non-profit organisation that fulfils a bridging function between academia, the police and the private security sector by organising conferences, courses and training programmes – and a webinar on adult vulnerable individuals organised by a Flemish publisher.[48] It should be noted, however, that such external initiatives reach only a limited number of police officers, given that participation is voluntary and that existing external training programmes have limited capacity. In addition, such initiatives only address vulnerability very briefly and do not profoundly enhance practitioners' skills in identifying and responding to vulnerability.[49]

Vulnerability has also received increasing attention in Flemish defence lawyers' training following the successful implementation of the EU-funded SUPRALAT project in Belgium.[50] SUPRALAT consists of an e-learning module (including PowerPoint presentations and reading materials) and two practical sessions (including discussions, exercises and role play) adhering to a train-the-trainer

46 *Salduz v Turkey* App no 36391/02 (ECtHR 27 November 2008) and subsequent case law; Directive 2013/48/EU of the European Parliament and of the Council on the Right of Access to a Lawyer in Criminal Proceedings and in European Arrest Warrant Proceedings and on the Right to Have a Third Party Informed upon Deprivation of Liberty and to Communicate with Third Persons and with Consular Authorities while Deprived of Liberty [2013] OJ L 294/1.
47 See https://www.policingandsecurity.be/en/ (accessed 10 March 2022).
48 Gompel & Svacina. Available at: http://ymlp.com/zg62oo (accessed 10 March 2022).
49 This information is based on personal conversations with trainers at the Belgian police academies to assess the attention given to suspect vulnerability.
50 SUPRALAT stands for 'Strengthening suspects' rights in pre-trial proceedings through practice-oriented training for lawyers'. For more information on this project, see http://www.salduzlawyer.eu/ (accessed 10 March 2022); but also Anna Pivaty, Miet Vanderhallen, Yvonne Daly and Vicky Conway, 'Contemporary Criminal Defence Practice: Importance of Active Involvement at the Investigative Stage and Related Training Requirements' (2020) *International Journal of the Legal Profession* 25.

approach, with the aim of improving the legal assistance provided in the context of police questioning. Since 2021, this training programme has been compulsory for defence lawyers seeking to enrol in the police station duty lawyer scheme of the Flemish Bar Association.[51] Although SUPRALAT serves a broader purpose – enhancing active assistance during police questioning – and is not specifically intended to train lawyers on vulnerability, it offers some guidance on assessment during the early stages of criminal proceedings. The programme contains elements relevant to identifying vulnerability, focusing on knowledge of the potential risk factors of false confessions and the inability to understand and exercise certain procedural rights (eg, the right to remain silent). The approach taken is thus one of a psychological perspective, focusing in particular on the suspect's individual characteristics, such as age (juvenility) and mental disorder, suggestibility and compliance.[52] In the near future, however, the training programme will be complemented by an additional practical session aimed at identifying vulnerability, using a recently developed tool intended to facilitate the identification of both individual and situational risk factors.[53]

The Netherlands

In the Netherlands, the Police Academy is legally accredited to provide training to all Dutch police officers.[54] However, limited attention is given to police questioning in basic compulsory training programmes[55] and most Dutch police detectives engaging in questioning have not yet received specialist training in the conduct of police interviews.[56]

---

51 *Uniform reglement verhoorbijstand in het kader van de permanentiedienst*, Article 1.
52 This information is based on participation in the programme, by both accessing the e-learning module and attending the practical sessions, and has also already been described in Lore Mergaerts, 'Defence Lawyers' Views on and Identification of Vulnerability in Criminal Proceedings' (2021) *International Journal of the Legal Profession* 1, 10–11.
53 It concerns a tool that has been developed as part of the PhD research of the author of this chapter. See Lore Mergaerts, *Kwetsbare Verdachten in de Strafprocedure. De Conceptualisering van Kwetsbaarheid en de Rol van de Advocaat bij de Vaststelling ervan tijdens het Vooronderzoek* (Boom Juridisch Antwerp 2021).
54 https://www.politieacademie.nl/en/Pages/ThePoliceAcademy.aspx (accessed 10 March 2022); https://www.politieacademie.nl/politieacademie (accessed 10 March 2022). In contrast to Belgium, the Netherlands has one central Police Academy (in one location, Apeldoorn).
55 For an overview of all courses, see https://www.politieacademie.nl/onderwijs/onderwijsaanbod/Pages/Default.aspx, accessed 10 March 2022. See also Martijn van Beek and Jos Hoekendijk, 'The Investigative Interviewing of Suspects in the Netherlands' in Dave Walsh, Gavin E Oxburgh, Allison D Redlich and Trond Myklebust (eds), *International Developments and Practices in Investigative Interviewing and Interrogation. Volume 2: Suspects* (Routledge 2016) 157, 157–59.
56 Koen Geijsen, Corine de Ruijter and Nicole Kop, 'Identifying Psychological Vulnerabilities: Studies on Police Suspects' Mental Health Issues and Police Officers' Views' (2018) *Cogent Psychology* 1, 3; Koen Geijsen, Corine de Ruijter and Henry Otgaar, 'Van Politieverhoorders naar Politie-Interviews' in Marc Bockstaele, Fréderic

Nonetheless, one of these specialist training programmes provided by the Dutch Police Academy is specifically aimed at interviewing vulnerable suspects. The programme aims to train police officers in preparing and conducting police interviews with vulnerable suspects, with a particular focus on interview techniques adapted to the specific vulnerability of the suspect. Furthermore, the programme addresses the legal provisions relevant to vulnerable suspects, but also draws attention to the characteristics and identification of vulnerability, 'such as an intellectual disability, functional cognitive disorder, attention deficit hyperactivity disorder and psychiatric disorders'.[57] Officers are also taught how to use information from relevant third parties (eg, healthcare professionals) when preparing and conducting interviews with vulnerable suspects. To enable detectives to apply this knowledge in practice, the programme also includes simulation exercises and a short internship (eg, in a psychiatric hospital or youth institution).[58]

It should be noted, however, that this programme concerns a specific follow-up course that can only be attended by experienced police detectives who already possess relevant specialist knowledge, skills and expertise about police questioning, obtained via other specialist training programmes provided by the Police Academy.[59] Consequently, not all officers engaging in questioning can attend. Preventing all officers involved in questioning from undertaking training in vulnerability is problematic, however, because specialist detectives are only called in once vulnerability has been identified. Therefore, all officers involved in the questioning process should have knowledge of vulnerability.

The Dutch Police Academy has overcome this problem, to some extent, by developing a questionnaire to screen for potential vulnerabilities prior to or during police questioning.[60] More specifically, the questions concern the person's living and employment status; weekly routine; education; physical condition; use of medication; memory; orientation in time, location and person; hobbies; financial management; and literacy and numeracy. While the name of the questionnaire – 'Indication of Vulnerability Questionnaire' – suggests that it includes indications

Declercq, Robin Kranendonk, Koen Geijsen and Auke Van Dijk (eds), *Verhoor van Kwetsbare Volwassenen* (Gompel & Svacina 2021) 35, 47.

57   https://www.politieacademie.nl/onderwijs/onderwijsaanbod/Pages/opleiding.aspx?code=4300913 (accessed 10 March 2022).

58   https://www.politieacademie.nl/onderwijs/onderwijsaanbod/Pages/opleiding.aspx?code=4300913 (accessed 10 March 2022); Martijn van Beek and Jos Hoekendijk, 'The Investigative Interviewing of Suspects in the Netherlands' in Dave Walsh, Gavin E Oxburgh, Allison D Redlich and Trond Myklebust (eds), *International Developments and Practices in Investigative Interviewing and Interrogation. Volume 2: Suspects* (Routledge 2016) 157, 159.

59   For the specific requirements to be admitted to this training programme, see https://www.politieacademie.nl/onderwijs/onderwijsaanbod/Pages/opleiding.aspx?code=4300913 (accessed 10 March 2022).

60   Nicole M Nierop and Paul Van den Eshof, *Het Horen van Kwetsbare Personen door de Politie. Onderzoeksrapport van de Werkgroep Verhoor Kwetsbare Personen* (Politie 2014) 13 and 53. The questionnaire can be used not only to screen for vulnerability, but for witnesses and victims as well.

of vulnerability in general, the questions exclusively address individual factors that may be indicative of an intellectual disability, mental disorder or functional cognitive disorder.[61]

Finally, vulnerability has received increased attention in the formal training programme provided by the Dutch Bar Association. The criminal law module, among other things, briefly addresses the (complex) interpretation of 'vulnerability' and the important role of the defence lawyer, including the need for a prompt identification.[62]

Comparative Remarks

While legal and practical changes have resulted in explicit references to vulnerability in the Belgian and Dutch Code of Criminal Procedure regulations on police questioning, the provisions enshrined in law differ. The provision in the Belgian Code of Criminal Procedure focuses on the need for adaptation of the information provided to vulnerable suspects regarding their legal rights and entitlements, while the Dutch Code of Criminal Procedure addresses the need for mandatory assistance for vulnerable suspects from the defence lawyer. As such, the emphasis placed differs between both jurisdictions; but it should be noted that a definition of 'vulnerability' is lacking in both Belgium and the Netherlands. Moreover, further guidance from the Public Prosecutor's Service on the definition and identification of vulnerability remains limited.

As for the responsibility for identifying vulnerability, it appears that the police have a primary role, although this is not explicitly enshrined in Belgian or Dutch law. It can, however, be considered a logical consequence of current practice: police officers are likely to be the first in touch with a potentially vulnerable suspect. Their responsibility to identify vulnerability – at least in the Netherlands – can also be delineated from the attention paid to vulnerability indicators in the training and checklist provided by the Dutch Police Academy. In contrast to the Belgian situation, the role and ultimate responsibility of the Dutch assistant public prosecutor in identifying and addressing vulnerability should be noted, as they are responsible for deciding on the need for the assistance of a defence lawyer and on the audio and visual recording of the police interview.

In both jurisdictions, however, the defence lawyer is increasingly important in identifying and responding to vulnerability following the expansion of access to a lawyer prior to and during police questioning. The defence lawyer has the important tasks of defending suspects and serving in their best interests, which become even more crucial for vulnerable suspects given that they require special care to understand their legal rights and improve their statements for the purpose of an

---

61 In Dutch, '*Vragenlijst indicatie kwetsbaarheid verdachte*' (Nicole M Nierop and Paul Van den Eshof, *Het Horen van Kwetsbare Personen door de Politie. Onderzoeksrapport van de Werkgroep Verhoor Kwetsbare Personen* (Politie 2014) 53.

62 Information obtained from the principal instructor of the criminal law module. For more general information on the training programme and its curriculum, see https://beroepsopleidingadvocaten.nl/ (accessed 14 March 2022).

effective defence. However, the defence role may be restricted because a suspect whose vulnerability has not been identified may have already waived their right of access to a lawyer, potentially due to their vulnerability or lack of understanding. Consequently, in reality, they may not be afforded this essential enhanced level of protection, while they should not be able to waive their right.

Moreover, in reality, Belgian police and defence lawyers may shift the responsibility onto each other; while the Dutch police might shift this responsibility onto the defence lawyer and the assistant public prosecutor and *vice versa*.[63] Their seemingly shared responsibility has the potential to facilitate the timely detection of vulnerability and the adequate implementation of special provisions; but this requires that all parties' responsibilities are well defined and made explicit, with ultimate responsibility resting with the police.[64]

To be able to adequately identify and address vulnerability, it is crucial that all parties involved possess the necessary knowledge and skills. In Belgium, to date, defence lawyers have been better equipped to deal with vulnerability than police officers. The attention given to vulnerability in the training programme for defence lawyers is also more advanced when compared with the training provided in the Netherlands. In contrast to Belgium, however, vulnerability does receive considerable attention in the specialist formal training provided by the Dutch Police Academy. While this training programme is laudable, it is regrettable that not all officers conducting police interviews are eligible to enrol. It is vital to teach and train all police officers in identifying vulnerability, as early identification is key to secure the attendance of a specialised police detective and thus afford protection to vulnerable suspects.

Conclusion

Vulnerability has received explicit attention in Belgium and the Netherlands following the case law of the ECtHR and EU Directive 2013/48/EU on access to a lawyer during the pre-trial stage of criminal proceedings. This European guidance has prompted changes to police questioning regulations and practices in both jurisdictions. However, it is evident from this chapter that clear legal provisions are required, accompanied by a clear, but not overly narrow, definition of 'vulnerability' incorporating both individual and situational factors. Further guidance on indicators of vulnerability and how it should be dealt with should be provided in training for all parties involved. Such training should not only advance participants' knowledge and awareness of vulnerability, but also prioritise acquiring the

---

63 See also Samantha Fairclough, 'Using Hawkins's Surround, Field and Frames Concepts to Understand the Complexities of Special Measures Decision Making in Crown Court Trials' (2018) *Journal of Law and Society* 457, 483.

64 See also Lore Mergaerts and Roxanna Dehaghani, 'Protecting Vulnerable Suspects in Police Investigations in Europe: Lessons Learned from England and Wales and Belgium' (2020) *New Journal of European Criminal Law* 313, 334. See also Lore Mergaerts, 'Defence Lawyers' Views on and Identification of Vulnerability in Criminal Proceedings' (2021) *International Journal of the Legal Profession* 1, 17.

necessary skills to identify and deal with vulnerability. It may even be worthwhile to organise joint training sessions with the police, lawyers and public prosecutors where attention is paid to the different roles and responsibilities of each. Such initiatives may reduce the risk of shifting responsibility and may contribute to further awareness raising.

4 The Identification of Psychological Vulnerabilities and Suspect Interviews

An Expert Witness Perspective

Kasia Uzieblo and Miet Vanderhallen

Introduction

June 2006: the dead body of a strangled man is found in a secluded place. The criminal investigation does not uncover any suspects. In 2007, the Belgian police distribute search warrant notices. In 2008, two years after the murder, the police finally arrest a suspect in the case following a father's report about his son being harassed and threatened. In total, three suspects are arrested: David,[1] a 23-year-old man, and two alleged troublemakers. In 2015, the court acquits the three defendants, despite David's repeated confessions. In his verdict, the judge emphasises the inappropriate pressure that might have led to David's confessions.

When this case was brought to trial, the defence requested our services as expert witnesses to analyse the case and assess the suspect's vulnerability and the veracity of the statements made in relation to his mental state. This chapter discusses David's case in order to raise awareness of the demanding task of expert witnesses in such cases and provide insights into the complex interplay of psychological vulnerabilities and the situational factors surrounding the police interview. To do so, we describe the working methods of expert witnesses and the challenges faced in the role. Using David's case, we illustrate the main steps and measures taken to diagnose vulnerability and to analyse the statements made by a vulnerable suspect. The criminal case is first explained in more detail; we then go on to explore the vulnerability of suspects in interviewing, illustrated through an assessment of the case.

The Case

In June 2006 the body of a man was found in a secluded place in Belgium. The victim had been strangled. A year later, the police distributed numerous search warrant notices in the region with detailed information on the crime. The local media reported frequently on the case, including on the *modus operandi* of the

---

1 The publication of the case study was approved by David's lawyers, David and his parents. In order to protect the anonymity of people involved, fictional names and dates were used, and several features of the crime were altered.

DOI: 10.4324/9781003205166-6

murder, without any leads being uncovered. In 2008, David's mother went to the local police station to address her concerns regarding the safety of her son. She was concerned that her son had been isolating himself after receiving threats from a group of acquaintances who had also threatened the family. The police suspected David's involvement in the murder based on his mother's story and arrested David and two others. David was placed in a cell with one of his co-suspects and the police installed a cell tap. Afterwards David was repeatedly interviewed about his possible involvement, during which he alternated between denials and (partial) confessions:[2]

- During the first police interview, which was videorecorded and conducted at night, David made incriminating statements. The interview lasted for nine hours and 53 minutes.
- The first interview with the investigating judge was not videorecorded and lasted for one hour and nine minutes. During this interview, David made incriminating statements about preparing and dumping the body.
- In the second police interview, which was not videorecorded and conducted in the evening, David denied the crime. The interview lasted for three hours and 40 minutes and was interrupted for medical reasons.
- The third police interview, which again was not videorecorded and was conducted in the evening and at night, lasted for seven hours and 45 minutes. During this interview, David fully confessed to the crime.
- The fourth and final police interview, which was videorecorded and which started in the afternoon and ended at night, lasted for 11 hours and nine minutes. During this interview, David fully confessed to the crime.

It is clear from this timeline that David moved from incriminating statements to a full confession, which was later retracted. Not all interviews were videorecorded, including the first full confession. Since substantial discrepancies were noted between the written records and the videorecorded interviews, it is questionable whether the written records of the unrecorded interviews were sufficiently accurate. The final videorecorded police interview was only conducted and recorded in response to David's lawyer's objections to the full confession given during the third police interview, which was not videorecorded. In 2009, David was assessed by a team of forensic behavioural scientists on behalf of the Public Prosecutor's Office. Notably, these experts were asked to assess whether David should be admitted under the judicial 'internment measure';[3] they were not asked to assess

---

2 Since these interviews took place preceding the implementation of legal assistance at the police station in Belgium, there was no lawyer present during the police interviews. For a discussion of the implementation of legal assistance in the police station (and the lawyer's role in identifying vulnerability), see Lore Mergaerts in Chapter 3 of this collection.

3 Internment is a legal security measure ordered by the criminal court for individuals who exhibit mental illness(es) and who have committed a crime. These individuals are deemed not to have been in control of their actions because of the mental illness(es) and are considered to be a danger to society.

possible psychological vulnerabilities and their potential impact on David's behaviour during the police interviews.

Vulnerability in Suspect Interviewing

David's lawyers requested a psychological assessment to ascertain the veracity of his statement in light of a possible psychological vulnerability. Gudjonsson defines a suspect's 'psychological vulnerability' as 'psychological characteristics or mental states which render a suspect prone, in certain circumstances, to providing information which is inaccurate, unreliable (or invalid) or misleading'.[4] Individual characteristics such as age are also considered personal risk factors for false confessions. These vulnerabilities are important because they may place the suspect at a disadvantage in terms of coping with the demands of the interview (including stress and detention); making informed decisions and understanding questions, as well as the implications of their answers; and providing the police with accurate information.[5] In a broader sense, the suspect's vulnerability also encompasses situational factors that render a suspect prone to providing inaccurate information such as a false confession. Psychological and situational factors,[6] such as an accusatory interview model and the use of oppressive techniques, are best considered potential risk factors for vulnerability and, as such, for false confessions. This broad approach of the suspect's vulnerability corresponds to Dehaghani's concept of interrogating vulnerability, arguing that every suspect is vulnerable because of the position they are in.[7]

We were tasked with two main requests: first, to assess personal risk factors (ie, assessing the suspect's psychological vulnerability); and second, to assess the veracity of the statements in light of the mental state of the suspect. The latter addressed the complex and dynamic process of the suspect's vulnerability, which resulted from a dynamic interplay between individual and situational risk factors, in relation to the reliability of the confession.

In order to assess both questions, we received and analysed the following case file documents:

- one report (2003) describing a psychosocial evaluation of David (at 14 years old) requested by a student guidance centre, which stated that David exhibited mild mental disability and characteristics of an autism spectrum disorder (ASD);
- an expert report (2008) describing a psychiatric evaluation for court;

4 Gisli H Gudjonsson, *The Psychology of Interrogations and Confessions. A Handbook* (Wiley 2003) 316.
5 Gisli H Gudjonsson, 'Psychological Vulnerabilities During Police Interviewing. Why Are They Important?' (2010) 15 *Legal and Criminological Psychology* 161.
6 Saul M Kassin and Gisli H Gudjonsson, 'The Psychology of Confessions. A Review of the Literature and Issues' (2004) 5 *Psychological Science in the Public Interest* 33.
7 Roxanna Dehaghani, 'Interrogating Vulnerability: Reframing the Vulnerable Suspect in Police Custody' [2020] *Social and Legal Studies* 1.

- a psychiatric report (2011) describing persecutory delusions in the suspect, for which he was prescribed medication;
- two videorecorded suspect interviews (October and November 2006);
- written records of six suspects interviews (October and November 2006);
- a written record of the cell tap (October 2006); and
- a written record of the crime reconstruction (October 2006).

The next sections of this chapter address the main steps undertaken to answer the two questions of the assignment. However, such a complex task presents great challenges. The following measures were taken to address some important overarching challenges. First, a multidisciplinary team of experts – across clinical psychology, forensic psychology and legal psychology – was assembled to provide the necessary expertise to address the complex nature of the task. Second, to prevent influencing one another's analyses, we conducted our tasks individually and thereafter merged tasks, reaching consensus by discussion. Third, owing to time constraints, access to the complete legal file was unavailable to us; instead, we focused our attention on the crucial documents (listed above). Information from secondary sources (eg, previous expert reports) was treated with caution and, where necessary, disregarded (eg, technical and autopsy reports). It is also necessary to acknowledge the bias that experts may face – the most obvious of which arises from the client's defence through possible allegiance bias[8] (ie, that experts for the defence are looking for psychological vulnerabilities or false confessions to rule the confession inadmissible). As protective measures, the respective instruments for assessing the suspect's psychological vulnerability were carefully chosen and a scientific model for the assessment of the veracity of the confession was adopted (see below). Still, the analysis should be treated with caution, given that even when objective measures and structured procedures are applied,[9] allegiance bias still might occur.[10]

Psychological Assessment: Did David Exhibit Psychological Vulnerabilities?

The way in which psychological vulnerability is theoretically framed determines to a large extent how the psychological assessment is approached. Typically, young age, mental disorders, significant impairments of intelligence and social functioning, and physical disabilities are considered vulnerabilities.[11] However,

8 Daniel C Murrie, Marcus T Boccaccini, Lucy A Guarnera and Katrina A Rufino, 'Are Forensic Experts Biased by the Sides that Retained Them?' (2013) 24 *Psychological Science* 1889.

9 Daniel C Murrie and Marcus T Boccaccini, 'Adversarial Allegiance among Expert Witnesses' (2015) 11 *Annual Review of Law and Social Science* 37.

10 Melanie Sauerland, Henry Otgaar, Enide Maegherman and Anna Sagana, 'Allegiance Bias in Statements Reliability Evaluations Is Not Eliminated by Falsification Instructions' (2020) 228 *Zeitschrift für Psychologie* 210.

11 Victoria Herrington and Karl Roberts, 'Addressing Psychological Vulnerability in the Police Suspect Interview' (2012) 6 *Policing: A Journal of Policy and Practice* 177.

Gudjonsson defines 'psychological vulnerability' in a broader sense and delineates four broad categories:

- diagnosable mental illnesses;
- an abnormal mental state not necessarily related to a history of mental illnesses (eg, phobic symptoms, panic attacks and withdrawal symptoms);
- limited intellectual abilities; and
- personality characteristics, including suggestibility, compliance and acquiescence.[12]

These categories are associated with cognitions, feelings and behaviours (eg, susceptibility to feelings of guilt, faulty reality monitoring, poor memory capacity and failure to appreciate the implications and consequences of answers given) that could make a suspect prone to providing inaccurate or misleading information. To obtain a holistic view of the suspect, Gudjonsson's scientific model was used to identify relevant risk factors.

Regarding the methodology, the current (forensic) psychological assessment complied to a large extent with the diagnostic cycle. In Flanders (Belgium) and the Netherlands, this model is often used in clinical practice, as it provides the basic methodological structure for conducting psychological assessments as objectively and reliably as possible. It can also be seen as a countermeasure against bias. This cycle comprises the following phases:

- observation (ie, the collection and grouping of empirical factual material);
- induction (ie, the formulation of hypotheses);
- deduction (ie, derivation of testable predictions from the hypotheses);
- testing, to investigate whether the predictions are confirmed by the obtained assessment outcomes; and
- an evaluation of the hypotheses and assessment outcomes to formulate conclusions.[13]

However, the implementation of the entire cycle is often considerably limited within a forensic context, due to lack of time and limited possibilities for clinical observation and testing. This was no different in this assessment, so we were required to keep the observation phase to a minimum and to formulate the hypotheses based mainly on the available file data.

Various sources and methods are ideally used to test the hypotheses.[14] These may include – but need not be limited to – file information; information obtained from other people who know the person in question (hetero-amnestic information); life course information; clinical observations; and measurements using

12 Gisli H Gudjonsson, *The Psychology of Interrogations and Confessions. A Handbook* (Wiley 2003).

13 Jan J F ter Laak and Marijn P M de Goede, *Psychologische Diagnostiek: Inhoudelijke en Methodologische Grondslagen* (Pearson Benelux B.V. 2003).

14 Adam P Natoli, 'More Methods Can Result in More Knowledge: Why Psychology Needs to Use Multi-method Approaches' (2019) *The PsyPAG Quarterly*.

psychological tests. Such a multi-method approach can yield richer case formulations than single-modality assessments and – especially in a forensic context – helps to check for possible tendentious answers (eg, socially desirable responding or malingering) and gaps in the stories of the suspect or convicted individual. Considering the practical constraints that were encountered during the current assessment (eg, time and limited access to third-party information), we made use of the available file information; interviews with the accused, as well as with his parents; and psychological tests administered to both the accused and his father.

In what follows, we summarise the outcomes from the psychological assessment, grouped according to Gudjonsson's scientific model.

Mental Disorder

Since we had to prioritise certain elements in our assessment, we did not administer psychological tests to investigate the presence of mental disorders. Up to the time of the current analysis, no in-depth assessment of the suspect had been carried out to determine whether a formal diagnosis of any mental disorders could be made. However, based on the file information, we could not completely rule them out either. First, (early) childhood characteristics of an ASD[15] were described in an earlier psychosocial assessment of the then 14-year-old suspect. More specifically, rigidity, a lack of imagination and communicative and social difficulties were observed in David. These clinical observations were much in line with our observations during the interviews with and testing of the suspect. Among other things, a difficulty in making and maintaining both eye contact and interpersonal contact with the assessor, limited reciprocity during interactions, an absence of spontaneous contact and little variation in his non-verbal behaviour were observed. Second, previous reports described a psychotic state, characterised by mainly apathetic and bizarre behaviour and paranoid thinking. The file described that these symptoms had elicited a high level of anxiety in David in 2014, which in turn had led to his hospitalisation. Notably, previous experts also associated this anxiety with David's history of bullying victimisation. These clinical observations of previous assessors were included in the report, given their potential relevance; but it was also indicated that these matters had not been formally investigated.

Intellectual (Dis)abilities

In David's file, reference was made several times to his limited intellectual abilities, as measured by different intelligence tests across his lifespan. Given that empirical studies have demonstrated that stability or interchangeability of IQ scores across

15 We acknowledge that there is a discussion about the terminology used to name these developmental conditions. Various professionals question whether autism should be viewed as a disorder and want to move away from the negative views associated with the term 'disorder'. They therefore prefer the term 'autism spectrum condition'. However, we decided to use the terms used in the original reports and the clinical definitions as described in the DSM-5 (see n 18).

instruments is lacking, especially in individuals exhibiting intellectual disability,[16] we decided to reassess David's intellectual abilities. More specifically, the Wechsler Adult Intelligence Scale – Fourth Edition[17] was administered. The obtained profile indicated the presence of a mild intellectual disability, with deficits mainly noted in – but not limited to – verbal comprehension and working memory. In addition, various deficits in his adaptive functioning (considered as an additional proxy for intellectual functioning)[18] were established through observation, file information and information obtained through the interviews. These problems were situated in the conceptual, social and practical domains, and demonstrated that David exhibited a limited ability to meet community standards of personal independence and social responsibility as expected at his age.

Personality Traits

Based on the literature and David's previous psychiatric/psychosocial assessments, we decided to investigate the presence of pathological personality traits, state and trait anxiety, compliance and suggestibility. Taking into account David's limited verbal abilities, a small number of short questionnaires was selected. This test battery included the Personality Inventory for DSM-5 – Brief Form,[19] which was administered for David (self-report) and his father (informant report); the State-Trait Anxiety Inventory;[20] the Gudjonsson Compliance Scale (GCS);[21] and the Gudjonsson Suggestibility Scale.[22] The assessment of David's personality traits suggested moderate levels of negative affect (indicating anxiety, emotional lability, hostility, separation anxiety and/or submissiveness); disinhibition (indicating being easily distracted and impulsive, and/or tending to take risks and behave irresponsibly); psychoticism (indicating eccentricity, cognitive perceptual dysregulation and/or unusual beliefs and experiences); and introversion (indicating depressive traits, suspiciousness, introversion, avoidance of intimacy and/or lack of joy). David's GCS score suggested a higher level of compliance, indicating greater

16 Petra Habets, Inge Jeandarme, Kasia Uzieblo, Karel Oei and Stefan Bogaerts, 'Intelligence Is in the Eye of the Beholder: Investigating Repeated IQ Measurements in Forensic Psychiatry' (2014) 28 *Journal of Applied Research in Intellectual Disabilities* 182.

17 David Wechsler, *Wechsler Adult Intelligence Scale: WAIS-IV; Technical and Interpretive Manual* (Pearson 2008).

18 American Psychiatric Association, *Diagnostic and Statistical Manual of Mental Disorders: DSM-5* (American Psychiatric Association 2013).

19 Paul van der Heijden, Theo Ingenhoven, Han Berghuis and Gina Rossi, *De Nederlandstalige bewerking van The Personality Inventory for DSM-5-Adult* (Uitgeverij Boom 2014).

20 Henk M Van der Ploeg, *Handleiding bij de Zelf-Beoordelingsvragenlijst. Een Nederlandstalige bewerking van de Spielberger State-Trait Anxiety Inventory* (Pearson Assessment and Information B.V. 2000).

21 Gisli H Gudjonsson, 'Compliance in an Interrogative Situation: A New Scale' (1989) 10 *Personality and Individual Differences* 535.

22 Gisli H Gudjonsson, 'A New Scale of Interrogative Suggestibility' (1984) 5 *Personality and Individual Differences* 303.

levels of fear or discomfort with persons in an authoritarian position, a tendency to avoid conflict and confrontation and/or an eagerness to please others. No indications for heightened levels of state and trait anxiety or for suggestibility were found.

In sum, David exhibited several psychological vulnerabilities. Deficits were mainly found in the domain of his intellectual abilities and personality traits. The current assessment neither dismissed nor confirmed the presence of ASD and of psychotic symptoms characterised by mainly paranoid thinking, for which indications were found in the clinical observations and the available files. However, the mere presence of the aforementioned problems was insufficient to state that David's answers could be inaccurate or misleading due to the established psychological vulnerabilities. To support any statements on David's interrogative vulnerability, an in-depth analysis of the interaction between psychological vulnerabilities and the concrete police context was essential, as discussed below.

Analysis of the Interviews: Were the Statements in Relation to David's Mental State Accurate?

As with the psychological assessment in such cases, a detailed roadmap for assessing the veracity of statements does not exist. In the literature, some general models are discussed, such as Gudjonsson's factors of assessment[23] and the verification/falsification approach.[24] To analyse the accuracy of David's statements, the experts partly used Gudjonsson's model[25] on factors that needed to be assessed:

- the circumstances of the arrest and custody;
- the characteristics of the defendant;
- his mental and physical state during custody;
- interrogative factors;
- an explanation of the alleged false confession; and
- the retraction.

Owing to reasons pertaining to feasibility, the assessment was delineated to the analysis of David's characteristics; his psychological and physical state during interviews and police detention; and the characteristics of the interview. In line with the foregoing, Van Koppen[26] argues that the core elements for analysis of statement accuracy – more specifically, testing the scenario of a false confession –

---

23 Gisli H Gudjonsson, *The Psychology of Interrogations and Confessions. A Handbook* (Wiley 2003).
24 Peter van Koppen, *Overtuigend Bewijs. Indammen van Rechterlijke Dwalingen* (Nieuw Amsterdam 2011).
25 Gisli H Gudjonsson, *The Psychology of Interrogations and Confessions. A Handbook* (Wiley 2003).
26 Peter van Koppen, *Overtuigend Bewijs. Indammen van Rechterlijke Dwalingen* (Nieuw Amsterdam 2011).

applies to the individual characteristics of the suspect, the characteristics of the interview and the presence of a perpetrator or intimate knowledge. The analysis was limited to the following aspects:

- a discussion of the possible risks about the accuracy of the confessions, namely the risk of a false confession (judgement on the value of the statements belonged to the court); and
- a discussion of the potential accuracy of the confession by means of intimate knowledge and support of the statements in other evidence, based on the analysis of the police interviews.[27]

Hypothesis 1: The Confession Was False

Under the heading of the first hypothesis, both personal and situational risk factors for a false confession were analysed.

Personal Risk Factors (Psychological Vulnerability)

During the assessment of the interviews, several risk factors observed in David's psychological assessment emerged. Among these, the most important were intellectual disabilities and personality characteristics.

INTELLECTUAL DISABILITIES

In general, suspects with intellectual disabilities might be unable to understand their legal rights, the (importance of) the questions or the consequences of their answers. This can result in them being particularly vulnerable and providing inaccurate information.[28] They also experience more problems with memory capacity and have a greater tendency to confabulate.[29] At different times during the videorecorded interviews, David illustrated difficulties in understanding (part of) the questions. For example, he did not understand concepts such as 'civil registry', 'critical' and 'attitude'.

Furthermore, David stated on multiple occasions that he was bad at writing, spelling and mathematics, as demonstrated when he was asked to spell his girlfriend's name or when he counted the number of his family members on his fingers. David's difficulties in understanding questions led to a lack of understanding on the part of the interviewer, who regularly stressed that David must think, even

---

27 Peter van Koppen, *Overtuigend Bewijs. Indammen van Rechterlijke Dwalingen* (Nieuw Amsterdam 2011).
28 Gisli H Gudjonsson, *The Psychology of Interrogations and Confessions. A Handbook* (Wiley 2003); Gisli H Gudjonsson, 'Psychological Vulnerabilities during Police Interviewing. Why Are They Important?' (2010) 15 *Legal and Criminological Psychology* 161; Gisli H Gudjonsson and Theresa Joyce, 'Interviewing Adults with Intellectual Disabilities' (2011) 5 *Advances in Mental Health and Intellectual Disabilities* 16.
29 Gisli H Gudjonsson and Theresa Joyce, 'Interviewing Adults with Intellectual Disabilities' (2011) 5 *Advances in Mental Health and Intellectual Disabilities* 16.

when he did not seem to understand something. This approach put more pressure on David to answer the questions.

People with intellectual disabilities experience difficulties in remembering things that happened in the recent past (ie, poor immediate recall) and in the more distant past (ie, poor delayed recall).[30] The latter was especially important given the time lapse between the facts (2006) and David's interviews (2008). Nevertheless, interviewers repeatedly questioned the legitimacy of David's 'I don't know' responses by asking whether he dared not give an answer. Although it is known that individuals with intellectual disabilities exhibit recall problems and are more prone to confabulation,[31] the interviewers frequently pressured David to amend his 'I don't know' responses into specific answers.

Furthermore, people with intellectual disabilities also experience problems in situating events in time and space, which is particularly important in the context of a suspect's interview.[32] Throughout both videorecorded interviews, the interviewer insisted on precise time and place indications. When David – usually after some urging – did respond to this, he seemed to be guessing:

INTERVIEWER: Since when do you know him?

DAVID: From when I rented that car for him.

INTERVIEWER: How long have you known that person?

DAVID: I think 2008. I don't know.

PERSONALITY CHARACTERISTICS

There are various relevant personality characteristics when assessing the veracity of suspect statements, the most researched of which are suggestibility, compliance and acquiescence.[33] David was compliant and eager to please the interviewers on

30 Isabel CH Clare and Gisli H Gudjonsson, 'Interrogative Suggestibility, Confabulation, and Acquiescence in People with Mild Learning Disabilities (Mental Handicap): Implications for Reliability during Police Interrogations' (1993) 32 *British Journal of Clinical Psychology* 295; William R Lindsay, Richard P Hastings and Anthony R Beech, 'Forensic Research in Offenders with Intellectual & Developmental Disabilities 2: Assessment and Treatment' (2011) 17 *Psychology, Crime and Law*, 97; Gisli H Gudjonsson, 'Memory Distrust Syndrome, Confabulation and False Confession' (2017) 87 *Cortex* 156.

31 Saul M Kassin, Steven A Drizin, Thomas Grisso, Gisli H Gudjonsson, Richard A Leo and Allison D Redlich, 'Police-Induced Confessions: Risk Factors and Recommendations' (2010) 34 *Law and Human Behavior* 3; William R Lindsay, Richard P Hastings and Anthony R Beech, 'Forensic Research in Offenders with Intellectual & Developmental Disabilities 2: Assessment and Treatment' (2011) 17 *Psychology, Crime and Law*, 97; Gisli H Gudjonsson, 'Memory Distrust Syndrome, Confabulation and False Confession' (2017) 87 *Cortex* 156.

32 Barbera Landau and Andrea Zukowski, 'Objects, Motions, and Paths: Spatial Language in Children with Williams Syndrome' (2004) 23 *Developmental Neuropsychology* 105.

33 Isabel CH Clare and Gisli H Gudjonsson, 'Interrogative Suggestibility, Confabulation, and Acquiescence in People with Mild Learning Disabilities (Mental Handicap): Implications for Reliability during Police Interrogations' (1993) 32 *British Journal of Clinical Psychology* 295.

several occasions, such as when an interviewer indicated that an incident with a firebomb had occurred and suggested that the bottle used could only have been filled by one person. David changed his answer regarding who filled this bottle from 'Both' to 'I don't know' to 'I'll take it' upon the interviewer's insistence.

In line with the results of the tests, David exhibited a limited degree of suggestibility during the videorecorded interviews. Few examples of acquiescence were found in the videorecorded interviews, mostly at times where David seemed to be fatigued. For example, when his statement was read out to him, even though he was clearly falling asleep, he agreed to the statement.

Situational Risk Factors

During the analysis of David's interviews by the police, various situational risk factors arose. First, interview techniques used by the interviewers interacted with the above-mentioned personal risk factors. Throughout the videorecorded interviews, the interviewers used various inappropriate techniques to increase the pressure on David. Two of the most common techniques were the use of negative feedback and maximisation. Negative feedback is some form of disapproval that can be overt or implicit.[34] Maximisation involves the use of harsh techniques that are confrontational and designed to emphasise the seriousness of the crime or situation,[35] and that increase the risk of a false confession.[36] Negative feedback mostly occurred when police received an unsatisfactory answer – for example, when David did not know the answer; when the answer was not in line with what David had previously stated; or when the answer was contradictory to the interviewers' knowledge of the case. Research illustrates that people with intellectual disabilities are more sensitive to negative feedback, and more inclined to give in to 'leading' questions and to change their answers.[37] In contrast, interviewers gave positive feedback or rewards (eg, coffee or fries) when David's answers met their expectations.

Besides negative feedback, the interviewers frequently used maximisation, which according to the literature also increases the risk of a false confession.[38]

---

34 Gisli H Gudjonsson, *The Psychology of Interrogations and Confessions. A Handbook* (Wiley 2003).
35 Saul M Kassin and Karlyn McNall, 'Police Interrogations and Confessions: Communicating Promises and Threats by Pragmatic Implication' (1991) 15 *Law and Human Behavior* 233.
36 Allyson J Horgan, Melissa B Russano, Christian A Meissner and Jacqueline R Evans, 'Minimization and Maximization Techniques: Assessing the Perceived Consequences of Confessing and Confession Diagnosticity' (2012) 18 *Psychology, Crime & Law* 65.
37 Caroline Everington and Solomon M Fulero, 'Competence to Confess: Measuring Understanding and Suggestibility of Defendants with Mental Retardation' (1999) 37 *Mental Retardation* 212; Michael J O'Connell, William Garmoe and Naomi ES Goldstein, 'Miranda Comprehension in Adults with Mental Retardation and the Effects of Feedback Style on Suggestibility' (2005) 29 *Law and Human Behavior* 359.
38 Richard A Leo, 'False Confessions: Causes, Consequences, and Implications' (2009) 37 *The Journal of American Academy of Psychiatry and the Law* 332; Gisli H Gudjonsson 'The Psychology of False Confessions' in Daniel G Lassiter and Christian A

Maximisation was used, for example, by stating that David's sister would also be negatively affected since her mobile phone was involved; that David 'should think about his parents'; and that there was 'more evidence to follow'.

Research illustrates that police over-rely on the use of such poor or inappropriate techniques when interviewing vulnerable suspects.[39] The fact that the police did not adjust their techniques to David's obvious vulnerabilities is even more worrisome. This may be because police officers tend to underestimate the base rate of psychological vulnerabilities among suspects.[40] Numerous cases demonstrate false confessions owing to a failure to identify psychological vulnerabilities.[41]

The use of these inappropriate techniques seems to arise from a presumption of guilt on behalf of the interviewers. This was particularly evident in the fourth police interview, in which the interviewers' main goal was to obtain a videorecording of the full confession that David had made in the third interview. While videorecording should be considered a protective measure, in this case the interview was characterised by a clear confirmation bias: the interviewers were trying to obtain a similarly detailed confession by sometimes reading parts of the earlier confession, requesting an admission from David. When David did not meet these requests, the interview was interrupted twice, whereby the interviewers and David left the interview room to have a break. During the break, one could hear parts of a conversation about facts which the interviewers were pressuring David to admit to. For example, the interviewers mentioned that no one would believe him if he made another denial. Similarly, in the first interview, there seemed to be a conversation in between changing DVDs[42] in which the police provided information to David about the car involved in moving the body.[43] On one of these occasions, David referred to information mentioned by the police which had not been observed in the previous recordings. Later, David made self-incriminating statements.

Meissner (eds), *Police Interrogations and False Confessions. Current Research, Practice and Policy Recommendations* (American Psychological Association 2010).

39 Laura Faruggia and Fiona Gabbert, 'Vulnerable Suspects in Police Interviewing: Exploring Current Practice in England and Wales' (2020) 17 *Journal of Investigative Psychology and Offender Profiling* 17. Koen Geijsen, Sophie Vanbelle, Nicolien Kop and Corine De Ruijter, 'The Interrogation of Vulnerable Suspects in the Netherlands: An Exploratory Study' (2018) 9 *Research and Practice* 34.

40 Koen Geijsen, Corine de Ruijter and Nicolien Kop, 'Identifying Psychological Vulnerabilities: Studies on Police Suspects' Mental Health Issues and Police Officers' Views' (2018) 5 *Cogent Psychology* 1.

41 Gisli H Gudjonsson, 'Psychological Vulnerabilities during Police Interviewing. Why Are They Important?' (2010) 15 *Legal and Criminological Psychology* 161; Saul M Kassin, Steven A Drizin, Thomas Grisso, Gisli H Gudjonsson, Richard A Leo and Allison D Redlich, 'Police-Induced Confessions: Risk Factors and Recommendations' (2010) 34 *Law and Human Behavior* 3; Sara C Appleby, Lisa E Hasel and Saul M Kassin, 'Police-Induced Confessions: An Empirical Analysis of Their Content and Impact' (2011) 19 *Psychology, Crime & Law* 111; Koen Geijsen, Corine de Ruijter and Nicolien Kop, 'Identifying Psychological Vulnerabilities: Studies on Police Suspects' Mental Health Issues and Police Officers' Views' (2018) 5 *Cogent Psychology* 1.

42 The videorecording of the police interview was saved on different DVDs.

43 The consecutive DVDs did not always match up.

Notably, these techniques occurred during prolonged police interviews at night – two interview characteristics which increase the incidence of false confessions.[44] Research on false confessions demonstrates that the risk of false confession increases as the length of the interview increases. More specifically, the interviews in which false confessions were obtained lasted for at least six hours.[45] When David confessed to the crime, he was respectively interviewed for nine hours and 53 minutes (night), seven hours and 45 minutes (evening and night) and 11 hours and nine minutes (evening and night). In relation to the timing and duration of these interviews, it also appeared – particularly during the first interview – that David was fatigued; he even tended to fall asleep at the end of the interview. Fatigue in the sense of sleep deprivation – which was mentioned by David[46] – can have different negative effects during suspect interviews. Sleep deprivation impairs both attention span and flexible thinking, and increases suggestibility to leading questions.[47] Recent research suggests that sleep deprivation predisposes suspects to making false confessions by impairing complex decision-making processes – specifically, the ability to anticipate risks and consequences of behaviour, to inhibit behavioural impulses and to resist suggestive influences.[48]

Hypothesis 2: The Confession Was True

In order to test whether a confession is accurate, it should be tested against intimate knowledge which the perpetrator would have.[49] A distinction must be made between weak and strong intimate knowledge.[50] Strong intimate knowledge (unknown information by the police) is preferred over weak intimate knowledge (information known to the police), since research demonstrates that false confessions quite often include weak intimate knowledge.[51] The police should then

---

44   Steven A Drizin and Richard A Leo, 'The Problem of False Confessions in the Post-DNA World' (2004) 82 *North Carolina Law Review* 891; Brandon L Garrett, 'The Substance of False Confessions' (2010) 62 *Stanford Law Review* 1051.

45   Steven A Drizin and Richard A Leo, 'The Problem of False Confessions in the Post-DNA World' (2004) 82 *North Carolina Law Review* 891.

46   During a cell tap, recorded prior to the first police interview, David mentioned to his cellmate that he was unable to sleep. A written record of this cell tap was included in the documents that were analysed.

47   Yvonne Harrison and James A Horne, 'The Impact of Sleep Deprivation on Decision Making: A Review' (2000) 6 *Journal of Experimental Psychology: Applied* 236.

48   Steven J Frenda, Shari R Berkowitzb, Elizabeth F Loftus and Kimberly M Fenn, 'Sleep Deprivation and False Confessions' (2015) 13 *Proceeding of the National Academy of Sciences of the United States of America* 2047.

49   Bartosz W Wojciechowski, Minna Grans and Moa Lidén, 'A True Denial or a False Confession? Assessing Veracity of Suspects' Statements Using MASAM and SVA' (2018) 13 *PLoS One* e0198211.

50   Han Israëls and Peter J van Koppen, 'Daderkennis, Politiekennis en Sturend Verhoren' (2016) 35 *Netherlands Journal of Legal Philosophy* 8.

51   Brandon L Garrett, 'The Substance of False Confessions' (2010) 62 *Stanford Law Review* 1051; Sara C Appleby, Lisa E Hasel and Saul M Kassin, 'Police-Induced Confessions: An Empirical Analysis of Their Content and Impact' (2011) 19

verify the information, check whether it is supported by other evidence[52] and consider the extent to which independent evidence corroborates the confession.[53]

In this case, the test for intimate knowledge was less straightforward, since intimate knowledge was present; but at the same time, various opportunities for contamination could be identified. In addition to the public information in the media and flyers distributed by the police, the interviewers seemed to have provided information before the first interview, as well as in between and during interviews, through suggestive questioning. Moreover, given the passage of time, rumours had been circulating in the village where the murder took place. During the interviews, David provided information that was both accurate (but possibly contaminated by police or other sources) and inaccurate (pointing to a risk of confabulation or repeating inaccurate rumours).

Owing to the complexity of the case, we were unable to identify what information was contaminated and what was not. The analysis revealed many potential problems in this area. Strong intimate knowledge and testing the confession to other independent evidence revealed potential problems, mostly indicating the absence of strong intimate knowledge and of supportive evidence. Firm conclusions could not be made due to the limited time provided to the experts to analyse the entire case file, prohibiting a thorough analysis of all relevant factors.

Conclusions and Recommendations

In this chapter, we described the identification process of psychological vulnerabilities in a murder case. The assessment procedure comprised two parts: an assessment of David's psychological vulnerability and an analysis of the veracity of David's statements in relation to his mental state. Notably, although both parts of the assessment were analysed independently at first, the findings from the second part of the assessment were largely in line with the outcomes of the psychological assessment. This level of agreement gave additional validation to both the clinical-psychological and legal-psychological observations.

Psychology, Crime & Law 111; Laura Nirider, Joshua Tepfer and Steven A Drizin, 'Combating Contamination in Confession Cases' (2012) 79 *The University of Chicago Law Review* 837; Richard A Leo, Peter J Neufeld, Steven A Drizin and Andrew E Taslitz, 'Promoting Accuracy in the Use of Confession Evidence: An Argument for Pretrial Reliability Assessments to Prevent Wrongful Convictions (2013) 85 *Temple Law Review* 759; Brandon L Garrett, 'Contaminated Confessions Revisited' (2015) 101 *Virginia Law Review* 395.

52 Richard A Leo, 'False Confessions: Causes, Consequences and Implications' (2009) 17 *Journal of the American Academy of Psychiatry and the Law* 249; Pieter Tersago, Miet Vanderhallen, Joëlle Rozie and Sara-Jane McIntyre, 'From Suspect Statement to Legal Decision Making: How Judges Weigh the Evidence?' (2020) 228 *Zeitschrift für Psychologie* 175.

53 Kassi Saul M Kassin, Steven A Drizin, Thomas Grisso, Gisli H Gudjonsson, Richard A Leo and Allison D Redlich, 'Police-Induced Confessions: Risk Factors and Recommendations' (2010) 34 *Law and Human Behavior* 3.

Nevertheless, no assessment strategy is flawless. Several constraints were faced during the process. A first important constraint concerned the lack of a standardised approach in relation to the psychological assessment and the analysis of the interviews. While knowledge regarding psychological vulnerabilities has increased over the past few decades, a limited number of well-validated and standardised psychological tests exist to assess relevant risk factors in suspects, and more specifically in suspects with intellectual disabilities. Also, the specific dynamics between various psychological vulnerabilities and the suspect interview context are not yet well understood. For instance, the extent to which the presence of deviant personality traits can make a suspect vulnerable during a police interview has been insufficiently examined. Hence, more research into the actual impact of psychological vulnerabilities on the accuracy of confessions and the development of validated and standardised assessment methodologies are needed.

Significant practical limitations are an additional obstacle. As mentioned earlier, we were limited in time, which is usually the case when carrying out expert assessments. This forces experts to prioritise, which can result in relevant hypotheses being missed or insufficiently explored, as was also experienced in the current assessment. In addition, bias cannot be completely ruled out. This is because although independence is guaranteed in such assessments, the information obtained is often (unintentionally) pre-selected. Such practical limitations can in turn (albeit partially) explain phenomena such as adversarial allegiance (ie, the presumed tendency for experts to reach conclusions that support the party that retained them).[54] In practice, these practical limitations can rarely be completely avoided; but it is necessary for the expert to be aware of these limitations and to acknowledge the possible impact of these limitations in their report.

Despite these limitations and barriers, it is important to pay more attention to cases such as David's. Research and practice reveal the issues with the identification of psychological vulnerabilities and their negative impact on the accuracy of the suspect's statements. Vulnerable suspects are often not recognised by police officers[55] and the base rate of suspect vulnerabilities is still underestimated.[56] Consequently, it is no surprise that a substantial number of police officers take no special precautions when interviewing vulnerable suspects.[57] Possible explanations

54 Daniel C Murrie, Marcus T Boccaccini, Lucy A Guarnera and Katrina A Rufino, 'Are Forensic Experts Biased by the Side That Retained Them?' (2013) 24 *Psychological Science* 1889.

55 Susan Young, Emily J Goodwin, Ottilie Sedgwick and Gisli H Gudjonsson, 'The Effectiveness of Police Custody Assessments in Identifying Suspects with Intellectual Disabilities and Attention Deficit Hyperactivity Disorder' (2013) 11 *BMC Medicine* 248; Koen Geijsen, Corine de Ruijter and Nicolien Kop, 'Identifying Psychological Vulnerabilities: Studies on Police Suspects' Mental Health Issues and Police Officers' Views' (2018) 5 *Cogent Psychology* 1.

56 Koen Geijsen, Corine de Ruijter and Nicolien Kop, 'Identifying Psychological Vulnerabilities: Studies on Police Suspects' Mental Health Issues and Police Officers' Views' (2018) 5 *Cogent Psychology* 1.

57 Koen Geijsen, Corine de Ruijter and Nicolien Kop, 'Identifying Psychological Vulnerabilities: Studies on Police Suspects' Mental Health Issues and Police Officers'

for these empirical findings as observed in Belgian practice include a lack of knowledge about psychological vulnerabilities and a lack of tools or structural support for identifying them. Similar observations are also made in other relevant professional groups, such as defence lawyers and clinicians. For example, Belgian forensic psychologists and psychiatrists are mostly familiar with evaluations to determine whether the judicial 'internment measure' may apply, but are unfamiliar with the concept of psychological vulnerabilities within the police context and have no or only limited knowledge on how to approach such evaluations. Such observations in Belgian practice emphasise the need for continuing education in all relevant professions (including, but certainly not limited to, police, defence lawyers, magistrates and behavioural experts), and the development of standardised tools and support services. Hence, it is important to describe cases such as David's in order to sensitise various audiences to the topic and to stimulate discussion about the needs and possible solutions both theoretically and in practice.

Views' (2018) 5 *Cogent Psychology* 1; Laura Farrugia, 'Identifying Vulnerability in Police Custody: Making Sense of Information Provided to Custody Officers' (2021) 80 *Journal of Forensic and Legal Medicine*.

Part 2

Responses to Suspect Vulnerability

5 Vulnerable Suspects, Access to a Lawyer and the Right to a Fair Trial in Ireland

Alan Cusack, Shane Kilcommins, Gautam Gulati and Colum Dunne

Introduction

It is well established internationally that children, as well as individuals with intellectual disabilities, face particular challenges in negotiating the forensic formalities adopted by police at the pre-trial stage of the criminal process.[1] Owing to limitations in cognitive and linguistic development, the testimonial accuracy of police-elicited accounts yielded from these individuals has been found to attract a heightened risk of narrative bias, which can vary depending upon the types of questions asked, the status of the person asking them and the formality of the arena in which the interrogation takes place. For persons suspected of crime, the distortive impact of these psychological vulnerabilities can result in serious punitive consequences.

In recognition of the unique challenges facing vulnerable suspects in police custody across Europe, a distinct line of Strasbourg jurisprudence has emerged in recent years that emphasises the need for all states to facilitate meaningful access to a lawyer during a suspect's period of detainment pursuant to the fair trial commitment enshrined in Article 6 of the European Convention on Human Rights (ECHR).[2] Most recently, this line of inculpatory logic found vocal expression in the Chambers of Strasbourg in *Doyle v Ireland* (51979/17),[3] which arose following a decision by Ireland's Supreme Court to interpret Article 6 as excluding a suspect's right to have a lawyer physically present during a police interview.[4] While, in the circumstances, the ECHR refused to overrule the Supreme Court's decision, it was nevertheless openly critical of the general nature of the prohibition against physical access to a lawyer which prevailed in Irish police custody settings. Against the backdrop of this recent critical Strasbourg pronouncement, this chapter seeks to understand the right to a fair trial in Ireland, with a particular emphasis on the position of vulnerable suspects of crime.[5]

---

1 See Louise Forde and Ursula Kilkelly, Chapter 6 of this collection, with specific regard to the right of access to a lawyer for children.
2 See the introduction to this collection.
3 *Doyle v Ireland* App no 51979/17 (ECHR, 23 May 2019).
4 *People (DPP) v Doyle* [2017] IESC 1.
5 For a more general reflection on the transformation of human rights laws regarding persons with disabilities in Ireland, see Donna McNamara, Chapter 1 of this collection.

DOI: 10.4324/9781003205166-8

Setting the Scene: The Right to Access a Lawyer in Ireland

Access to a solicitor while detained in police custody has long been regarded in Ireland as an important means of equalising relations between the accused and the state in the detention process.[6] Accordingly, for over a quarter of a century, Irish law has recognised a suspect as having a constitutional right of reasonable access to a solicitor while detained in such custody.[7] The parameters of this constitutional entitlement, however, have traditionally been 'narrowly construed by the courts'.[8] For example, it was held that as long as members of *An Garda Síochána* (Ireland's national policing body) made *bona fide* attempts to contact a solicitor, they were entitled to proceed to question a detained suspect.[9] Indeed, even where contact had been made with a solicitor, and assuming that they were available to come to the station, there was nothing to prevent the *Gardaí* from questioning the detained suspect in the interim period before the solicitor's arrival.[10] Moreover, even when the solicitor presented themselves at the station, they were not entitled to sit in on the interrogation, as the right to reasonable access was historically deemed not to extend to having a solicitor physically present during the questioning.[11]

Recently, however, the Irish Supreme Court took the opportunity to reappraise the parameters of this right in two high-profile cases: *People (DPP) v Gormley and White*[12] and *People (DPP) v Doyle*.[13] In the former case, the Supreme Court recognised a suspect as having a constitutional right of reasonable access to legal advice prior to being interrogated, but 'left over to a future case the question of whether a suspect is entitled to have a lawyer present during questioning'.[14] This question ultimately fell to be determined in the latter case of *People (DPP) v Doyle*,[15] which concerned an appeal against a conviction for murder. It was the appellant's contention that the criminal proceedings leading to his conviction had been unfair as he had been denied an opportunity to have his lawyer present at his

---

6 See generally Liz Campbell, Shane Kilcommins, Catherine O'Sullivan and Alan Cusack, *Criminal Law in Ireland* (Clarus Press 2020).

7 *People (DPP) v Healy* [1990] 2 IR 73. The detainee also has the correlative entitlement, pursuant to Section 5 of the Criminal Justice Act 1984, to be informed of this right of access.

8 Liz Campbell, Shane Kilcommins, Catherine O'Sullivan and Alan Cusack, *Criminal Law in Ireland* (Clarus Press 2020) 405.

9 Section 5A of the Criminal Justice Act 1984, as inserted by Section 9(a) of the Criminal Justice Act 2011, prohibits the questioning of a detainee until they have had the opportunity to consult with their solicitor. This section has not yet commenced.

10 *People (DPP) v Buck* [2002] 2 IR 268.

11 See generally Vicky Conway and Yvonne Daly, 'From Legal Advice to Legal Assistance: Recognising the Changing Role of the Solicitor in the Garda Station' (2019) *Irish Judicial Studies Journal*.

12 [2014] IESC 17.

13 [2017] IESC 1.

14 Liz Heffernan, *Evidence in Criminal Trials* (2nd ed, Bloomsbury Professional 2020) 229.

15 [2017] IESC 1.

fifteenth police interview, during the course of which he confessed to the crime. In dismissing this appeal, the Supreme Court definitively ruled that the constitutional right under Irish law to a trial in due course of law (pursuant to Article 38.1 of *Bunreacht na hÉireann*) did not incorporate an entitlement to have a lawyer physically present during questioning.[16]

This Supreme Court ruling was not, however, the end of the tale and important questions remained unaddressed with regard to the reconcilability of Irish pre-trial practice with the requirements of Article 6 of the ECHR.[17] Most notably, the ruling by the Supreme Court appeared to contradict the tone and tenor of the Grand Chamber's ruling in *Salduz v Turkey*, where it declared:

> the Court finds that in order for the right to a fair trial to remain sufficiently 'practical and effective', Article 6 § 1 requires that, as a rule, access to a lawyer should be provided as from the first interrogation of a suspect by the police, unless it is demonstrated in the light of the particular circumstances of each case that there are compelling reasons to restrict this right. Even where compelling reasons may exceptionally justify denial of access to a lawyer, such restriction – whatever its justification – must not unduly prejudice the rights of the accused under Article 6.[18]

This passage represented the first clear delineation of the two-step approach which is now routinely taken by the European Court of Human Rights (ECtHR) in any examination of a challenge relating to an individual's entitlement to access a lawyer. Under this binary test, the ECtHR considers first, whether there are compelling reasons in a given case to justify a restriction on the right of access to a lawyer; and second, whether in the particular circumstances of a case the national proceedings can be considered to be fair overall.

When viewed through the lens of this binary assessment, the Supreme Court ruling in *Doyle* is arguably open to – and in fact became the target of – justified

---

16 See, for instance, the dicta of Charleton J at paras 49–50: 'It must also be remembered that there is a practice in this jurisdiction of informing people as to their rights both orally and in writing, having a custody officer whose duty it is to ensure that questioning is carried on fairly and for a reasonable time only, not at night unless the suspect requests this, and that an arrested person has access to legal advice before any questioning begins. But, those rights to be meaningful must be consistently applied. Otherwise, the State might find itself in a Miranda environment. They were applied here. Any issues as to brutality, psychological pressure, the crafty planting through suggestive questioning of every detail of the crime prior to any admission in the mind of the arrestee so that the confession statement becomes apparently trustworthy, unfairness or the coercion of the suggestible are visible and susceptible to judicial scrutiny as a result of the presence of video-recording in interview rooms … It cannot therefore be concluded that it is a necessary part of the right to a trial in due course of law under Article 38.1 of the Constitution that a lawyer should be present for the interviewing of a suspect in Garda custody.'
17 See *Averill v UK* (2001) 31 EHRR 36.
18 (2009) 49 EHRR 19 at 55. The recent decision in *Beuze v Belgium* (2019) 69 EHRR 1 is also instructive. See also *Ibrahim v United Kingdom* (2015) 61 EHRR 9.

juridical criticism.[19] In later proceedings maintained by the same applicant in Strasbourg,[20] the ECtHR determined that no compelling reasons existed to justify the 'general nature' of the restriction in Ireland, as it was not based on an 'individual assessment of the applicant's circumstances'.[21] However, this Irish practice was ultimately upheld by the ECtHR on the second limb of the test, on the reasoning that the overall fairness of the applicant's trial had not been 'irretrievably prejudiced' by this restriction.[22]

In arriving at this conclusion under the second limb of the binary test, the ECtHR had regard to a range of considerations, including the vulnerability of the applicant; allegations of ill treatment; the existence of other inculpatory evidence; the public interest in prosecuting the crime; and the existence of procedural safeguards such as electronic recording of interviews. While ultimately, the ECtHR upheld Irish pre-trial procedure on this occasion, Heffernan notes that this outcome rested on 'the extant access that this applicant had been afforded, the existence of ample other evidence in the case and the range of safeguards'.[23] Going forward, it is submitted that these same indices of fairness – articulated by the ECtHR in *Doyle* – may provide rich scope for challenges to any future admissions made during the course of a police interrogation in Ireland where a lawyer is not present, particularly in cases involving a vulnerable suspect.[24]

Vulnerability in Custody: Locating *Doyle* in a National and International Context

As the dust from the *Doyle* decision settles, the reconfigured contours of Ireland's pre-trial procedure landscape have yet to be charted definitively. However, one distinctive feature of the post-*Doyle* era can perhaps already safely be assumed: the emergence henceforth of a greater judicial tolerance for a more expansive conceptualisation of the exigencies of Article 6 of the ECHR. Crucially, at the heart of the re-imagined indicia of fairness must now, following *Doyle* (as well as the preceding cases of *Beuze*,[25] *Simeonovi*[26] and *Ibrahim*[27]), lie an express judicial

---

19 See generally Liz Heffernan, *Evidence in Criminal Trials* (2nd ed, Bloomsbury Professional 2020) 684.

20 *Doyle v Ireland* App no 51979/17 (ECHR, 23 May 2019).

21 *Doyle v Ireland* App no 51979/17 (ECHR, 23 May 2019), para 92.

22 See *Doyle v Ireland* App no 51979/17 (ECHR, 23 May 2019), para 102: 'The Court finds that, in the circumstances of the present case, notwithstanding the very strict scrutiny that must be applied where, as here, there are no compelling reasons to justify a restriction of the accused's right of access to a lawyer, when considered as a whole the overall fairness of the trial was not irretrievably prejudiced.'

23 Liz Heffernan, *Evidence in Criminal Trials* (2nd ed, Bloomsbury Professional 2020) 687.

24 See generally Liz Campbell, Shane Kilcommins, Catherine O'Sullivan and Alan Cusack, *Criminal Law in Ireland* (Clarus Press, 2020) 417.

25 *Beuze v Belgium* (2019) 69 EHRR 1.

26 *Ibrahim v United Kingdom* (2015) 61 EHRR 9.

27 (2018) 66 EHRR 2.

consideration of, *inter alia*, a detainee's vulnerability. While ultimately in *Doyle*, the ECtHR declined to classify the applicant as vulnerable, this decision was arguably attributable to the idiosyncratic facts of the high-profile case in hand, including the fact that the applicant was an 'adult and a native English speaker', and was 'physically and mentally strong throughout the interviews'.[28] However the likelihood of the ECtHR taking an equally non-interventionist approach in a case involving a more ostensibly deserving vulnerable suspect – such as an adult with an intellectual disability – is significantly less certain.

It would seem this is for good reason.[29] Owing to limitations in cognitive functioning and linguistic fluency, suspects with intellectual disabilities have been found to face pronounced challenges in negotiating the forensic formalities adopted by police at the pre-trial stage of the criminal process.[30] People with intellectual disabilities, for example, have been found in many instances to experience broad deficits in memory encoding, storage and retrieval, which can inhibit their ability to deliver accurate accounts of eyewitness events at trial.[31] Moreover,

---

28 *Doyle v Ireland* App no 51979/17 (ECHR, 23 May 2019) § 85.

29 See generally, Alan Cusack, 'The Pre-Trial Position of Vulnerable Victims of Crime in Ireland' in Penny Cooper and Linda Hunting (eds) *Addressing Vulnerability in Justice Systems* (Wildy, Simmonds and Hill Publishing) 185–218; Gautam Gulati, Alan Cusack, Brendan D Kelly, Shane Kilcommins and Colum P Dunne, (2020b) 'Experiences of People with Intellectual Disabilities Encountering Law Enforcement Officials – A Narrative Systematic Review' (2020) 71 *International Journal of Law and Psychiatry*, 101609; Gautam Gulati, Alan Cusack, John Bogue, Anne O'Connor, Valerie Murphy, Darius Whelan, Walter Cullen, Cliona McGovern, Brendan D.Kelly, Elizabeth Fistein, Shane Kilcommmins and Colum P Dunne, 'Challenges for People with Intellectual Disabilities in Law Enforcement Interactions in Ireland; Thematic Analysis Informed by 1537 Person-Years' Experience' (2021) 75 *International Journal of Law and Psychiatry*, 101683.

30 See generally Alan Cusack, 'Victims of Crime with Intellectual Disabilities and Ireland's Adversarial Trial: Some Ontological, Procedural and Attitudinal Concerns' (2017) 68(4) *Northern Ireland Legal Quarterly* 433–449 at 445; Alan Cusack, 'Beyond Special Measures: Challenging Traditional Constructions of Competence and Cross-Examination for Vulnerable Witnesses in Ireland' (2020) 4(2) *Irish Judicial Studies Journal*, 98, 103; Joanne Morrison, Rachel Forrester-Jones, Jill Bradshaw and Glynis Murphy, 'Communication and Cross-Examination in Court for Children and Adults with Intellectual Disabilities: A Systematic Review' (2019) 23(4) *International Journal of Evidence and Proof*, 366; Andrew Sanders, Jane Creaton, Sophia Bird and Leanne Weber, *Victims with Learning Disabilities: Negotiating the Criminal Justice System* (University of Oxford Centre for Criminological Research 1997); Christopher Williams, *Invisible Victims: Crime and Abuse against People with Learning Disabilities* (Jessica Kingsley Publishers 1995).

31 Marguerite Ternes and John C Yuille, 'Eyewitness Memory and Eyewitness Identification Performance in Adults with Intellectual Disabilities' (2008) 21 *Journal of Applied Research in Intellectual Disabilities* 519–531; Mark R Kebbell, Chris Hatton, Shane D Johnson and Caitriona ME O'Kelly, 'People with Learning Disabilities as Witnesses in Court: What Questions Should Lawyers Ask?' (2001) 29 *British Journal of Learning Disabilities* 98; Nitza B Perlman, Kristine I Ericson, Victoria M Esses and Barry J Isaacs, 'The Developmentally Handicapped Witness: Competency as a Function of Question Format' (1994) 18 *Law and Human Behaviour* 171.

studies suggest that these individuals can be more suggestible, more acquiescent, more likely to confabulate and more likely to engage in nay-saying than their counterparts within the general population.[32] There is also evidence to suggest that such persons are more likely to obfuscate generic details about an alleged incident; that they will entertain a final option bias in response to closed multiple choice questions; that their knowledge of the legal process is poor; and that they struggle routinely to comprehend legal terminology.[33]

In light of the pronounced cognitive and communicative challenges that persons with intellectual disabilities face in responding to allegations of criminal wrongdoing, there is – it is submitted – a particularly urgent need for criminal justice systems to mainstream strict procedural safeguards in their pre-trial interactions with any individuals drawn from this constituency:[34]

> Any failure to adapt forensic procedures at the pre-trial stage of the criminal process to take account of the ontological realities of intellectual impairment, poses not only a material risk of eliciting inaccurate testimony, but also a wider, more pressing danger of securing a wrongful conviction through the admission of false, self-inculpatory evidence.[35]

32 Gautam Gulati, Alan Cusack, John Bogue, Anne O'Connor, Valerie Murphy, Darius Whelan, Walter Cullen, Cliona McGovern, Brendan D Kelly, Elizabeth Fistein, Shane Kilcommmins and Colum P Dunne, 'Challenges for People with Intellectual Disabilities in Law Enforcement Interactions in Ireland; Thematic Analysis Informed by 1537 Person-Years' Experience' (2021) 75 *International Journal of Law and Psychiatry*, 101683; Kristine I Ericsson and Nitza B Perlman, 'Knowledge of Legal Terminology and Court Proceedings in Adults with Developmental Disabilities' (2001) 25(5) *Law and Human Behaviour* 529; Marguerite Ternes and John C Yuille, 'Eyewitness Memory and Eyewitness Identification Performance in Adults with Intellectual Disabilities' (2008) 21 *Journal of Applied Research in Intellectual Disabilities* 519–531; Laird W Heal and Carol K Sigelman, 'Response Biases in Interviews of Individuals with Limited Mental Ability' (1995) 39(4) *Journal of Intellectual Disability Research* 331.
33 Kristine I Ericsson and Nitza B Perlman, 'Knowledge of Legal Terminology and Court Proceedings in Adults with Developmental Disabilities' (2001) 25(5) *Law and Human Behaviour* 529; Nigel Beail, 'Interrogative Suggestibility, Memory and Intellectual Disability' (2002) 15 *Journal of Applied Research in Intellectual Disabilities* 129; Mark R Kebbell, Chris Hatton, Shane D Johnson and Caitriona ME O'Kelly, 'People with Learning Disabilities as Witnesses in Court: What Questions Should Lawyers Ask?' (2001) 29 *British Journal of Learning Disabilities* 98.
34 Gisli H Gudjonsson, *The Psychology of Interrogations and Confessions* (Wiley, 2003); Gisli H Gudjonsson, 'Psychological Vulnerabilities During Police Interviews. Why are they Important?' (2010) 15 *Legal and Criminological Psychology* 161; Janice Leggett, Wendy Goodman and Shamim Dinani, 'People with Learning Disabilities' Experiences of Being Interviewed by the Police' (2007) 35 *British Journal of Learning Disabilities* 168.
35 Alan Cusack, Gautam Gulati, Colum P Dunne and Shane Kilcommins, 'Policing Vulnerability: An Inquiry into the Pre-Trial Treatment of Suspects with Intellectual Disabilities in Ireland' (forthcoming) *Policing: An International Journal*.

One of the clearest Irish examples of the dangers associated with adopting an improper or disability-neutral approach to investigative interviewing, especially in circumstances where a suspect is vulnerable, is the case of Dean Lyons. This case arose after Lyons – a 24-year-old heroin addict, described as being 'borderline learning disabled'[36] – falsely confessed to a double murder. A number of weeks following Lyons' confession, Mark Nash admitted to the murders.[37] A Commission of Investigation into the Dean Lyons Case was subsequently established to consider the forensic developments which had contributed to the elicitation of his false admission of guilt.[38] While the commission ultimately concluded that there had been no deliberate attempt at the investigative stage of the proceedings to undermine the rights of Dean Lyons, it noted that inappropriate leading questions were inadvertently asked of him by interviewing *Gardaí*, which equipped him with the information to maintain a credible (albeit false) confession. It was also noted that Lyons was abnormally and exceptionally suggestible, and had an abnormal tendency to yield to leading questions.[39] There was also evidence to suggest that he had a long track record of making up stories that were wholly false and being able to tell these stories in a convincing manner.[40] Following the confession by Nash, the charges against Lyons for the murders were withdrawn on 29 April 1998, by which point he had spent in excess of eight months in prison. Lyons died in Manchester on 12 September 2000. A formal apology was issued to his family by *An Garda Síochána* on 24 March 2005.[41]

While miscarriage of justice cases such as the Lyons affair offer a stark reminder of the dangers associated with the failure to adapt forensic procedures at the pre-trial stage of the criminal process to take account of the 'ontological realities of intellectual impairment',[42] it is important to emphasise that the exigencies of Article 6 of the ECHR do not automatically preclude a rigorous forensic

---

36 George Birmingham, *Report of the Commission of Investigation (Dean Lyons Case) Set up Pursuant to the Commissions of Investigation Act 2004* (2006). Available at: http://www.justice.ie/en/JELR/Dean%20Lyons%20Commission%20of%20Investigation.pdf/Files/Dean%20Lyons%20Commission%20of%20Investigation.pdf (accessed 31 October 2021).

37 *Nash v Director of Public Prosecutions* [2015] IESC 32.

38 George Birmingham, *Report of the Commission of Investigation (Dean Lyons Case) Set up Pursuant to the Commissions of Investigation Act 2004* (2006).

39 George Birmingham, *Report of the Commission of Investigation (Dean Lyons Case) Set up Pursuant to the Commissions of Investigation Act 2004* (2006) 7.

40 George Birmingham, *Report of the Commission of Investigation (Dean Lyons Case) Set up Pursuant to the Commissions of Investigation Act 2004* (2006) 6.

41 In the aftermath of the publication of the commission's findings, and in contemplation of the publication of similar concerns by the Morris Tribunal, an entirely new interview model – the *Garda Síochána* Interview Model – was introduced in Irish policing operations. See generally Geraldine Noone, 'An Garda Síochána Model of Investigative Interviewing of Witnesses and Suspects' in John Pearse (ed) *Investigating Terrorism: Current Political, Legal and Psychological Issues* (Wiley-Blackwell 2015).

42 Alan Cusack, 'Victims of Crime with Intellectual Disabilities and Ireland's Adversarial Trial: Some Ontological, Procedural and Attitudinal Concerns' (2017) 68(4) *Northern Ireland Legal Quarterly* 433, 448.

interrogation of vulnerable suspects. Neither the psychological vulnerabilities of such persons nor any related limitations in social functioning present evidentiary or rights-based challenges that are insurmountable within a modern criminal process.[43] As Gudjonsson points out, there is no empirical basis for treating as unreliable the evidence of a witness simply because its author presents it with a number of psychological vulnerabilities: 'Persons with moderate learning disability may well be able to give reliable evidence pertaining to basic facts, even when they are generally highly suggestible and prone to confabulation.'[44]

However, for best evidence to prevail – and to secure unequivocal compliance with the imperatives of Article 6 of the ECHR – the forensic design of proceedings (including, importantly, the availability of targeted procedural safeguards) would appear from a very recent Strasbourg case – *Hasáliková v Slovakia*[45] – to be key.

Safeguarding Vulnerability: *Hasáliková v Slovakia* (2021)

This case concerned a Slovak national who was serving a 15-year sentence in Levoča Prison following her conviction of a 'particularly serious' murder. The primary source of evidence levied against the applicant was a series of inculpatory (albeit contradictory) statements elicited from her co-accused during the pre-trial proceedings, as well as a series of repeated confessions that the applicant had made to a range of criminal justice professionals (including an investigator, a medical expert and a pre-trial judge). These pre-trial admissions were tendered in the presence of the applicant's court-appointed counsel in circumstances where she had been provided with written information about her rights as well as information concerning the charges against her. In her proceedings before the ECtHR, the applicant contended that the criminal proceedings in Slovakia leading to her conviction had been unfair, thereby constituting breaches of Article 6, Article 5 and Article 17 of the ECHR.

At trial, it had emerged that the applicant had a 'slight intellectual disability ... with infantile features and simplistic thinking'.[46] Moreover, expert psychological evidence suggested that she was 'also very naïve, emotionally immature and easily influenced'.[47] It was the applicant's case that there had been a failure to adjust the

---

43 Alan Cusack, 'Addressing Vulnerability in Ireland's Criminal Justice System: A Survey of Recent Statutory Developments' (2020) 24(3) *International Journal of Evidence and Proof* 280; Alan Cusack, 'Reforming Ireland's Adversarial Trial for Victims of Crime with Intellectual Disabilities' in Orla Lynch, James Windle, and Yasmin Ahmed (eds) *Giving Voice to Diversity in Criminological Research* (Bristol University Press 2021) 233–252.

44 Gisli H Gudjonsson, *The Psychology of Interrogations and Confessions* (Wiley 2003) 334. See further Marguerite Ternes and John C Yuille, 'Eyewitness Memory and Eyewitness Identification Performance in Adults with Intellectual Disabilities' (2008) 21 *Journal of Applied Research in Intellectual Disabilities* 519. See also Miet Vanderhallen and Kasia Uzieblo, Chapter 4 of this collection.

45 *Hasáliková v Slovakia* App no 39654/15 (ECHR, 24 June 2021). A request by the applicant to refer this ruling to the Grand Chamber is currently pending.

46 *Hasáliková v Slovakia* App no 39654/15 (ECHR, 24 June 2021) § 21.

47 *Hasáliková v Slovakia* App no 39654/15 (ECHR, 24 June 2021) § 21.

Slovakian pre-trial framework to take account of her intellectual disability. Speci-fically, it was contended that in the absence of special treatment and assistance, the applicant had been unable to understand the various procedural steps involved in her detention, as well as the written information provided to her by the autho-rities; and consequently any inculpatory admissions were unreliable on account of her 'traumatising situation'.[48] In addition, the applicant maintained that she had been denied an opportunity to appoint her own lawyer prior to her first police interview and had also been denied an opportunity to attend the interview of her co-accused and to cross-examine him in court.

In ruling that there had been no violation of Articles 6(1) and 6(3) of the ECHR, the ECtHR placed a heavy emphasis upon the fact that the applicant had been notified of the charges against her upon her arrival at the police station; and had been presented with information about her right to legal assistance, her right to silence and her right to select a legal representative within 30 minutes of being notified of the charges. Moreover, given that the applicant had signed a statement confirming that she had fully understood this information, as well as a copy of her interview record (together with her court-appointed lawyer), and in light of the fact that she had failed to object to her limited freedom to instruct a lawyer, the ECtHR refused to give 'weight to the applicant's allegation that she was limited in her right to choose a lawyer'.[49]

Meanwhile, with regard to the applicant's ancillary allegation concerning the failure by Slovakian authorities to recognise and respond to her individual vulner-ability, the ECtHR took the opportunity to explicitly repeat the centrality of assessing a suspect's vulnerability in the context of any allegation of pre-trial pro-cedural unfairness:

> The Court observes in this context that, when assessing the impact of procedural failings at the pre-trial stage on the overall fairness of the criminal proceedings, it has to examine, among other things, whether the applicant was particularly vulnerable, for example, by reason of age or mental capacity.[50]

In the unique circumstances of the case, however, the majority of the ECtHR refused to recognise the Slovakian authorities as being under an obligation to make appropriate adjustments for the applicant, as there were insufficient indi-cators of her vulnerability.[51] Significantly, in arriving at this – arguably

---

48 *Hasáliková v Slovakia* App no 39654/15 (ECHR, 24 June 2021) § 46.
49 *Hasáliková v Slovakia* App no 39654/15 (ECHR, 24 June 2021) § 65.
50 *Hasáliková v Slovakia* App no 39654/15 (ECHR, 24 June 2021) § 67.
51 '[The applicant] was not suffering from any mental illness or disorder and had been able to recognise the dangerousness of her actions and foresee their consequences. Furthermore, the Court has to take account of the fact that she was an adult and lit-erate and had been assisted by a lawyer from her very first questioning, during which she confirmed that she fully understood the charges and did not require any further explanation … the applicant did not point to any indication in the records of her

controversial –[52] finding, the ECtHR was ostensibly influenced by the operational presence of a range of safeguards that operated to prevent misdecision and false confessions:

> The Court is ... convinced that there were no defects in the pre-trial stage of the proceedings and that the applicant's statements were obtained lawfully, following the application of the legislative framework in place, and after the applicant had received information about her procedural rights as well as legal advice. There was thus no reason for the courts to exclude her pre-trial statements from the evidence and not use them against her at the trial.[53]

Patently, then, national authorities are not inhibited by the exigencies of the ECHR from engaging in a rigorous forensic interrogation of vulnerable detainees, provided that this interrogation is scaffolded by a procedural framework that safeguards the right to a fair trial. In adopting this approach, the *Hasálikova* judgment can be seen to represent a principled attempt by the authorities in Strasbourg to regulate 'the relatively hidden arena of the interview room' by reconciling the public interest in investigating crime on the one hand with the countervailing need to guard against procedural impropriety on the other. Yet the capacity of Ireland's pre-trial process to appropriately balance these competing interests is anything but certain at the time of writing. Indeed, while the fairness of Ireland's pre-trial machinery may ultimately have been upheld in *Doyle*, the invulnerability of the applicant in that case conspired to ensure that the court focused almost exclusively on the issue of access to a lawyer, obviating the need for a broader consideration of the adequacy of other ancillary safeguards that exist under Irish law in order to protect child suspects and individuals with an intellectual disability.

---

interviews and examinations that she had had difficulty understanding or expressing herself. Nor did the court having interviewed the applicant during the investigation notice anything particular. Had the applicant considered herself unprepared for the interviews or in need of any further explanation or assistance, it was incumbent on her and her lawyer to bring such concerns to the attention of the authorities.' *Hasálikova v Slovakia* App no 39654/15 (ECHR, 24 June 2021) § 68.

52 It is important to note that two members of the chamber – President Ksenija Turković and Judge Lorraine Schembri Orland – offered dissenting judgments in the case which centred upon broader conceptualisations of 'vulnerability' in the context of judicially assessing the adequacy of national counterbalancing measures as required pursuant to Articles 6(1) and 6(3) of the ECHR. For an excellent critical analysis of the narrow construction of vulnerability, as entertained by the majority of the chamber, see Roxanna Dehaghani, 'Not Vulnerable Enough? A Missed Opportunity to Bolster the Vulnerable Accused's Position in Hasálikova V. Slovakia' *Strasbourg Observers*, 23 November 2021. Available at https://strasbourgobservers.com/2021/11/23/not-vulnerable-enough-a-missed-opportunity-to-bolster-the-vulnerable-accuseds-position-in-hasalikova-v-slovakia/ (accessed 15 March 2022).

53 *Hasálikova v Slovakia* App no 39654/15 (ECHR, 24 June 2021) § 72.

Safeguards for Vulnerable Suspects in Ireland

The Responsible Adult Safeguard

For adults with intellectual disabilities, one of the most important safeguards enshrined in Irish law is the recognition of a right to be accompanied by a 'responsible adult' during the course of an investigative interview. Specifically, pursuant to Regulation 22(1) of the Criminal Justice Act, 1984 (Treatment of Persons in Custody in Garda Síochána Stations) Regulations, 1987 ('Custody Regulations'), any adult detainee whom the member in charge 'suspects or knows to be mentally handicapped' must not, save with the authority of that member, be questioned in relation to an offence or asked to make a written statement 'unless a parent or guardian is present'.[54] Derogations from this standard are both envisaged and tolerated by the legislation.[55] These exceptions, however, will assist members of *An Garda Síochána* only in extremely narrow circumstances where overriding interests related to the protection of life, the protection property or procedural efficiency are at stake.[56] Moreover, before any derogation from the 'responsible adult' safeguard will be countenanced, a member in charge must, as a matter of first recourse (unless it is impractical to do so), arrange for 'the presence during questioning of … the other parent or another guardian … an adult relative, or … some other responsible adult other than a member'.[57] Regulation 22(2) of the Custody Regulations expressly provides that where the member in charge arranges for the presence of 'some other responsible adult other than a member', the responsible adult referred to in that provision must, where practicable, 'be a person who has experience in dealing with the mentally handicapped'.[58]

In many respects the 'responsible adult' safeguard enshrined in the Custody Regulations is analogous to the 'appropriate adult' safeguard that currently operates in England and Wales.[59] Prompted by public disquiet at the treatment of two

54 Regulation 22(1) of the Criminal Justice Act, 1984 (Treatment of Persons in Custody in Garda Síochána Stations) Regulations, 1987 read in conjunction with Regulation 13(1) of the Criminal Justice Act, 1984 (Treatment of Persons in Custody in Garda Síochána Stations) Regulations, 1987.

55 See generally Alan Cusack, 'An Overview of the Legal Position of Vulnerable Suspects and Defendants in Ireland' *Irish Criminal Justice Agencies Annual Conference* (Dublin, 4 June 2021).

56 Regulation 13(1) of the Criminal Justice Act, 1984 (Treatment of Persons in Custody in Garda Síochána Stations) Regulations, 1987.

57 Regulation 13(2) of the Criminal Justice Act, 1984 (Treatment of Persons in Custody in Garda Síochána Stations) Regulations, 1987.

58 Regulation 22(2) of the Criminal Justice Act, 1984 (Treatment of Persons in Custody in Garda Síochána Stations) Regulations, 1987.

59 See generally, Roxanna Dehaghani, 'He's Just Not That Vulnerable: Exploring the Implementation of the Appropriate Adult Safeguard in Police Custody' (2016) 55(4) *The Howard Journal* 396; Roxanna Dehaghani and Chris Bath, 'Vulnerability and the Appropriate Adult Safeguard: Examining the Definitional and Threshold Changes within PACE Code C' (2019) 3 *Criminal Law Review* 213; Gautam Gulati, Alan Cusack, Brendan D Kelly, Shane Kilcommins and Colum P Dunne, 'Experiences of

child suspects and one adult with an intellectual disability who confessed under duress to being involved in the death of Maxwell Confait in 1972,[60] as well as the publication of the Royal Commission on Criminal Procedure report in 1981,[61] the 'appropriate adult' safeguard was introduced for the purpose of safeguarding the 'rights, entitlements and welfare of juveniles and vulnerable persons'.[62] According to paragraph 11.15 of Code C,[63] a person of any age who is suspected by an officer to either be 'vulnerable' or a juvenile (ie, under 18 years of age) must not – save in limited circumstances – 'be interviewed regarding their involvement or suspected involvement in a criminal offence or offences, or asked to provide or sign a written statement under caution or record of interview, in the absence of the appropriate adult'. According to Dehaghani and Bath:

> The AA [appropriate adult] performs a number of different, but overlapping and complementary, functions. He or she must support, advise and assist the suspect; ensure that the police act properly and fairly, informing a senior officer if not; assist with communication whilst respecting the right to silence; and ensure rights are protected, respected and understood by the suspect.[64]

The appropriate adult has a role not only in interviews, but whenever the suspect is given or asked to provide information or participate in any procedure:

> This includes when warnings in relation to adverse inferences are given, when rights and entitlements are explained, when samples—such as fingerprints, photographs and DNA—are to be taken, when strip or intimate searches are to be conducted, and during charge, bail and police cautions.[65]

In Ireland, by contrast, there is considerably less clarity with regard to the parameters of a responsible adult's operational authority. The origins of this ambiguity must – at least in part – be traced to the vagueness of Ireland's subsisting statutory

People with Intellectual Disabilities Encountering Law Enforcement Officials – A Narrative Systematic Review' (2020) 71 *International Journal of Law and Psychiatry* 101609.

60 Christopher Price and Jonathan Caplan, *The Confait Confessions* (Marion Boyars, 1977).

61 Roxanna Dehaghani, 'He's Just Not That Vulnerable: Exploring the Implementation of the Appropriate Adult Safeguard in Police Custody' (2016) 55(4) *The Howard Journal* 396.

62 Code C: Code of Practice for the Detention, Treatment and Questioning of Persons by Police Officers (2018), para 1.7A.

63 Code C: Code of Practice for the Detention, Treatment and Questioning of Persons by Police Officers (2018).

64 Roxanna Dehaghani and Chris Bath, 'Vulnerability and the Appropriate Adult Safeguard: Examining the Definitional and Threshold Changes within PACE Code C' (2019) 3 *Criminal Law Review* 213, 214.

65 Roxanna Dehaghani and Chris Bath, 'Vulnerability and the Appropriate Adult Safeguard: Examining the Definitional and Threshold Changes within PACE Code C' (2019) 3 *Criminal Law Review* 213, 214.

and policy framework, which has failed not only to replicate the detailed standards contained in the Code of Practice, but also to address the unmet operational need among members of *An Garda Síochána* for a detailed guidance note on the operation of the safeguard.[66] Equally, the absence of a dedicated Irish training body for individuals tasked with fulfilling this role can be seen to have played a key role in preserving the hidden status of this facility within Ireland's criminal justice framework.[67]

The Notice of Rights

In addition to the 'responsible adult' safeguard, the Custody Regulations seek to further offset the power imbalances in Ireland's police interview room by recognising the right of suspects to be provided with a notice of rights. Specifically, Regulation 8(2) insists that 'a member in charge shall without delay give the arrested person or cause him to be given a notice' containing specified information relating to the right to consult a solicitor and the right to have notification of custody sent to another person. Where the arrested person is 'mentally handicapped'[68] or a child under 18 years of age, the notification of custody is mandatory and is accompanied by a request 'to attend at the station without delay'.[69]

In order to comply with this requirement, it is now the practice of *An Garda Síochána* to issue a Notice of Rights: Form C72(s) – Information to Persons in Custody to all arrested persons in *Garda* custody. However, this form is not without its shortcomings. In its current format, for instance, the document fails to contain a complete summary of an arrested person's rights. The right to silence and the right to an interpreter, for example, are currently absent from the document. Moreover, many of the limited rights that are enumerated in the text of the notice of rights are framed in an unclear manner, incorporating reference to other statutory provisions. In addition, the absence of a detailed or easily read explanation of relevant rights further undermines the accessibility of the document.[70]

---

66 See generally, Alan Cusack, 'An Overview of the Legal Position of Vulnerable Suspects and Defendants in Ireland', Irish Criminal Justice Agencies Annual Conference (Dublin, 4 June 2021).

67 Alan Cusack, 'An Overview of the Legal Position of Vulnerable Suspects and Defendants in Ireland', Irish Criminal Justice Agencies Annual Conference (Dublin, 4 June 2021).

68 Regulation 22(2) of the Criminal Justice Act, 1984 (Treatment of Persons in Custody in Garda Síochána Stations) Regulations, 1987.

69 Regulation 8(1)(c)(ii) of the Criminal Justice Act, 1984 (Treatment of Persons in Custody in Garda Síochána Stations) Regulations, 1987 as amended by Regulation 3 of Criminal Justice Act 1984 (Treatment of Persons in Custody in Garda Síochána Stations) (Amendment) Regulations 2006.

70 Alan Cusack, 'An Overview of the Legal Position of Vulnerable Suspects and Defendants in Ireland', Irish Criminal Justice Agencies Annual Conference (Dublin, 4 June 2021).

A Note on the Custody Regulations

Owing to these significant procedural lacunae in the due process framework architected by the Custody Regulations, the degree to which the needs of vulnerable suspects are meaningfully addressed by this statutory instrument is uniquely ambiguous. This concern is heightened, moreover, by the porous lawful authority of the regulations themselves.[71] According to Section 7(3) of the Criminal Justice Act 1984:

> A failure on the part of any member of the Garda Síochána to observe any provision of the regulations shall not of itself render that person liable to any criminal or civil proceedings or of itself affect the lawfulness of the custody of the detained person or the admissibility in evidence of any statement made by him.

Accordingly, the elicitation of any evidence from a suspect in contravention of the safeguards enshrined in the regulations, does not automatically render the relevant proofs inadmissible; nor does it render the individual's detention unlawful. Rather, in such circumstances, the admissibility of any inculpatory evidence will fall to be determined on a case-by-case basis at the discretion of the presiding trial judge.[72] This *ad hoc* approach, it is submitted, provides an unruly template for securing a lasting consensus around the pre-trial safeguards that must be observed in order to vindicate the due process rights of all suspects – and in particular, those who are vulnerable – within the Irish justice system.[73]

Conclusion

Irish courts, much like their international counterparts, have long recognised that the constituent elements of a fair trial are not immutable.[74] This logic, which initially found expression in Strasbourg in *Beuze*,[75] has evolved (through subsequent affirmations in *Simeonovi*[76] *Ibrahim*[77], *Doyle*[78] and, most recently, *Hasálikova*)[79] to become the cornerstone of a line of projectionist judgments from the ECtHR that asserts unequivocally that the fairness of criminal proceedings can only truly

---

71 In this regard, the legal authority of the Custody Regulations mimics the non-binding authority of the commitments enshrined in Code C in England and Wales. See Code of Practice for the Detention, Treatment and Questioning of Persons by Police Officers (2018), s 67(10).
72 See *DPP v Spratt* [1995] 1 IR 585.
73 See, for example, *People (DPP) v Darcy* (unreported, Court of Criminal Appeal, 29 July 1997).
74 See, for example, *Heaney v Ireland* [1994] 2 ILRM 420, 430.
75 *Beuze v Belgium* (2019) 69 EHRR 1.
76 *Ibrahim v United Kingdom* (2015) 61 EHRR 9.
77 (2018) 66 EHRR 2.
78 *Doyle v Ireland* App no 51979/17 (ECHR, 23 May 2019).
79 *Hasálikova v Slovakia* App no 39654/15 (ECHR, 24 June 2021).

be gauged by assessing national pre-trial measures through the lens of a non-exhaustive matrix of factors. Chief among these will be a consideration of a suspect's vulnerability.

With this in mind, the appropriateness of reified Irish pre-trial procedure is no longer certain. Indeed, if the ECtHR was tolerant of the Irish legal system's encroachment on a suspect's right of access to a lawyer in the high-profile case of *Doyle* (which, it is important to reiterate, involved a physically and mentally strong suspect), it is difficult to see the ECtHR being equally sympathetic to any identical restriction in future cases that involve a more vulnerable detainee. The vagueness, moreover, of Ireland's 'responsible adult' framework – in addition to the absence of an accessible Notice of Rights Form and the discretionary status of the Custody Regulations – all pose further urgent questions with respect to the capacity of Ireland's extant mainstream pre-trial formalities to meet the exacting procedural exigencies of Article 6 of the ECHR. It is also difficult to reconcile these failures of provision with the state's constitutional obligation under Article 38.1 of *Bunreacht na hÉireann* to secure a trial in due course of law for all Irish citizens.[80]

With the recent publication of the *Hasálikova*[81] judgment by the ECtHR – in addition to the reservations articulated by the ECtHR with regard to the provision of pre-trial legal assistance in *Doyle* – Irish criminal justice stakeholders have been presented with uniquely instructive insight into the level of procedural armament that is prescribed by Article 6 of the ECHR. These judgments, it is submitted, should act as emboldening reference points for Irish policy makers and police officials, encouraging them to urgently reimagine the subsisting repository of pre-trial safeguards in order to ensure that Ireland's criminal process is in a position not only to withstand any further future scrutiny in Strasbourg, but also – more importantly – to vindicate and protect the human rights of some of the most vulnerable members of Irish society.

---

80 See, for instance, *Heaney v Ireland* [1994] 2 ILRM 420; *People (DPP) v Gormley and White* [2014] 1 ILRM 377.
81 *Hasálikova v Slovakia* App no 39654/15 (ECHR, 24 June 2021).

6 Children's Rights and Police Questioning

The Right to a Lawyer

Louise Forde and Ursula Kilkelly

Introduction

When children come into conflict with the law, the police are normally their first point of contact with the criminal justice system. For children suspected of involvement in offending behaviour, a police interview can be their first experience of the justice process. While anyone can be vulnerable in this situation, children's young age and lack of maturity and understanding can make them particularly sensitive to the pressures of that environment. Moreover, research has suggested that a range of factors can influence children's ability to make good decisions: they can be more suggestible than adults;[1] their stage of development can impact how they respond to questions;[2] and they tend to be focused on immediate, short-term benefits.[3] These difficulties can be exacerbated when children have difficulty understanding the language used,[4] or have communication, intellectual or other difficulties with comprehension.[5] The vulnerabilities that children experience in

1 Kaitlyn McLachlan, Ronald Roesch and Kevin S Douglas, 'Examining the Role of Interrogative Suggestibility in Miranda Rights Comprehension in Adolescents' (2011) 35(3) *Law and Human Behavior* 165.

2 Kathryn Monahan, Laurence Steinberg and Alex R Piquero, 'Juvenile Justice Policy and Practice: A Developmental Perspective' (2015) 44(1) *Crime and Justice* 577; Thomas Grisso, Laurence Steinberg, Jennifer Woolard, Elizabeth Cauffman, Elizabeth Scott, Sandra Graham, Fran Lexcen, Nicholas Dickon Reppucci and Robert Schwartz, 'Juveniles' Competence to Stand Trial: A Comparison of Adolescents' and Adults' Capacities as Trial Defendants' (2003) 27(4) *Law & Human Behavior* 333.

3 Hayley MD Cleary, 'Applying the Lessons of Developmental Psychology to the Study of Juvenile Interrogations: New Directions for Research, Policy, and Practice' (2017) 23(1) *Psychology, Public Policy, and Law* 118.

4 Richard Rogers, Jennifer A Steadham, Chelsea E Fiduccia, Eric Y Drogin and Emily V Robinson, 'Mired in Miranda Misconceptions: A Study of Legally Involved Juveniles at Different Levels of Psychosocial Maturity' (2014) 32 *Behavioral Sciences & the Law* 104.

5 Maxine Winstanley, Roger T Webb and Gina Conti-Ramsden, 'Psycholinguistic and Socioemotional Characteristics of Young Offenders: Do Language Abilities and Gender Matter?' (2019) 24 *Legal and Criminal Psychology* 195; Kaitlyn McLachlan, Ronald Roesch and Kevin S Douglas, 'Examining the Role of Interrogative Suggestibility in Miranda Rights Comprehension in Adolescents' (2011) 35(3) *Law and Human Behavior* 165; Kelly Howard, Clare McCann and Margaret Dudley, '"It's

DOI: 10.4324/9781003205166-9

their interaction with the justice system make it particularly important that they have access to appropriate advice and assistance, especially legal advice and representation. For the reasons above, this is especially acute in the context of police questioning.

The right to access legal assistance is a fundamental aspect of the rights of persons accused of or charged with criminal offences and is recognised under international instruments such as the International Covenant on Civil and Political Rights (ICCPR) and the European Convention on Human Rights (ECHR).[6] Specific to children, Article 40(2) of the United Nations Convention on the Rights of the Child (UNCRC) recognises that any child who is suspected, accused or alleged to have infringed the penal law has a right to 'legal or other appropriate assistance' in the preparation of their defence. The child's right to access legal advice has been reinforced further in instruments such as the European Guidelines on Child-Friendly Justice;[7] EU Directive 2016/800 on procedural safeguards for children who are suspects or accused persons in criminal proceedings;[8] and internationally in the UN Committee on the Rights of the Child's revised General Comment.[9]

Important as these standards are, it is only through the implementation of procedural safeguards that rights are fully realised for children in conflict with the law. In order for children to have their legal rights and interests adequately protected when they are being interviewed by police, their right to access legal advice should not only be protected in law, but also be available and accessible in practice. Despite this, research has shown that children in such situations often do not benefit from the right to access legal advice, while it conversely suggests great benefit to children when they do.[10]

Really Good … Why Hasn't It Happened Earlier?" Professionals' Perspectives on the Benefits of Communication Assistance in the New Zealand Youth Justice System' (2020) 53(2) *Australian & New Zealand Journal of Criminology* 265.

6 See the introduction and Alan Cusack, Shane Kilcommins, Gautam Gulati and Colum Dunne, Chapter 5 of this collection. See also Jantien Leenknecht, Chapter 2 of this collection, regarding the implementation of child-specific rights in different jurisdictions.

7 Council of Europe: Committee of Ministers, *Guidelines of the Committee of Ministers of the Council of Europe on child-friendly justice* (adopted by the Committee of Ministers on 17 November 2010 at the 1098th meeting of the Ministers' Deputies) CM/Del/Dec(2010)1098/10.2.

8 Directive (EU) 2016/800 of the European Parliament and of the Council of 11 May 2016 on procedural safeguards for children who are suspects or accused persons in criminal proceedings.

9 UN Committee on the Rights of the Child (2019), *General Comment No. 24: Children's rights in juvenile justice* CRC/C/GC/24; this has replaced the previous UN Committee on the Rights of the Child, *General Comment No. 10: Children's rights in juvenile justice* (2007) CRC/C/GC/10.

10 Vicky Kemp, '"No Time for a Solicitor": Implications for Delays on the Take Up of Legal Advice' (2013) 3 *Criminal Law Review* 184; Vicky Kemp, Pascoe Pleasence and Nigel J Balmer, 'Children, Young People and Requests for Police Station Legal Advice: 25 years on from PACE' (2011) 11(1) *Youth Justice* 28; Katie Quinn and

This chapter aims to consider the application of the child's right to a lawyer in the context of police questioning, taking account of the particular vulnerabilities and needs of children in such situations. The chapter begins by considering the child's right to 'legal and other assistance' under the UNCRC and their entitlement to legal advice under other human rights instruments. The chapter then explores the role played by lawyers acting for children with regard to police questioning, as well as the barriers that may prevent that access being effective. The complex question of whether the child has a right to waive their right to a lawyer is also considered from a children's rights perspective. In considering these issues, the chapter draws on original research exploring children's experiences of their rights during police questioning which was conducted by the authors in Ireland in 2020 with the support of the Policing Authority.[11]

International Standards

The UNCRC is a binding international legal treaty that sets out the rights to which children are entitled in all areas of their lives. Article 40 of the UNCRC makes specific provision for the rights of children in conflict with the law and Article 40(2) details the procedural rights that apply when children are suspected, accused or alleged to have committed a criminal offence. In addition, Article 12(1) of the UNCRC guarantees a child's right to be heard in all matters that affect them; and Article 12(2) recognises the right of the child to be heard in any judicial proceedings that affect them, either directly or through a representative in a manner consistent with national law. Article 40(2)(b)(ii) provides that children should have access to 'legal *or* other appropriate assistance' (emphasis added), which must be available from the outset of the proceedings.[12] The wording of this provision suggests that legal assistance is not guaranteed to children in justice proceedings, causing the Committee on the Rights of the Child to express concern that as a result, children enjoy 'less protection' than adults in this area under international law.[13]

When looking to understand the basis for this provision, the drafting of the UNCRC offers an explanation.[14] During the drafting process, a proposed text

John Jackson, 'Of Rights and Roles: Police Interviews with Young Suspects in Northern Ireland' (2007) 47(2) *The British Journal of Criminology* 234; Ursula Kilkelly and Louise Forde, *Children's Rights and Police Questioning: A Qualitative Study of Children's Experiences of Being Interviewed by the Garda Síochána* (Policing Authority, 2021).

11 Ursula Kilkelly and Louise Forde, *Children's Rights and Police Questioning: A Qualitative Study of Children's Experiences of Being Interviewed by the Garda Síochána* (Policing Authority, 2021). See Miranda Bevan, Chapter 7 of this collection, for an exploration of children's rights during police questioning in England and Wales.

12 UN Committee on the Rights of the Child (2019) *General Comment No. 24: Children's rights in the child justice system* (CRC/C/GC/24) at para 49.

13 UN Committee on the Rights of the Child (2019) *General Comment No. 24: Children's rights in the child justice system* (CRC/C/GC/24) at para 62.

14 See further Nigel Cantwell, 'The Origins, Development and Significance of the United Nations Convention on the Rights of the Child' in Jaap Doek, Nigel Cantwell

from Canada gave explicit recognition to children's due process rights, including the right to information using appropriate language; the right to be presumed innocent; the right to a fair hearing by an independent tribunal within a reasonable time; and the right to legal assistance.[15]

However, not all states parties agreed. Delegates from the United Kingdom and Finland, for instance, raised concerns about the right to legal assistance, arguing that other assistance – such as from social workers – would be appropriate.[16] The proposal to include representation by non-lawyers as well as lawyers was also raised by Germany and the Netherlands.[17] It was suggested by the Dutch delegation, for instance, that assistance should only be given to the child if the interests of justice required it.[18] The assumption seemed to be, therefore, that if a welfare-focused system of justice were in place, formal legal assistance would not be necessary. The text finally adopted, recognising the child's right to 'legal or other assistance', thus represented a compromise between these various perspectives.

However, in the years since the adoption of the UNCRC, there has been greater recognition of the importance of the child's right to legal assistance. Following a similar observation of the Human Rights Committee in 2007,[19] the Committee on the Rights of the Child emphasised in 2019 that the right to legal assistance is 'a minimum guarantee in the criminal justice system for all persons' under Article 14(3)(d) of the ICCPR, which includes children.[20]

Other international instruments have also stressed the importance of the child's right to legal assistance. Access to legal advice from the earliest stages of proceedings, including during police questioning, has been held by the European Court of Human Rights to be essential to protecting the right to participate effectively in criminal proceedings under Article 6 of the ECHR.[21] The European Guidelines on Child-Friendly Justice state unequivocally that whenever a child is apprehended by the police, they should be 'provided with access to a lawyer'; and that a child should only be questioned in the presence of a lawyer or one of their

and Sharon L de Detrick, *The United Nations Convention on the Rights of the Child: A Guide to the* Travaux Préparatoires (Martinus Nijhoff Publishers, 1992), p 19.

15 Office of the High Commissioner for Human Rights, *Legislative History of the Convention on the Rights of the Child: Volume II* (United Nations, 2007) at p 746.

16 Document *E/CN.4/1986/39* at para 98 as reprinted in Office of the High Commissioner for Human Rights, *Legislative History of the Convention on the Rights of the Child: Volume II* (United Nations, 2007) at pp 464 and 466.

17 Document *E/CN.4/1986/39* at para 98 as reprinted in Office of the High Commissioner for Human Rights, *Legislative History of the Convention on the Rights of the Child: Volume II* (United Nations, 2007) at para 577, at p 498.

18 Document *E/CN.4/1986/39* at para 98 as reprinted in Office of the High Commissioner for Human Rights, *Legislative History of the Convention on the Rights of the Child: Volume II* (United Nations, 2007) at para 578, at p 498.

19 Human Rights Committee (2007) *General Comment No.32: Article 14: Right to equality before courts and tribunals and to a fair trial* (CCPR/C/GC/32) at para 42.

20 UN Committee on the Rights of the Child (2019) *General Comment No. 24: Children's rights in the child justice system* (CRC/C/GC/24) at para 50.

21 *Martin v Estonia* Case No 35985/09 (First Section) 30 May 2013; *Salduz v Turkey* (2000) 49 EHRR 19.

parents or another trusted adult. The guidelines provide detailed guidance on legal counsel and representation, emphasising the child's entitlement to their own legal representation and legal aid, and the need for lawyers to be knowledgeable about children's rights and related matters.[22]

Similarly, EU Directive 2016/800 on procedural safeguards for children who are suspects or accused persons in criminal proceedings emphasises the extent and scope of the child's right to legal assistance, with Article 6 requiring that member states 'ensure that children are assisted by a lawyer'. This mandatory language is reinforced elsewhere in the directive, which recognises the need to ensure that this assistance is provided 'without undue delay' and before the point where the child is questioned by police. Moreover, Article 6(4) details the type of assistance that should be provided by a lawyer, including ensuring that the child has legal assistance during police questioning and that lawyers can participate actively during the questioning processes. It is clear that any limited derogation must comply with the child's right to a fair trial in full consideration of the child's best interests.

The emphasis placed on the importance of adequate legal assistance and the increased guidance on how to exercise this right underscore the importance of the right to legal advice for children in conflict with the law at the international level. This has most recently been reiterated by the Committee on the Rights of the Child. In its revised General Comment in 2019, the committee highlights that the right to legal representation is a minimum guarantee.[23] It recommends that states provide free and effective legal representation for all children who are facing criminal charges.[24] The support of practitioners throughout all stages of the criminal justice process is also fundamental to realise the child's right to participate effectively in the proceedings.[25] While 'other appropriate assistance' from well-trained officers may be acceptable, the committee seems to limit this to situations where children are diverted to programmes or are in systems which do not result in convictions, criminal records or deprivation of liberty; even in these circumstances, it is stressed that the person tasked with providing this assistance should have sufficient knowledge of the legal aspects of the child justice process.[26] Significantly, the committee recommends that children not be permitted to waive their right to legal representation 'unless the decision is made voluntarily and under impartial judicial supervision'. Despite the relatively weak wording of Article 40(2)(b)(ii) of the UNCRC, taken together, these contemporary legal standards regard the provision of legal assistance as essential to the effective realisation of

---

22 Ton Liefaard, 'Child-Friendly Justice: Protection and Participation of Children in the Justice System' (2016) 88(4) *Temple Law Review* 905.

23 UN Committee on the Rights of the Child (2019) *General Comment No. 24: Children's rights in the child justice system* (CRC/C/GC/24) at para 50.

24 UN Committee on the Rights of the Child (2019) *General Comment No. 24: Children's rights in the child justice system* (CRC/C/GC/24) at para 51.

25 UN Committee on the Rights of the Child (2019) *General Comment No. 24: Children's rights in the child justice system* (CRC/C/GC/24) at para 46.

26 UN Committee on the Rights of the Child (2019) *General Comment No. 24: Children's rights in the child justice system* (CRC/C/GC/24) at para 50.

children's rights in criminal proceedings, except in the very specific circumstances outlined by the committee.

Challenges in Implementing the Right of the Child to Access Legal Advice in Practice

Empirical studies from the United States, the United Kingdom and elsewhere have shed light on both the importance to children of having access to adequate legal assistance and the practical difficulties that children can experience exercising this right. Research has highlighted the vulnerability of children during police questioning and revealed the serious consequences that they may experience navigating this process without adequate support. While it is important that children may be more likely to make a false confession during the course of police questioning,[27] there are also other consequences of children's lack of maturity and inexperience in this setting. Gooch and von Berg, for example, have highlighted that children may be more inclined to comply with police requests in the hope of being allowed to leave the police station more quickly.[28] In addition, research has found that children's powerlessness in this situation can make them inclined to cooperate more readily with police officers and other adults in authority.[29] Children's cognitive immaturity may also impact on their legal capacity in this context.[30]

These vulnerabilities can be further heightened by emotional and mental health concerns, low IQ, low literacy levels, special educational needs and communication difficulties.[31] Where children have experienced abuse, trauma, loss or neglect,

27 Megan Glynn Crane, 'Childhood Trauma's Lurking Presence in the Juvenile Interrogation Room and the Need for a Trauma-informed Voluntariness Test for Juvenile Confessions' (2017) 62 *South Dakota Law Review* 626, 627; Emily Haney-Caron, Naomi ES Goldstein and Constance Mesiarik, 'Self-Perceived Likelihood of False Confession: A Comparison of Justice-Involved Juveniles and Adults' (2018) 45(12) *Criminal Justice and Behaviour* 1955.

28 Kate Gooch and Piers von Berg, 'What Happens in the Beginning, Matters in the End: Achieving Best Evidence with Child Suspects in the Police Station' (2019) 19(2) *Youth Justice* 85, 88–89.

29 Hayley MD Cleary, 'Police Interviewing and Interrogation of Juvenile Suspects: A Descriptive Examination of Actual Cases' (2014) 38(3) *Law and Human Behaviour* 271, 272; Barry C Feld, 'Police Interrogation of Juveniles: An Empirical Study of Policy and Practice' (2006) 97(1) *The Journal of Criminal Law and Criminology* 219, 244; Barry Feld, 'Real Interrogation: What Actually Happens when Cops Question Kids' (2013) 47(1) *Law and Society Review* 1, 24–2.

30 Jodi L Viljoen and Ronald Roesch, 'Competence to Waive Interrogation Rights and Adjudicative Competence in Adolescent Defendants: Cognitive Development, Attorney Contact, and Psychological Symptoms' (2005) 29(6) *Law and Human Behaviour* 723,

31 Kate Gooch and Piers von Berg, 'What Happens in the Beginning, Matters in the End: Achieving Best Evidence with Child Suspects in the Police Station' (2019) 19(2) *Youth Justice* 85, 89; Megan Glynn Crane, 'Childhood Trauma's Lurking Presence in the Juvenile Interrogation Room and the Need for a Trauma-informed Voluntariness Test for Juvenile Confessions' (2017) 62 *South Dakota Law Review* 626.

mental health issues or substance abuse, these factors can also increase their vulnerability.[32] Children's level of understanding – both of the specific questions they are being asked and of the process and the potential consequences of that process – can be further impacted where they experience communication difficulties of any kind. Police questioning processes rely heavily on the suspect having sufficient language and related skills to successfully navigate this process,[33] and it is therefore of concern that a range of studies have documented high levels of cognitive disabilities and communication difficulties among children in conflict with the law.[34] Children being interrogated about criminal activity – especially where the matter is very serious or where questioning is by necessity complex or technical – can experience very significant challenges during police questioning. All of this highlights the importance of ensuring that the child has access to effective legal advice and assistance sufficient to safeguard their legal rights and promote good decision making through their participation in the criminal process.

Despite the strong recognition and clear importance of the child's legal rights in this area, children continue to experience difficulties claiming their rights. The matter is undoubtedly complicated by the fact that the child may, in many cases, choose not to seek access to a lawyer. For instance, several studies have found that children often decide not to avail of their right to legal assistance during the course of police questioning,[35] with some indications that the rate of waiver is very high. In one US study, for instance, 80% of young people waived their Miranda rights;[36] while another suggested that this number could be as high as 90%.[37]

32 Megan Glynn Crane, 'Childhood Trauma's Lurking Presence in the Juvenile Interrogation Room and the Need for a Trauma-informed Voluntariness Test for Juvenile Confessions' (2017) 62 *South Dakota Law Review* 626.

33 Stavroola AS Anderson, David J Hawes and Pamela C Snow, 'Language Impairments among Youth Offenders: A Systematic Review' (2016) 65 *Children and Youth Services Review* 195, 196; Jodi L Viljoen and Ronald Roesch, 'Competence to Waive Interrogation Rights and Adjudicative Competence in Adolescent Defendants: Cognitive Development, Attorney Contact, and Psychological Symptoms' (2005) 29(6) *Law and Human Behaviour* 723, 736–7.

34 Kathy Ellem and Kelly Richards, 'Police Contact with Young People with Cognitive Disabilities: Perceptions of Procedural (In)justice' (2018) 18(3) *Youth Justice* 230; Stavroola AS Anderson, David J Hawes and Pamela C Snow, 'Language Impairments among Youth Offenders: A Systematic Review' (2016) 65 *Children and Youth Services Review* 195; see further Pamela C Snow, Dixie D Sanger, Laura M Caire, Patricia A Eadie and Teagan Dinslage, 'Improving Communication Outcomes for Young Offenders: A Proposed Response to Intervention Framework' (2014) 50(1) *Language and Communication Disorders* 1.

35 Hayley MD Cleary, 'Police Interviewing and Interrogation of Juvenile Suspects: A Descriptive Examination of Actual Cases' (2014) 38(3) *Law and Human Behaviour* 271, 279; Vicky Kemp, Pascoe Pleasence and Nigel J Balmer, 'Children, Young People and Requests for Police Station Legal Advice: 25 Years on from PACE' (2011) 11(1) *Youth Justice* 28.

36 Barry C Feld, 'Police Interrogation of Juveniles: An Empirical Study of Policy and Practice' (2006) 97(1) *Journal of Criminal Law and Criminology* 219, 255.

37 Barry Feld, 'Real Interrogation: What Actually Happens when Cops Question Kids' (2013) 47(1) *Law and Society Review* 1, 11–12.

Similarly, in the United Kingdom, a 2011 study highlighted difficulties in determining the extent to which the introduction of legislative guidance designed to better protect detainees' rights while in police custody had benefited children.[38] This study raised particular concern that younger children –aged 10 to 13 – were least likely to request and receive legal advice.[39] It was also noted as a matter of concern that 43% of young people did not request a solicitor despite subsequently being charged.[40]

Children deciding whether to access legal advice may make this decision independently or in consultation with a parent, guardian or other adult. The reasons for choosing to waive the right to a lawyer may thus depend on the individual circumstances, and may be impacted by the availability of a lawyer to attend the police station (promptly) and the eagerness on the part of detainee to leave the police detention.[41] Reductions in legal aid may also be important.[42] For others, the perceived minor nature of the offence or their sense of the evidence against them might influence the decision.[43] Regardless, it would appear that for many children tasked with making this decision, they simply do not understand what assistance a lawyer might usefully provide during police questioning.[44]

Whatever the reason, the fact that many children who face police questioning opt not to access their right to legal advice raises real questions about the extent to which they enjoy the legal safeguards to which they are entitled. It is for this reason that the question of whether a child can legitimately waive their right to legal advice has become the subject of debate.[45] Feld has highlighted children's legal autonomy to waive this right,[46] drawing attention to the need to ensure that

---

38 Vicky Kemp, Pascoe Pleasence and Nigel J Balmer, 'Children, Young People and Requests for Police Station Legal Advice: 25 Years on from PACE' (2011) 11(1) *Youth Justice* 28.

39 Vicky Kemp, Pascoe Pleasence and Nigel J Balmer, 'Children, Young People and Requests for Police Station Legal Advice: 25 Years on from PACE' (2011) 11(1) *Youth Justice* 28.

40 Vicky Kemp, Pascoe Pleasence and Nigel J Balmer, 'Children, Young People and Requests for Police Station Legal Advice: 25 Years on from PACE' (2011) 11(1) *Youth Justice* 28, 37.

41 Vicky Kemp, '"No Time for a Solicitor": Implications for Delays on the Take Up of Legal Advice' (2013) 3 *Criminal Law Review* 184.

42 Bethany A'Court and Raymond Arthur, 'The Role of Lawyers in Supporting Young People in the Criminal Justice System: Balancing Economic Survival and Children's Rights' (2020) 42(4) *Journal of Social Welfare and Family Law* 498.

43 Layla Skinns, *Police Powers and Citizens' Rights: Discretionary Decision-Making in Police Detention* (Routledge, 2019), 125.

44 Vicky Kemp, Pascoe Pleasence and Nigel J Balmer, 'Children, Young People and Requests for Police Station Legal Advice: 25 Years on from PACE' (2011) 11(1) *Youth Justice* 28, 38–39.

45 Jodi L Viljoen and Ronald Roesch, 'Competence to Waive Interrogation Rights and Adjudicative Competence in Adolescent Defendants: Cognitive Development, Attorney Contact, and Psychological Symptoms' (2005) 29(6) *Law and Human Behaviour* 723.

46 Barry C Feld, 'Police Interrogation of Juveniles: An Empirical Study of Policy and Practice' (2006) 97(1) *Journal of Criminal Law and Criminology* 219, 228.

protections are in place to guide the child's decision making in this regard. To understand the issue further, the next section considers children's experiences of accessing legal advice in Ireland drawing on an original, empirical study of children's experiences of their rights during police questioning.[47]

Children's Experiences of Exercising their Right to Legal Advice in Ireland

Funded by the Policing Authority, the study involved individual interviews with four groups of participants – children, parents or guardians, lawyers and members of *An Garda Síochána* (the police) – who had experienced the child interview process. In total, 20 children aged between 14 and 18 were interviewed, as well as 12 members of *An Garda Síochána*, four lawyers and three parents or adults who had acted in a caring and supportive role for children who were being questioned by *Gardaí*. The children who took part all had some experience of being interviewed by the police and were identified through Oberstown Children Detention Campus (the national detention centre), Garda youth diversion projects and other youth groups working with children in conflict with the law. Parents and adults in a supportive role were also identified through facilitator groups working with children in conflict with the law; while members of *An Garda Síochána* who participated in the research were identified in cooperation with the *Garda* Research Unit. Efforts were made to include participants from different geographical regions of the country and with different levels of experience of police interviews with children. Ethical approval was granted by the Social Research Ethics Committee in University College Cork; and a youth advisory group (made up of four young people aged 14 to 18) helped to develop the question frames used for the children who participated in this study.[48] While the research explored a number of issues relating to children's experiences of police questioning, this section specifically focuses on children's experiences of their right to access legal advice and assistance.

The Children Act 2001 governs the treatment of children in conflict with the law in Ireland and recognises the child's right to access legal advice. The legislation places a general obligation on members of *An Garda Síochána* to:

> act with due respect for the personal rights of the children and their dignity as human persons, for their vulnerability owing to their age and level of maturity

---

47 Ursula Kilkelly and Louise Forde, *Children's Rights and Police Questioning: A Qualitative Study of Children's Experiences of being interviewed by the Garda Síochána* (Policing Authority, 2021); this report, containing the full results of the study, is available at www.policingauthority.ie.

48 Full details of methodology are found in Ursula Kilkelly and Louise Forde, *Children's Rights and Police Questioning: A Qualitative Study of Children's Experiences of being interviewed by the Garda Síochána,* (Policing Authority, 2021); this report, containing the full results of the study, is available at www.policingauthority.ie.

and for the special needs of any of them who may be under a physical or mental disability.[49]

It also requires them to ensure the integrity of the investigation process. The act contains a number of specific procedural requirements, including that the child be informed of their entitlement to a lawyer. The member in charge of the *Garda* station who bears specific responsibility for ensuring the welfare of those in police custody is responsible for notifying the child of their entitlement to consult with a lawyer prior to being questioned. If a child or their parent or guardian requests legal advice, the member in charge of the station must notify a solicitor as soon as practicable and provide the child with the name of a solicitor if necessary.[50] A reasonable time must be allowed to facilitate this consultation before questioning can take place.[51] More generally, it is important to note that the right of an accused person to access a solicitor is a right under the Irish Constitution, although this has historically been limited to access to a lawyer prior to inter-view.[52] While there is no statutory entitlement for a child, therefore, to have a lawyer present with them during the police interview, it is now common practice to allow a solicitor to be present if this is requested.[53]

In the study, all of the child participants had been advised of their right to consult with a solicitor prior to being questioned, although the issue of whether this right was exercised was more complex. While many children had accessed legal assistance, others had not. When children were asked why they had chosen not to exercise their right to a solicitor, a range of reasons emerged, many of which echoed the findings of the research set out above.[54] For instance, a number of children pointed to the risk of delay as a key reason, referring to waiting for a lawyer as 'a whole lot of hassle', adding 'I just want to get home as quick as I can' (Child 11). Another child explained: 'I never even bothered ringing my solicitor most of the time ... because I always wanted to get out of there as fast as possible' (Child 1).

The issue of delay was also cited by both lawyers and guardians/carers for children in police custody as a major reason why children chose not to exercise their right to legal advice (Lawyer 2; Caring Role 2).

Aside from delay, however, other reasons also emerged. In some cases, it was suggested that children did not fully understand the potential consequences of

---

49 Section 55 of the Children Act 2001 (No. 24 of 2001).
50 Section 60 of the Children Act 2001.
51 Section 61 of the Children Act 2001.
52 *DPP v Healy* [1990] 2 IR 73; *Lavery v Member in Charge, Carrickmacross Garda Station* [1999] 2 IR 390; see also *DPP v Gormley and DPP v White* [2014] IESC 17, [2014] 2 IR 591 and *DPP v Doyle* [2017] IESC 1.
53 *An Garda Síochána, Code of Practice on Access to a Solicitor by Persons in Garda Custody* (An Garda Síochána, April 2015).
54 Layla Skinns, *Police Powers and Citizens' Rights: Discretionary Decision-Making in Police Detention* (Routledge, 2019) at p.125; Vicky Kemp, '"No Time for a Solicitor": Implications for Delays on the Take Up of Legal Advice' (2013) 3 *Criminal Law Review* 184–202.

their situation (Lawyer 4); while some children considered that the offence they were accused of was not serious enough to warrant a solicitor's advice. As one child said: '[I]t's only like thefts and stuff, I don't think I need a solicitor for that' (Child 2); while another suggested: '[T]here was nothing really serious about it, like. I was doing fine without it' (Child 17). In a number of cases, where children had prior experience of being interviewed by *Gardaí* in relation to other suspected offences, children felt that they did not need legal advice because they had been through the experience before (Child 5; Child 7). Adults who had supported children highlighted that children may not know the name of a solicitor to contact in those situations (Caring Role 2). In other cases, children did not give a clear reason as to why they had refused legal advice (Child 4).

It is notable that *Garda* participants in the study were very supportive of children exercising their right to access legal advice and noted that when a child was concerned, they would often 'overemphasise that it is important that they do seek legal advice prior to coming into an interview room' (Garda 8). Although whether a solicitor was present in an interview room depended on the circumstances of the individual case, the *Gardaí* were generally supportive of them being there. Significantly, while the *Gardaí* regarded this as an important safeguard for the child, they also considered that it brought greater transparency to the process and allowed them to 'concentrate on the interviews' (*Garda* 1).

When children did exercise their right to consult a solicitor, the children often reported this as positive. One child said that he had found it 'very, very helpful', and had felt that there was someone 'fighting it with me' (Child 15). This feeling of having someone on their side (Child 9) and advising them on what to say and what not to say during a *Garda* interview (Child 12) was particularly useful. For others, solicitors were a very important source of information (Child 7); one child felt that they would 'tell you more about the interview and all than the Guards will' (Child 10). In other cases, having a lawyer present made children feel safer while they were being interviewed by *Gardaí* (Child 7). On the whole, the children who exercised their right to consult with a solicitor found this to be a hugely beneficial experience, reflecting the importance of ensuring that children being questioned by the police have access to a lawyer.

It is interesting that a number of participants in this study – both lawyers and children – raised the issue of whether it should be possible for children to waive their entitlement to legal advice. One lawyer expressed the opinion that 'no child should be allowed to refuse a solicitor unless it's done in a manner in which they are fully informed, and their parents are fully informed' (Lawyer 2); while another commented, in respect of her clients who regularly refused the right to consult with a solicitor, that the right should be 'automatic' and thus that 'a child cannot be questioned without a solicitor' (Lawyer 4).

Interestingly, a number of the children in the study raised the question of whether children should ever be questioned without prior legal advice or having a solicitor present. Some children who had waived their right to legal advice said that with the benefit of hindsight, they would have made a different decision

(Child 2; Child 19). Another child expressed the view that children should not be able to refuse the assistance and advice of a solicitor:

> I think that a solicitor should be mandatory because when you're younger you're just going to say, 'No, I don't want a solicitor, I just want to get out of here,' but then you're just going ... they're delighted with that then because you're just going yourself into a ball of shit, like. (Child 1)

While more research is certainly needed to tease out these issues in more detail, the experiences and views of the children in the study about accessing legal advice raise important issues about how best to promote more effective access to a lawyer prior to police questioning.

One other issue worthy of mention in this context is the need to ensure that lawyers who assist children in the police station are specially trained. International standards set by the Committee on the Rights of the Child emphasise the need for continuous and systematic training for all professionals working with children in conflict with the law.[55] This sentiment was echoed by the lawyers who took part in the study in Ireland. While solicitors noted the lack of formalised, specialised training for lawyers who represent children, they expressed a desire for additional training (Lawyer 2; Lawyer 3), highlighting the complexity of the issues that arise when assisting children and the importance of ensuring that vulnerable people are provided with effective assistance (Lawyer 4; Lawyer 2).

Conclusion

The importance of ensuring that children have access to effective legal assistance and of considering how this right is implemented in practice is vital to ensure that children's rights are adequately protected when they are interviewed by police. This is important both to safeguard the rights of the child and to promote the integrity of the criminal process. The particular vulnerabilities that children experience due to their age, maturity and inexperience, and in many cases due to communication or learning difficulties, make realising this right to the fullest extent possible all the more pressing.

The crucial nature of this right is reflected in the international standards in this area. While the UNCRC itself requires children to be provided with 'legal or other appropriate assistance', under Article 40(2), the Committee on the Rights of the Child has made it clear that adequate legal assistance is of central importance, and that other types of assistance should be considered only in situations where children are not facing criminal charges or convictions. In addition, the proliferation of other international instruments which highlight the importance of legal assistance for children during police questioning – including the European Guidelines on Child-Friendly Justice and EU Directive 2016/800 on procedural safeguards

---

55 UN Committee on the Rights of the Child, *General Comment No. 24, Children's rights in the child justice system* (2019) (CRC/C/GC/24) at para 39.

for children who are suspects or accused persons in criminal proceedings – reinforce the need to ensure that children have adequate access to legal advice and assistance during the course of police questioning. The recommendation by the Committee on the Rights of the Child that children should be able to waive their right to legal advice only in circumstances where this is done voluntarily and under impartial judicial supervision is particularly noteworthy.[56] This strongly indicates that children should be supported in accessing legal assistance prior to being questioned by police in order to ensure that their rights are adequately protected. At the very least, measures should be adopted to ensure that this is a fully informed decision.

Although a full-scale international study is required to scope out these issues in more detail, it is evident nonetheless that greater efforts are required to ensure that children's legal rights are protected in the domestic legal system. Apart from ensuring that all children who exercise this right have prompt access to a specially trained lawyer, these measures should also include making available to children accessible and child-friendly information that helps them to exercise their rights in their own legal interests. The potentially serious consequences of proceeding to be questioned without legal assistance or representation should be made very clear. This raises complex questions involving the availability of adequately trained and knowledgeable lawyers who can assist children, and in relation to access to legal aid. While many children choose not to avail of their right to access legal advice, it is clear from the documented experiences of children that there are many benefits for those who do so. This growing body of research, the emphasis on the importance of legal advice in an increasing number of international standards and guidelines available, and the views and perspectives of children with lived experiences and who are most directly affected by this issue indicate the benefits and the importance of ensuring that children's right to access legal advice and assistance is properly respected and realised.

---

56 UN Committee on the Rights of the Child, *General Comment No. 24, Children's rights in the child justice system* (2019) (CRC/C/GC/24) at para 51.

7 Behind Closed Doors

Protections for Child Suspects in Police Custody

Miranda Bevan

Introduction

Police custody is a hidden world. What occurs for children behind its closed doors is critically important, not only for the outcome of the criminal justice process, but also for the child's ongoing attitudes towards the police and authority more generally. Yet in England and Wales, the child suspect[1] is rarely glimpsed in empirical research; nor are their experiences often scrutinised in court. In particular, how successfully the protections which should be afforded to them address the acute vulnerability they experience in the custody block, and the extent to which they are supported to participate effectively in the process, have not been comprehensively explored.[2] This chapter aims to begin the process of bringing this hidden world into the light by providing a critical assessment of the protections for child suspects in England and Wales, both on paper and from the perspective of the child in practice.

Arguably, the police custody phase ought to trigger the most substantial protections of all youth justice processes in England and Wales. First, the child is detained on the suspicion of criminal behaviour alone,[3] and many will never even be charged with an offence. As Andrew Ashworth has argued, processes pre-trial should impose the 'minimum burdens' on suspected individuals.[4] Second, the child suspect is in acute legal jeopardy – what they say, or do not say, in interview is liable to be determinative of the case against them,[5] and admissions made will frequently result in an out-of-court disposal without recourse to the courts.[6]

---

1 'Child suspect' and 'young suspect' are used here to denote a 10 to 17-year-old detained in police custody following an arrest.
2 See Louise Forde and Ursula Kilkelly, Chapter 6 of this collection, for an exploration of children's rights during police questioning in Ireland.
3 Police and Criminal Evidence Act 1984 (PACE), Section 24.
4 Andrew Ashworth, *The Criminal Process: An Evaluative Study* (1st edn, OUP 1994) 31.
5 Frank P Belloni and Jacqueline Hodgson, *Criminal Injustice: An Evaluation of the Criminal Justice Process in Britain* (Macmillan 2000).
6 The overall caution rate for children in the year to March 2019 was 24% (Ministry of Justice (MOJ)/Youth Justice Board, *Criminal Justice Statistics Quarterly*, England and Wales, April 2018 to March 2019).

DOI: 10.4324/9781003205166-10

Third, children who find themselves in police custody are likely to be particularly vulnerable on a number of measures. By virtue of the strikingly low, and oft-criticised, minimum age of criminal responsibility in England and Wales,[7] children as young as 10 may find themselves in police custody facing a criminal allegation. However, across the age bracket, the child suspect's natural developmental immaturity is liable to compromise their ability to engage in legal processes, to manage the strain of detention and to make the decisions required of them in that setting.[8] To compound their difficulties, children in conflict with the law in England and Wales are recognised as a group experiencing significantly raised prevalence of dispositional vulnerabilities, such as communication disorders,[9] developmental disorders[10] and learning disability;[11] and they are more likely to have experienced childhood adversities, such as violence within the family,[12] bereavement[13] or exclusion from school,[14] and to be in the care of the local authority.[15] Finally, the power imbalance between child and state in police detention is at its most extreme. The child suspect is, for the most part, alone in the coercive – and often unfamiliar – custody environment, and at the beginning of a wider adversarial process. While the distinction between adversarial and inquisitorial systems is increasingly less stark,[16] in England and Wales there remains no judicial oversight of any aspect of this closed process pre-charge. The protections afforded to a suspect lie in the hands of the custody officer (CO),[17] who, while independent of the investigation, is nonetheless a police officer and –

---

7   Children and Young Persons Act 1933 (CYPA), Section 50. See, for example, Barry Goldson, 'COUNTERBLAST: "Difficult to Understand or Defend": A Reasoned Case for Raising the Age of Criminal Responsibility' [2009] 48 *Howard Journal of Criminal Justice* 514.

8   Thomas Grisso and others, 'Juveniles' Competence to Stand Trial: A Comparison of Adolescents' and Adults' Capacities as Trial Defendants' [2003] 27 *Law and Human Behavior* 333; Michael Lamb and Megan Sim, 'Developmental Factors Affecting Children in Legal Contexts' (2013) 13 *Youth Justice* 131.

9   Marc Woodbury-Smith, 'Conceptualising Social and Communication Vulnerabilities among Detainees in the Criminal Justice System' [2020] 100 *Research in Developmental Disabilities* 103611.

10 Nathan Hughes and others, *Nobody Made the Connection: The Prevalence of Neurodisability in Young People Who Offend* (Children's Commissioner 2012).

11 Nancy Loucks, *No One Knows: Offenders with Learning Difficulties and Learning Disabilities – A Review of Prevalence and Associated Needs* (Prison Reform Trust 2007).

12 Ingrid Obsuth and others, 'Violent Poly-Victimization: The Longitudinal Patterns of Physical and Emotional Victimization Throughout Adolescence (11–17 Years)' [2018] 28 *Journal of Research on Adolescence* 786.

13 Nina Vaswani, 'The Ripples of Death: Exploring the Bereavement Experiences and Mental Health of Young Men in Custody' [2014] 53 *Howard Journal of Crime and Justice* 341.

14 Charlie Taylor, *Review of the Youth Justice System in England and Wales* (MOJ 2016).

15 Her Majesty's Inspectorate of Prisons, *Children in Custody 2018–19* (2020), 2.

16 Jacqueline S Hodgson, *The Metamorphosis of Criminal Justice: A Comparative Account* (OUP 2020).

17 PACE, Sections 36–37.

from a child's perspective in particular – a part of the prosecution. Given all these factors, it is hard to overstate the importance of robust and effectively implemented protections for child suspects.

With these issues in mind, the next section of this chapter assesses the protections available on paper for children in police custody, contrasting the minimal adjustment of the adult custody process to accommodate children with the more significant differentiation provided for the child defendant post-charge. The third section draws on a mixed-methods qualitative research study to consider the implementation and efficacy of those adjustments in practice, from the perspective of the child suspect. In brief concluding observations, I consider the extent to which the child suspect's rights, particularly those guaranteed by the United Nations Convention on the Rights of the Child[18] (UNCRC), are protected and review the implications of these findings.

Protections on Paper for Child Suspects

In England and Wales, the primary aim of the youth justice system – distinct from that applicable to adults – is to 'prevent offending by children and young persons';[19] and both the police and the courts have a duty to 'safeguard and promote the welfare of children and young people'.[20] The child's rights under the UNCRC are also engaged. Particularly relevant here are the child's rights to fair treatment within the justice system (Article 40) – especially the right to participate effectively in the proceedings and the right to child-friendly accommodations.[21] Also key are the child's right not to be detained save as a measure of 'last resort' and for the 'shortest appropriate period'; and the right to be treated in detention with 'humanity and respect' and in a manner which 'takes into account the needs of persons of his or her age' (Article 37).

For child defendants, this differentiated approach is reflected in a distinct legal framework and a court experience which, for the vast majority, is very different from that of an adult defendant. Children are separated from adult defendants both in transportation to court and while awaiting and after their hearing.[22] Save for those charged with 'grave' crimes[23] and in other limited circumstances,[24] children are dealt with in the youth court, which is specially adapted to meet their needs.[25] Its specialisation is reflected both in processes and in physical

18 Ratified by the United Kingdom and entered into force September 1990.
19 Crime and Disorder Act 1998 (CDA), Section 37.
20 Children Act 2004, Section 11. See also CYPA, Section 44.
21 Committee on the Rights of the Child, *General Comment No. 24 (2019) on children's rights in the child justice system* (CRC/C/GC/24), 46.
22 CYPA, Section 31.
23 Powers of Criminal Courts (Sentencing) Act 2000, Section 91.
24 For example, where the child is jointly charged with an adult, Magistrates' Courts Act 1980, Section 24.
25 CYPA, Part 3. For details, see Kate Aubrey-Johnson, Shauneen Lambe and Jennifer Twite, *Youth Justice Law and Practice* (Legal Action Group 2019), 426ff.

arrangements. There is no public access to the court[26] and courtroom layout is modified to reduce inhibitions[27] – including, in the majority of cases, allowing the child to sit alongside their lawyer and any adult supporter, rather than in the dock.[28] District judges and magistrates are required to have special training,[29] and to use adjusted language and different modes of address; while for sentence, the presence of a specialist youth offending team (YOT) representative is required. Different, more stringent requirements are in place before the court can deprive a child of liberty on remand;[30] and there is a strong emphasis on completion of youth justice processes as swiftly as possible.[31]

Whether tried in the youth or the Crown court, the child's right to participate effectively in the proceedings is recognised in the Criminal Procedure Rules (CrimPR)[32] (and Criminal Practice Directions (CrimPD)),[33] which require 'every reasonable step' to be taken to facilitate the participation of young and vulnerable defendants. There is undoubtedly an inequity between the protections available to a child defendant and those afforded to child prosecution witnesses and complainants, for whom much more generous statutory provision is made in terms of special measures.[34] Nonetheless, although there is no statutory right in force,[35] a child defendant can be assisted in giving their evidence by an intermediary (a specialist communication facilitator), and for the whole trial if necessary.[36] Additionally, where a child defendant is questioned, advocates are expected to adapt their questioning to the child rather than the child having to cope with adult phraseology,[37] and specific training to equip advocates for this is expected.[38] Although available evidence suggests that trial protections for young defendants are not always implemented, or implemented effectively,[39] in practice there is

26 CYPA 1933, Section 47.
27 Judicial College, Youth Court Bench Book (June 2020), para 13.
28 Magistrates' Association Protocol, para 3; Criminal Practice Direction 3G.8.
29 CYPA, Section 45(3); Justices of the Peace Rules, SI 709/2016, Rule 30.
30 Legal Aid, Sentencing and Punishment of Offenders Act 2–12, Sections 98–102.
31 Judicial College, Youth Court Bench Book (June 2020), para 2.
32 Criminal Procedure Rules 2020 No 759 ('CrimPR'), Rule 3.8(3)(b) – applicable in both youth and Crown Court.
33 CrimPD October 2015 as amended April 2016, November 2016, January 2017, April 2018, October 2018, April 2019, October 2019, May 2020 and October 2020, 3D.2.
34 Youth Justice and Criminal Evidence Act 1999, Sections 16ff. For discussion see, for example, Samantha Fairclough, 'Speaking Up for Injustice: Reconsidering the Provision of Special Measures through the Lens of Equality' [2018] *Criminal Law Review* 4.
35 Section 104 of the Coroners and Justice Act 2009 has never been brought into force.
36 *C v Sevenoaks Magistrates' Court* [2009] EWHC 3088 (Admin) and Crim PD 3F.12ff. See most recently *R v Dean Thomas* [2020] EWCA Crim 117 and *TI v Bromley Youth Court* [2020] EWHC 1204 (Admin).
37 *R v Lubemba* [2014] EWCA Crim 2014 [45].
38 *R v Grant Murray* [2017] EWCA Crim 1228, although not mandated.
39 Lord Carlile, *Independent Parliamentarians' Inquiry into the Operation and Effectiveness of the Youth Court* (2014); Charlie Taylor, *Review of the Youth Justice System in England and Wales* (MOJ 2016).

nonetheless at least a statutory framework (in the CYPA), supported by the CrimPR, the CrimPD and case law, which provides for a significantly differentiated process at trial.

But the position is very different for a child detained as a suspect in police custody, to whom the legal framework affords scant protection. Unlike the youth court judge or magistrate, the CO who is responsible for the child's welfare and who oversees the process in custody[40] is not required to have any specialist youth training; nor are the staff who deal with most of the child's needs. In contrast to most child defendants, the child suspect does not experience fully separate facilities; nor are there more stringent requirements for their detention. The same test for authorising detention – namely, that detention is 'necessary to secure or preserve evidence' or to 'obtain evidence by questioning'[41] – applies to children and adults alike. No reference is made in the legislation to the child's right to be detained only as a 'last resort' and for the 'shortest appropriate period'.[42] Indeed a single initial time limit of 24 hours applies to all detainees.[43] The statutory requirement for separation in the criminal process[44] is confined to adults who have been 'charged' and so does not bite in relation to most adult detainees. In contrast to the statutory arrangements for child defendants in the youth court,[45] the child in police custody is barely glimpsed in primary legislation. There is a statutory duty to inform 'as soon as is practicable' a parent (or other person responsible for the child's welfare) of the child's arrest and whereabouts;[46] and if the child suspect is a girl, she must be 'under the care of' a woman during her detention,[47] although this does not require constant attention. Once charged, a child refused bail is statutorily required, subject to very limited exceptions, to be transferred from the police station to local authority accommodation before being produced to court.[48] However, there is no requirement to remove a child suspect to more suitable accommodation overnight pre-charge or where a child is detained for a suspected breach of bail conditions.[49]

All other adjustments and protections for child suspects are contained within secondary legislation – predominantly the Codes of Practice which accompany PACE, particularly Code C,[50] or in guidance prepared by the College of Policing,

---

40 PACE, Section 37.
41 PACE, Section 37
42 UNCRC, Article 37(b).
43 PACE, Section 41.
44 CYPA 1933, Section 31.
45 CYPA 1933, Part 3.
46 PACE, Section 57.
47 CYPA 1933, Section 31.
48 PACE, Section 38(6).
49 See *R (on the application of BG) v Chief Constable of the West Midlands* [2014] EWHC 4374 (Admin).
50 Code C: Revised Code of Practice for the Detention, Treatment and Questioning of Persons by Police Officers ('Code C'), published August 2019 (in force at the time of writing).

'Authorised Professional Practice (Detention and Custody)' (APP).[51] However, these are limited adaptations of the adult process, rather than a child-specific regime.[52] The most substantial protection is the provision of support from an 'appropriate adult' (AA), who must attend the police station[53] and be with the child for significant events in the process, such as for the explanation of legal rights,[54] for strip and intimate searching,[55] and for interview.[56] The AA must fulfil a number of functions: advising and assisting the child; ensuring that due process is observed; helping the child to understand and exercise their rights; and enabling communication between child and police.[57] The role on paper is complex and demanding; but Code C specifies that, in the first instance, it should be fulfilled by a parent or guardian,[58] who by their nature are untrained for the task. Where family members are unable to act, the role will generally be fulfilled by a representative of the local authority or the YOT;[59] or by a lay volunteer, often unknown to the child.

Beyond the AA role, child-specific protections are limited to a prohibition on a child being detained with an adult in a cell, and not in an adult cell at all unless no other 'secure' or 'more comfortable' accommodation is available.[60] The 'Notes for Guidance' which accompany Code C (NFG) additionally suggest that staff should check on a child in their cell 'more frequently' than on other detainees.[61] Otherwise, the APP and Code C simply require 'special care' to be taken, for example when questioning a child;[62] and include more general exhortations for procedures to be strictly followed and detention times to be kept to a minimum for children, avoiding in particular detention overnight.[63] In contrast to the Crim PR and the Crim PD, PACE and Code C place no positive onus on the CO, or on interviewing officers, to enable the effective participation of a child suspect, despite the applicability of the principle in police custody following *Panovits v Cyprus*.[64] Interviewing officers are not expected to be trained in child-friendly questioning techniques;[65] there is no specific

---

51 This is guidance only to which officers should 'have regard'; 'There may, however, be circumstances when it is perfectly legitimate to deviate from APP, provided there is clear rationale for doing so.' Available at: https://www.app.college.police.uk/abou t-app (accessed 11 August 2021).

52 See also Jantien Leenknecht, Chapter 2 of this collection, on the implementation of child-specific rights.

53 Code C 3.15.

54 Code C 3.17.

55 Code C Annex A.

56 Code C 11.15.

57 Code C 1.7A.

58 Code C 1.7(b).

59 Code C 1.7(b).

60 Code C 8.8.

61 NFG 9B.

62 NFG 11C.

63 For example, APP (Children and Young Persons) 2.

64 (2008) 27 BHRC 464, [67].

65 Kate Gooch and Piers von Berg, 'What Happens in the Beginning, Matters in the End: Achieving Best Evidence with Child Suspects in the Police Station' [2019] 19 *Youth Justice* 85.

requirement for modified language or modes of address to be used; and there is no framework to enable intermediary assistance to be provided.[66] While free legal advice is available to all suspects, child suspects are required to opt for that advice,[67] as adults are – although the AA can request a solicitor to attend on their behalf.[68] Thus, unlike the heavily differentiated approach taken in the youth court, the child suspect in police custody effectively undergoes the same procedures in essentially the same environment as an adult suspect. Even more stark is the contrast with the treatment of child complainants and prosecution witnesses, who are interviewed in separate specialist facilities and questioned by officers who are specially trained to elicit their best evidence.[69]

Protections in Practice for Child Suspects

How then are these limited protections implemented in practice for children in police custody in England and Wales? Surprisingly, there has been very little empirical examination of how these protections function for, and are experienced by, children in police custody. What glimpses we have of the child suspect in England and Wales tend to feature as part of wider all-ages research in custody;[70] involve very small numbers of children and young people;[71] be purely quantitative;[72] or touch on police custody experiences only as part of more general research.[73] I draw here on a mixed methods qualitative study which, for the first time in England and Wales, has explored the experiences of a substantial number of children and young people recently detained as children in police custody.

Methods

Semi-structured interviews were conducted with children and young people who had recent and/or repeated experience of detention as 10 to 17-year-olds in police custody in England and Wales (n=41). I refer to them collectively as 'young

---

66 In contrast to Northern Ireland, see John Taggart, '"I am not beholden to anyone … I consider myself to be an officer of the court": A Comparison of the Intermediary Role in England and Wales and Northern Ireland' [2021] 2 *International Journal of Evidence and Proof* 141.
67 Code C 3.5(a)(i).
68 Code C 6.5A.
69 MOJ, 2011, *Achieving Best Evidence in Criminal Proceedings: Guidance on interviewing victims and witnesses, and guidance on using special measures.*
70 See Satnam Choongh, *Policing as Social Discipline* (OUP 1997).
71 See Vicky Kemp and Jacqueline Hodgson, 'Chapter 4. England and Wales Empirical Findings' in Miet Vanderhallen and others (eds), *Interrogating Young Suspects: Procedural Safeguards from an Empirical Perspective*, vol 2 (Intersentia 2016). This involved a focus group with five children and analysis of 12 police interviews.
72 Layla Skinns, *Overnight Detention of Children in Police Cells* (The Howard League 2011).
73 Neal Hazel, Ann Hagell and Laura Brazier, *Young Offenders' Perceptions of Their Experiences in the Criminal Justice System* (ESRC 2003).

participants' and individually by pseudonym. The sample group covered a range of ages: 10 to 14 years (n=5); 15 to 16 years (n=19); 17 to 18 years (n=15); and over 18 (n=2). It included eight girls and 14 BAME[74] young people. Young participants had varying levels of experience in police custody: some had only one detention experience (n=6); some had several (two to four episodes, n=18); while others had been detained more frequently (five or more episodes, n=17). Fully informed consent was obtained from all young participants, and from an adult with parental responsibility where the participant was under 16; and care was taken to ensure ongoing consent throughout the interview. On average, interviews lasted just over 43 minutes.

Young participant interviews were supplemented by 192 hours of observations conducted in six police custody blocks across three force areas, comprising a major regional metropolitan force and two county forces. Observations involved tracking all young suspects passing through the block; observing processes and conditions within the block; and holding informal interviews and discussions with police officers and staff (n=96),[75] healthcare practitioners (n=14), solicitors (n=9),[76] independent custody visitors (ICVs) (n=3) and AAs (n=11).[77] Further separate semi-structured interviews were conducted with additional AAs (n=11), solicitors (n=4) and ICVs (n=3). Numerical signifiers are used for all adult participants. All the interviews and fieldnotes were transcribed in full and subjected to thematic analysis, the material being coded using a hybrid approach combining both deductive and inductive methods.[78]

Protections from the Child's Perspective

Lack of Separation from Adult Detainees

In contrast to the separation achieved in the youth court, in police custody children were frequently waiting to be booked in alongside, or in sight of, adult detainees. Their presence could be extremely distressing: 'I'm just starin' at them, like, scared, but tryin' to act not scared ... so I'm starin' at them thinkin', "Who's this?" and, "Who's that?" "Which one of these is gonna be the one to hurt me or kill me?"' (Elijah). Young participants often felt inhibited by the presence of arrested adults, when they were booked into custody and asked health and welfare

---

74 It should be acknowledged that this term may be problematic, particularly as it is a 'catch-all' that may not reflect the complexity of how race and ethnicity are categorised and experienced.

75 Officers include COs, investigating officers and inspectors. Staff are referred to as (CA) (custody assistant), although different titles were given for this role in different force areas.

76 Legal representatives are referred to as solicitors, although this group also encompasses accredited police station representatives.

77 Including familial AAs (FAAs) and volunteer AAs (VAAs).

78 Jennifer Fereday and Eimear Muir-Cochrane, 'Demonstrating Rigor Using Thematic Analysis: A Hybrid Approach of Inductive and Deductive Coding and Theme Development' [2006] 5 *International Journal of Qualitative Methods* 80.

questions during risk assessment, particularly when the adult was known to them as a local offender or (for girls) was of a different gender. Once in the cell, anguished or angry shouting and screaming from adults in nearby cells could be deeply disturbing, preventing sleep and raising anxiety levels: 'For someone's first time in the cell it can be quite frightening ... all these people around you acting all crazy' (Jake).

Unnecessary Detentions and Lack of Prioritisation

Although some COs expressed a growing unwillingness to authorise the detention of children,[79] there were still a significant number of children detained in circumstances which did not meet the strict 'necessity' test.[80] While this sometimes arose from the failure of third-party services in the community, more commonly their detention was simply more convenient to the investigation or, sometimes, because officers felt that a period in the cell would be a 'deterrent' (CO43); could set them 'on the right path' (CO34); or was favoured for its social disciplinary impact, 'like the naughty step' (CO12).[81] Likewise, the exhortations in Code C and the APP to prioritise child suspects and keep detention times to a minimum could have some impact, particularly for 10 to 14-year-olds. However, during fieldwork I observed no systematic arrangements for prioritising children and generally, without legislative time limits, these aspirations for reduced detention periods were not realised. Almost three-quarters of young participants described detention lasting more than 10 hours, including 11 recounting episodes of over 30 hours on at least one occasion (often for breach of bail). On observation the mean pre-charge detention time, where the full episode could be tracked (in 33 cases), was 11.75 hours, with 18 detention episodes lasting over 10 hours. The statutory requirement to find alternative accommodation for children refused bail[82] was only met once on observation; and many children, pre-and post-charge, were detained overnight.

Delays in the early stages, where a child could wait an hour or more in handcuffs to be booked in, could be exhausting and have a detrimental effect on their ability to take in important rights information and participate in the early custody processes. For many young participants, their desire to rush through the process in the hope of hastening their release meant that they did not have the patience to engage effectively with risk assessment; nor would they query any of the complex rights information provided. As Riley explained: 'You just say you understand it ... Even if I don't understand, I'd say I understand ... Just to skip time.' Desperation to avoid long periods in detention was a substantial driver in refusing legal advice. In England and Wales, uptake of legal advice among children is strikingly low,

79 See also in Roxanna Dehaghani, 'Automatic Authorisation: An Exploration of the Decision to Detain in Police Custody' [2017] *Criminal Law Review* 187.
80 PACE, Section 37.
81 Also observed in Satnam Choongh, *Policing as Social Discipline* (OUP 1997).
82 PACE, Section 38(6).

with 43% of children who went on to be charged in one study not requesting legal advice, and 10 to 13-year-olds emerging as the least likely group (of all ages) to opt for a solicitor.[83] While, on observation, legal advice was routinely offered to all suspects, uptake by children was low and largely in line with previous research. By far the most common reason given by children for refusal was the delay a solicitor was considered inevitably to cause: 'I didn't want one ... I just wanted to get out' (Alex). The right to request legal advice at a later stage and the repetition of the offer on arrival of the AA rarely overcame young participant concerns about extending their time in custody. Nor did COs often adapt the offer to enable child suspects to understand the benefits of legal advice, despite being encouraged to do so in the APP,[84] revealing a tendency to align with the case construction objectives of interviewing officers rather than prioritising their role as independent guardians of suspect rights.[85]

The Compromised Appropriate Adult Role

The AA role was rarely performed as envisaged on paper. In the first instance, although timely notification of arrest was routinely achieved,[86] the AA's arrival was frequently heavily delayed by the CO – often deliberately so – in order to coincide with the investigating officers being ready for interview. Many young participants and young suspects on fieldwork waited many hours, often overnight, before seeing their AA.[87] Once present, the AA's ability to fulfil the role was often undermined by minimal support from the CO. Frequently COs provided familial and untrained AAs with very little information about the role, their rights and duties, hampering their ability to provide the assistance expected. AAs of all types complained of very limited access to the child, being required by COs to wait separately, often outside the block, once they had had an initial meeting. Conceptual difficulties with the role also emerged. The composite and complex nature of the role meant that no single AA was likely to have the skills to fulfil both its welfare and due process aspects – aspects which were, in any event, often in conflict. Familial AAs could often provide support and reassurance; and some, particularly younger participants spoke movingly of the comfort a parent could provide: 'Just to have my Mum there – it means a lot to me' (Michael). However, familial AAs themselves often described feeling out of their depth, lacking an understanding of the process and the child's rights, and feeling too intimidated to ask questions or to challenge the CO:

---

83 Vicky Kemp, Pascoe Pleasence and Nigel Balmer, 'Children, Young People and Requests for Police Station Legal Advice: 25 Years on from PACE' [2011] 11 *Youth Justice* 28.

84 APP (Children and Young Persons), 3.3.

85 See for similar Michael McConville, Andrew Sanders and Robert Leng, *The Case for the Prosecution* (Routledge 1991).

86 PACE, Section 57.

87 See for similar, Tim Bateman, *A Night in the Cells: Children in Police Custody and the Provision of Non familial Appropriate Adults* (Children's Commissioner 2017).

I'd not been in that situation before so I just went along with everything, you know, what they did and they have to do and thought 'Do I need a solicitor?' I don't know. So, I'm not really clued up with it all, you know what I mean? (FAA5)

By contrast, non-familial AAs tended to be well informed about the role and the child's rights and thus equipped for due process duties, but were often unknown to the child or had a prior relationship (as social worker or YOT officer), which could itself be problematic. As a result, young participants frequently reported feeling unable to engage with them: 'I just remember her being old and I just didn't pay much attention to her … a complete stranger, I just don't want her' (Cole). This could be particularly the case for BAME young participants: '[T]hey brought someone, some next white guy I don't even know who he was, I'm not going to feel comfortable around him, he felt like a police officer himself' (Zayn). The AA's lack of privilege[88] limited substantially what non-familial AAs felt they could discuss with child suspects and meant that they were rarely present to support children in legal consultation.

Minimal Adjustment of Detention Conditions

The notable lack of adjustment to accommodate young suspects was most striking in relation to the conditions of detention itself. While the prohibition on detention in a cell with an adult was always met, on observation children were routinely held in adult cells, enabled by the permissive nature of the provision.[89] Young participants were strikingly consistent in their overwhelmingly negative response to their time in the cell: 'It's just horrible – it's just four walls innit … it's freezing. It smells, it's just not a nice place to be' (Sadie). Where children were detained in 'juvenile detention rooms', as alternative accommodation, these were internally identical to adult cells, distinguishable sometimes only by signage or by having a differently configured door. Checks were routinely conducted more frequently for detained children;[90] but while some staff tried to engage with young suspects, more often the check involved only a glance through the spyhole in the door or hatch, sometimes with the offer of a drink. Such checks were more likely to disturb children trying to sleep, or raise false hopes of release, than to support wellbeing.

Detention conditions were rarely adjusted to account for child suspects' youth or vulnerabilities. Stripped of all personal possession except their clothing, and provided with minimal distraction items (on observation never more than reading material, which was itself often not age appropriate), young participants struggled to cope with the confinement and lack of stimulation: '[S]taring at nothing' (Jackson); '[L]ooking at four walls. Every two seconds going round and round'

---

88 NFG 1E.
89 Code C 8.8.
90 NFG 9B.

(Simon). Coping with boredom could be 'right hard' (Nathan); but for some it was near intolerable: 'I mean it would be bad for an hour but the length I was in there, it was terrible ... I think if I had to go in now I'd cry. I would actually cry' (Tom). For those with additional vulnerabilities, detention could be seriously destabilising. Zoe, for example, stated: 'I have ADHD and they wouldn't give me my medication until I see a doctor ... and I was bugging out like, I was actually going crazy. I can't be in a small room for too long.' The experience was physically and emotionally exhausting, often made more stressful as a result of uncertainty about what was happening and when they would be released. Young suspects were routinely not made aware of provisions which could have mitigated their isolation and uncertainty, such as the right to speak to an AA 'at any time'[91] or their entitlement to request a phone call.[92] Notably, care by a female officer[93] was not apparent in practice to female participants, and several reported recoiling from the offer to speak to a female officer because it was routinely linked to the offer of sanitary products. Many young participants experienced a sense of loss of control, lapsing into a state of resigned helplessness; but for some, frustration could boil over into anger and defiance: 'I was only in there for five hours and that whole five hours I was just agging them, just terrorizing the beast, just kicking the door' (Luke).

COs and staff were not equipped, in terms of training or resources, to take a child-friendly approach. Thus, many failed to appreciate where adjustments were required in respect of particular conditions, such as an autism spectrum condition, or to make the link between problematic behaviour and vulnerability. As a result, officers tended to fall back on normative assumptions about vulnerability, so that too frequently only those young suspects who were 'upset and tearful' (CA11), who performed their vulnerability,[94] were accorded more sympathetic treatment. Even where vulnerability was identified, risk management mechanisms understandably prevailed and there were very limited resources for addressing such needs in custody. A history of self-harm, for example, would invariably result simply in greater levels of surveillance or the removal of items of clothing, reducing the risk of a serious incident but often proving more traumatic for the child. Children who responded in a less compliant, more problematic way appeared to lose the right to a welfare-focused approach. Described pejoratively – for example, as 'absolutely foul' (CA3, CA4) – they were not considered to merit sympathetic, child-friendly treatment. CA41 described: 'If they're awake I'll speak to them and ask if they want a drink. People (fellow CAs) will say, "What are you doing talking to them?"' (CA41). Locked in oppositional relations with the police, some young participants expressed a corresponding reluctance to accept support from officers and staff – even from healthcare professionals, who were considered to be working with the police.

91 Code C 3.18.
92 Code C 5.6.
93 CYPA 1933, Section 31.
94 Roxanna Dehaghani, '"Vulnerable by Law (But Not by Nature)": Examining Perceptions of Youth and Childhood "Vulnerability" in the Context of Police Custody' (2017) 39 *Journal of Social Welfare and Family Law* 454.

A Failure to Enable Effective Participation

Such traumatic and draining experiences had a negative impact on young participants' legal decision making and their ability to participate effectively in interview. Sandor, for example, described feeling 'just too out of it ... just really, really emotional and afraid and tired' by the time his interview began. Some young participants, solicitors and AAs were positive about interviewing officers who were calm, friendly and asked 'straightforward questions' (FAA5) in an 'understandable and understanding' (VAA3) way. However, a significant number of young participants complained of questioning methods which they felt were designed to 'get you mixed up' (Rezar); to 'catch you out' (Aidan, Dexter); to 'trip', 'trick' and 'twist' their words. Such reactions accord with the repeated identification of persuasive and oppressive interview techniques in previous research.[95]

Some young participants explained that they no longer tried to answer questions as a result, preferring to make no comment. Others felt unable to give a good account of themselves or even pressurised into a false confession to bring the interview to a close: '[Y]ou'll be that pressured that you might 'ave to lie and say, 'Yeah, fair enough, I did do it' ... Just to get it over with' (Logan). No participant, lay or professional, had experienced a child being supported by an intermediary in interview. COs and interviewing officers placed reliance on AAs to support those with more profound communication needs. However, none of the non-familial AAs encountered in this study had a specialist background in supporting speech and language difficulties. Meanwhile, familial AAs often felt unable to intervene, struggled with their own language difficulties or were a source of inhibition for young participants, who were frequently unwilling to speak freely about their behaviour in front of family members.

Conclusion

This brief analysis has identified a framework of protections for child suspects which, on paper, is of a different order to that available to child defendants and falls even further short of the support provided to child witnesses and complainants. The review of this framework in practice, from the perspective of the child, reveals that even these scant protections are not always implemented and, where they are implemented, are frequently ineffective. The data suggests that the child's right to be detained only as a 'last resort' and for the 'shortest appropriate period' (Article 37) is often not being realised in police custody; nor do child suspects commonly experience adaptation of the processes to meet their needs and enable their effective participation (Article 40).

The ramifications of this lack of adjustment are profound and far reaching. Young participants' accounts of their police interviews raise issues about the

---

95 Vicky Kemp and Jacqueline Hodgson, 'Chapter 4. England and Wales Empirical Findings' in Miet Vanderhallen and others (eds), *Interrogating Young Suspects: Procedural Safeguards from an Empirical Perspective*, vol 2 (Intersentia 2016), 153–58; Sarah Medford, Gisli H Gudjonsson and John Pearse, 'The Efficacy of the Appropriate Adult Safeguard During Police Interviewing' [2003] 8 *Legal and Criminological Psychology* 253.

fairness and reliability of the evidence elicited from them in such circumstances. At the same time, and equally concerningly, many young participants experienced their detention as disrespectful and punitive, and considered that the police would deliberately 'long out' (Harper) the process for that purpose. We should be unsurprised, in light of the work of procedural justice scholars,[96] that young participants related a reduction in the legitimacy of the police in their eyes as a result of what they perceived to be this unfair and disrespectful treatment in custody:

> ... it's the sort of thing where if I needed them I wouldn't even bother ... I just wouldn't wanna call 'em, just because I don't think they're that nice people. Since I was in there for so long and they were useless when I was in there, I just don't really think they're that trustworthy ... (Tom)

Additionally, far from a harsh experience setting a young suspect 'on the right path', young participants revealed a sense of resentment and alienation liable to foster further offending, reflecting Lawrence Sherman's defiance theory:[97]

> ... by putting you in a room, making you sit by yourself, it's not going to make you accept, reflect on the thing you've done. It's going to make you think like, 'You lot treat me like shit.' I might as well do worse things in there. I don't know, it makes you entirely a bit different ... (Carter)

The custody process for children is, as a result, revealed to be frequently counterproductive and liable to frustrate the aims and principles of the youth justice process.

As Steyn LJ observed in *R v G*:[98] 'Ignoring the special position of children in the criminal justice system is not acceptable in the modern civil society.' Procedures that undermine the rights of children in the earliest stage of prosecution taint the whole process and do not serve the interests of complainants and victims. The analysis has revealed a web of factors driving this problematic position-- structural, institutional and individual – which pose challenges for reform. But overlaying these factors, the invisibility of the child suspect experience – in the legal framework, in the courts and in empirical research – has allowed the inadequacy of protections for them to persist for too long. Academics, lawyers and other criminal justice practitioners have raised the profile of, and thereby secured better protection for, vulnerable defendants in the courts in recent years. A similar journey of reform for child suspect protections is long overdue.

---

96 Tom R Tyler and Yuen J Huo, *Trust in the Law: Encouraging Public Cooperation with the Police and Courts* (Russell Sage Foundation 2002); Tom R Tyler, *Why People Obey the Law* (YUP 1990).

97 Lawrence W Sherman, 'Defiance, Deterrence, and Irrelevance: A Theory of the Criminal Sanction' (1993) 30 *Journal of Research in Crime and Delinquency* 445.

98 [2003] UKHL 50, [53].

8 The Right to an Interpreter

Taking Stock, Looking Forward

Heidi Salaets, Katalin Balogh and Stefan Aelbrecht

Introduction: Foreign Language Vulnerability

> Imagine a family on holiday in a foreign country where they do not speak the local language. An unfortunate accident happens; nobody in the family is injured, but the accident causes the death of a civilian of that country. The police arrest the parents on suspicion of causing unlawful death and they are kept in custody indefinitely. Their children are put into youth care. Nobody in the family knows what is happening because communication between the parties is impossible: there is no common language.

Other chapters in this collection engage extensively with the overarching concepts of vulnerability and resilience.[1] Here, we focus on foreign language vulnerability, which concerns situations in which a person finds themselves unable to communicate directly with (legal) authorities as a result of (special) language needs. Central to our understanding of vulnerability is Mergaerts' broader conceptualisation – namely the (in)ability to exercise procedural rights.[2] If an individual is unable to understand procedures or cannot be understood (in both a general and a linguistic sense), they cannot exercise their rights. A professional interpreter – that is, a trained and accredited interpreter – can provide the necessary linguistic assistance to enable the understanding required for the effective exercise of these procedural rights.

This chapter delves into the legal basis for the right to an interpreter[3] and illustrates how foreign-language vulnerability compounds with other aspects of vulnerability, such as age, impairments, disorders and deprivation of liberty. It then discusses the role of the interpreter and draws on data from empirical case studies in Belgium which provide insight into how effective the implementation of

---

1 See the introduction and Miet Vanderhallen and Kasia Uzieblo, Chapter 4 of this collection.
2 Lore Mergaerts and others, 'Challenges in Defining and Identifying a Suspect's Vulnerability in Criminal Proceedings: What's in a Name and Who's to Blame?' in Penny Cooper and Linda Hunting (eds) *Access to Justice for Vulnerable People* (Wildy, Simmonds & Hill Publishing 2018) 48–71.
3 References to an 'interpreter' are always to a professional interpreter. We explicitly mention when this is not the case.

DOI: 10.4324/9781003205166-11

the right to an interpreter is in practice. The specific focus here is on two types of vulnerable individuals: minors and prisoners.

In the case of minors, this vulnerability involves a lack of social, biological, sexual and legal maturity that prevents them from understanding their rights.[4] This is in line with their evolving capacities, and involves striking a balance between the recognition of children as active agents and their entitlement to protection in accordance with their relative immaturity and youth.[5] For prisoners, vulnerability emerges from the isolation they face: a closed-off existence that is largely limited to their cell. Both types of vulnerability are exacerbated by the aforementioned foreign-language vulnerability. While care must be taken to avoid the pitfall of quantifying vulnerability ('more', 'less', 'extremely', 'particularly', 'highly'),[6] it is nevertheless important to pay attention to language as an important layer of vulnerability, and to how language abilities (or lack thereof) interact with and potentially exacerbate other aspects of vulnerability.[7]

The insights from these studies indicate that there are common issues among these groups regarding the impartiality, trustworthiness and perceived linguistic competences of the interpreter. The chapter concludes by providing some recommendations for reform.

The Right to an Interpreter

An interpreter plays a paramount role in ensuring that suspects, accused persons,[8] victims[9] and asylum seekers[10] can understand the proceedings and exercise their right to a fair trial.[11] From a legal perspective, the right to interpretation is enshrined in EU Directive 2010/64 on the right to interpretation and

---

4 György Virág, 'Interpreted Interviews with Highly Vulnerable Children' in Katalin Balogh and Heidi Salaets (eds), *Children and Justice: Overcoming Language Barriers* (Intersentia 2015) 77–93.

5 See United Nations Convention on the Rights of the Child, Article 5.

6 Martha Fineman, 'The Vulnerable Subject and the Responsive State' (2011) 60 *Emory Law Journal* 269.

7 See also Kim Turner and Claire Westwood, Chapter 9 of this collection.

8 Directive 2010/64/EU of the European Parliament and of the Council of 20 October 2010 on the right to interpretation and translation in criminal proceedings [2010] OJ L 280/1.

9 Directive 2012/29/EU of the European Parliament and of the Council of 25 October 2012 establishing minimum standards on the rights, support and protection of victims of crime, and replacing Council Framework Decision 2001/220/JHA [2012] OJ L 315/57.

10 Directive 2013/32/EU of the European Parliament and of the Council of 26 June 2013 on common procedures for granting and withdrawing international protection [2013] OJ L 180/60.

11 Commission Recommendation of 27 November 2013 on procedural safeguards for vulnerable persons suspected or accused in criminal proceedings 2013/C 378/02, OJ C 378/8; see also Directive 2010/64/EU, recital 27 and Directive 2012/13/EU, recital 26.

translation[12] in criminal proceedings, which was adopted as part of the EU Roadmap for strengthening the procedural rights of suspected or accused persons in criminal proceedings.[13] Directive 2010/64/EU sets out minimum rules and seeks to harmonise the legal architecture of EU member states, meaning that:

> the protection should never fall below the standards provided by the [European Convention on Human Rights] ECHR or the Charter as interpreted in the case-law of the European Court of Human Rights or the Court of Justice of the European Union.[14]

Hence, this chapter draws upon this legal framework with reference to the ECHR, European Court of Human Rights (ECtHR) case law and EU Directive 2010/64, where relevant.

The duty to provide interpretation to an individual who does not speak the language of the proceedings rests with the state. It requires that authorities ensure that people involved in the proceedings can follow them and make themselves understood. Interpretation should be provided in a language in which the accused has sufficient command for the purpose of their defence. This does not mean that defendants should necessarily be able to follow the proceedings in their native language. Rather, the benchmark is whether the accused is informed in detail of the nature and the cause of the accusation against them; and whether they can defend themselves – notably by being able to put their version of the events before the court.[15]

The right to an interpreter for a person who does not understand or speak the local language is paramount at all stages of criminal proceedings before investigative and judicial authorities – including police questioning, court hearings and any necessary interim hearings – unless it is demonstrated that there are compelling reasons to restrict this right.[16] However, since a case has not yet come before the ECtHR requiring it to consider the restriction of the right to an interpreter, it is not clear what reasons would be deemed sufficient in this regard.

Despite the interpreter's importance, the absence of an interpreter does not unequivocally result in a violation of the right to a fair trial. The specific circumstances and facts of each case are important elements in determining whether a

---

12 Interpreting – which involves immediate, on-the-spot or distance oral or signed linguistic assistance – is distinct from translation, which concerns written communication.

13 Resolution of the Council of 30 November 2009 on a Roadmap for strengthening procedural rights of suspected or accused persons in criminal proceedings (Text with EEA relevance) (2009/C 295/01).

14 Directive 2010/64/EU of the European Parliament and of the Council of 20 October 2010 on the right to interpretation and translation in criminal proceedings [2010] OJ L 280/1, recital 32.

15 Article 6 ECHR, paragraph 3 (a, e). See also *Hermi v Italy*, no 18114/02, § 70, 28 June 2005; and *Mustafa Güngör v Turkey*, no 40853/05, 12 October 2010

16 *Baytar v Turkey*, no 45440/04, § 50, 14 October 2014; and *Diallo v Sweden*, no 13205/07, §25, 5 January 2010.

violation of Article 6 of the ECHR has occurred.[17] Arguably, this could be the case if an interpreter in a given language is unavailable; or if the person in question has waived their right to an interpreter, which can only be done knowingly and after full consideration, presupposing that the person has been informed about this right in a language that they understand.[18] Importantly, however, a lawyer cannot waive the right to an interpreter in the name of their client.[19]

The ECHR has refined the requirements on the need for an interpreter by explicitly referring to the applicant as being vulnerable when addressing a potential violation of the right to an interpreter.[20] The authorities must assess the interpreting needs of the defendant if there is reason to suspect that the defendant is not sufficiently proficient in the language of the proceedings, irrespective of whether a complaint has been made by or on behalf the defendant.[21] An interpreter will usually translate from and into the defendant's mother tongue or preferred language. However, if the defendant speaks an additional language and this is used for translation instead (eg, because an interpreter is not available in their native language), the defendant's proficiency in that alternative language should be ascertained and verified before the decision is taken to use that language for the purposes of interpreting. This decision cannot be based solely on nationality, assumptions or a lack of cooperation; and significantly more than a few rather basic statements in an alternative language are needed to establish that someone is sufficiently well versed in that language to use it for translation purposes.[22] The ECtHR has suggested that assessments of proficiency could be based on asking open-ended questions and/or consulting the person in question.[23] It has also drawn attention to the importance of noting in the record any procedure used and decision taken with regard to the verification of interpreting needs, any notification of that right to an interpreter and any assistance provided by an interpreter.[24]

---

17 Nikos Vogiatzis, 'Interpreting the Right to Interpretation under Article 6(3)(e) ECHR: A Cautious Evolution in the Jurisprudence of the European Court of Human Rights?' (2022) 22(1) *Human Rights Law Review* 1.

18 *Dvorski v Croatia* [GC], no 25703/11, § 101, ECHR 2015; and *Ibrahim and Others v United Kingdom* [GC], nos 50541/08 and three others, § 272, 13 September 2016

19 *Kamasinski v Austria*, no 9783/82, § 80, 19 December 1989.

20 *Vizgirda v Slovenia*, no 59868/08, §100, 28 August 2018

21 See, for example, *Brozicek v Italy*, 19 December 1989, Series A no 167 and *Cuscani v United Kingdom*, no 32771/96, § 38, 24 September 2002; *Vizgirda v Slovenia*, no 59868/08, §81, 28 August 2018. See also Directive 2010/64/EU, Article 2(4): 'Member States shall ensure that a procedure or mechanism is in place to ascertain whether suspected or accused persons speak and understand the language of the criminal proceedings and whether they need the assistance of an interpreter.'

22 *Hermi v Italy*, no 18114/02, § 71, 28 June 2005; *Vizgirda v Slovenia*, no 59868/08, §84, 28 August 2018

23 Inspiration could be sought in the National Institute of Child Health and Human Development Protocol on the International Evidence-Based Investigative Interviewing of Children; *Vizgirda v Slovenia*, no 59868/08, §84, 28 August 2018.

24 *Vizgirda v Slovenia*, no 59868/08, §84–85, 28 August 2018.

For the right to an interpreter to be practical and effective, it is the duty of the authorities (ie, the prosecution, law enforcement and judicial authorities)[25] to ensure the quality and adequacy of the interpretation provided. This interpretation is in line with Directive 2010/64/EU, which requires member states to take concrete measures to ensure that the interpretation provided sufficiently safeguards the fairness of the proceedings.

Other research has shown that there is considerable divergence from, and 'flat' transposition of, Directive 2010/64/EU. In addition, the directive has had only a very limited effect on national proceedings.[26]

Legal Interpreter Role and Existing Research

This section outlines the role of the legal interpreter in theory, before examining the existing (albeit limited) research available on this role and its effectiveness in practice. As outlined below, although legal interpreters are considered to be 'merely' responsible for communication during the legal process, their role is more complex and users' expectations can be more challenging than one might expect.

As a starting point, legal interpreters are part of the legal system but are not involved in the decision-making process. They are governed by a series of ethical and professional principles, including professional competence, accuracy, impartiality, confidentiality, protocol and demeanour (using the same grammatical person as the speaker or sign-language user), and professional secrecy.[27] These principles essentially require the interpreter to act as a metaphorical 'machine', 'conduit' or 'glass pane'. In other words, the 'code of conduct' requires the interpreter to be as invisible as possible and to leave the floor to the primary participants of the encounter by merely serving as the 'linguistic bridge' between the authorities and

---

25 *Knox v Italy*, no 76577/13, 24 January 2019.

26 Steven Cras and Luca De Matteis, 'The Directive on the Right to Interpretation and Translation in Criminal Proceedings', (2010) 4 *The European Criminal Law Associations Forum* 153; Maciej Fingas, 'The Right to Interpretation and Translation in Criminal Proceedings – Challenges and Difficulties Stemming from the Implementation of the Directive 2010/64/EU', (2019) 9(2) *European Criminal Law Review* 175; Lore Mergaerts, *European Safeguards for Vulnerable Suspects and Defendants: Good Intentions, but with Limited Effect in National Proceedings* (Report from the Commission to the European Parliament and the Council, 2020) on the implementation of Directive 2010/64/EU of the European Parliament and of the Council of 20 October 2010 on the right to interpretation and translation in criminal proceedings [2018]
   COM/2018/857.

27 European Association for Legal Interpreters and Translators, 'EULITA Code of Professional Ethics' (2013). Available at: https://www.eulita.eu/wp-content/uploads/files/EULITA-code-London-e.pdf (accessed 4 June 2022). Belgium respects these principles and has implemented them by via the Royal Decree of 18 April 2017 (http://www.ejustice.just.fgov.be/cgi_loi/change_lg.pl?language=nl&la=N&cn=2017041816&table_name=wet, last accessed 4 June 2022) , published in the *Official Gazette* of 31 May 2017 (http://www.ejustice.just.fgov.be/mopdf/2017/05/31_1.pdf#Page17, last accessed 4 June 2022).

the layperson(s) involved in the criminal proceedings. To this end, interpreters should use direct speech to stimulate the dialogue between the two primary participants in the exchange that they are translating. This means that they should use the first-person 'I' form in the translation when relaying what the party has said (eg, 'I was attacked', rather than translating as 'The defendant says he was attacked'). In contrast, the interpreter will refer to their own person in the third person (eg, 'The interpreter needs to ask for clarification').[28]

Interestingly, there is substantial evidence from interpreting studies (a discipline that examines interpreters in a range of settings, including the legal one) that, in practice, interpreters do not act in this machine-like, invisible way.[29] Instead, the empirical insights indicate that interpreters across various settings (eg, legal, medical, asylum-seeking, social) interact with the primary participants – for example, by regulating turn taking and by acting as gatekeepers in the communication. This is a significant finding for the legal context discussed in this chapter, given the importance of communication in the legal decision-making process, from the first encounter with the police/asylum authorities to the proceedings before the court/decision body. Written and oral/signed communications are essential to be able to determine an appropriate outcome and possible sentence. As we know, interpreters are the gatekeepers of communication between a foreign language-speaking suspect, victim or witness and the police or legal actor (judge/lawyer/prosecutor). If linguistic and cultural issues cause a failure in communication between these parties, the interpreter is the only one who understands and sees this miscommunication occurring. The interpreter's code of conduct tells them to act in a machine-like way and to continue translating while staying out of the process itself. However, the interpreter is, of course, a human being who is actually present in the encounter, and who can use their common sense to avoid major miscommunications by explaining transparently to each party what has gone wrong in the communication and how to reset it. In other words, the interpreter is not a translation machine that merely transfers words from one language in another, but instead is more present in the encounter.[30]

With regard to the accuracy and completeness of the interpreter's translation, there is sometimes a mismatch between the expectations of users and the requirements of interpreters in practice. Service users, such as legal practitioners, may expect the translation to be literal – that is, a word-for-word translation. However, this does not correspond to the linguistic and cultural realities of language. Hertog (2015) states this in a very clear way:

> One particular requirement for interpreters is legal professionals' insistence that, because justice is at stake and the interpreted rendition becomes the

28 European Association for Legal Interpreters and Translators, 'EULITA Code of Professional Ethics' (2013). Available at: https://www.eulita.eu/wp-content/uploads/files/EULITA-code-London-e.pdf (accessed 4 June 2022).

29 Cecilia Wadensjö, *Interpreting as Interaction* (Longman, 1998).

30 Raffaela Merlini, 'Dialogue Interpreting' in Franz Pöchhacker (ed), *Routledge Encyclopedia of Interpreting Studies* (Routledge 2015), 102 ff.

official record, the exchanges between the parties are translated 'verbatim' and that legal interpreters are absolutely accurate and impartial ... But statements do not flow 'literally' from one language into another in equal number and sequence, 'verbatim' is not synonymous with accuracy and impartiality does not entail invisibility.[31]

Instead, accuracy and completeness are understood as faithful instead of literal translation, meaning that the general thrust of what is said is communicated between the parties. More broadly, however, it is the faithfulness of the translation – affirming the importance of trust and integrity in the interpreters' ethical code – that is important. Setton summarises this as follows:

> Fidelity or 'faithfulness' has been a key meme of discourse on translation and interpreting since earliest time, and has traditionally been seen as the primary criterion of quality. Fidelity and its equivalent terms in various languages are associated with notions of trust and integrity, and thus also engage the interpreter's professional ethics. ... In contemporary usage, the 'faithfulness' of a translation is sometimes more narrowly understood to refer to its accuracy and completeness.[32]

A considerable body of research on the role and function of interpreters in the legal context has developed since the 1990s. This research predominantly focuses on interpretation in criminal proceedings and investigates both the pre-trial and trial contexts. It also considers other topics, such as the quality and training of legal interpreters. Hertog provides a comprehensive overview of this research and states that 'the landmark study is Berk-Seligson's (1990) linguistic-ethnographic analysis of English/Spanish dialogues in various US courts',[33] which is considered as the starting point of 30 years of intensive research on legal interpreting. We do not have space to provide a comprehensive overview of the existing literature of legal interpretation. Key findings from this literature include, among other things, that quality still constitutes a challenge because adequate training is far from ensured in many countries; that the legal interpreter's role is continuously the subject of debate and critical reflection because of its complexity; and that new technology has become an additional challenge on top of the existing ones.

The findings from these studies are, of course, relevant to all laypeople in criminal proceedings who need an interpreter. This chapter is specifically interested in foreign-language vulnerability in addition to vulnerabilities stemming from status as a minor in criminal proceedings or status as a prisoner. For the latter

---

31 Erik Hertog, 'Legal Interpreting' in Franz Pöchhacker (ed) *Routledge Encyclopedia of Interpreting Studies* (Routledge 2015) 232 ff.

32 Robin Setton, 'Fidelity' in Franz Pöchhacker (ed), *Routledge Encyclopedia of Interpreting Studies* (Routledge 2015) 161ff.

33 Erik Hertog, 'Legal Interpreting' in Franz Pöchhacker (ed), *Routledge Encyclopedia of Interpreting Studies* (Routledge 2015) 230 ff.

group, we look at the criminal proceedings before imprisonment. The existing research in relation to these groups is scant.

For minors, Matthias and Zaal[34] found that interpreters in South Africa for child witnesses[35] were often 'inappropriate' because they were in a hurry to get through the case or were exhibiting improper non-verbal behaviour, 'such as laughing or frowning at the child to show disbelief of what the child was saying'.[36] Fontes[37] highlighted language-related pitfalls for interpreters in working with diverse families in child advocacy centres[38] in the United States; while Keselman and others[39] showed that children's voices were excluded from interaction or at least controlled by interpreters for Russian asylum-seeking children in Sweden. One example is that children who asked to have the interactions between the interpreter and the asylum worker translated received the answer, 'That is not necessary for you to know!'[40] This shows that children are often treated in a patronising way and are not respected as fully fledged participants in the conversation.

Findings also indicate why it is important, for instance, to be aware of the effect that suggestibility (which is affected by the use of leading or closed questions) might have on children: on their memory; on their nonverbal behaviour; on how suggestibility can create false symptoms or false statements; and on how this at least justifies the need to verify children's forensic interviews – especially where they take place in another language and an interpreter is an intermediary.[41] Indeed, research focusing on monolingual interview techniques (without a foreign-language component) has resulted in, among other things, the development of the Protocol of the National Institute of Child Health and Human

---

34 Carmel Matthias and Noel Zaal, 'Hearing Only a Faint Echo? Interpreters and Children in Court' (2002) 18(3) *South African Journal on Human Rights* 350 ff

35 Regarding vulnerability, we make no distinction between child victims, witnesses or accused persons, since they are all minors and by definition indicated as vulnerable. See Directive (EU) 2016/800 of the European Parliament and of the Council of 11 May 2016 on procedural safeguards for children who are suspects or accused persons in criminal proceedings [2016] OJ L132/1.

36 Carmel Matthias and Noel Zaal, 'Hearing Only a Faint Echo? Interpreters and Children in Court' (2002) 18(3) *South African Journal on Human Rights* 359.

37 Lisa A Fontes, *Child Abuse and Culture. Working with Diverse Families* (The Guilford Press 2005).

38 A children's advocacy centre is a community-based, child-focused facility where children alleged to be victims of abuse or neglect are interviewed and receive medical exams, if necessary, therapy and other critical services in a non-threatening and child friendly environment. See https://fncac.org (accessed 4 June 2022).

39 Olga Keselman and others, '"That Is Not Necessary for You to Know!" Negotiation of Participation Status of Unaccompanied Children in Interpreter-Mediated Asylum Hearings' (2010) 12(1) *Interpreting* 83 ff.

40 Olga Keselman and others, That Is Not Necessary for You to Know!" Negotiation of Participation Status of Unaccompanied Children in Interpreter-Mediated Asylum Hearings' (2010) 12(1) Interpreting 83 ff.

41 Henry Otgaar and Mark L Howe, *Finding the Truth in the Courtroom. Dealing with Deception, Lies, and Memories* (OUP 2018).

Development ('NICHD Protocol')[42] by Lamb and colleagues[43] for evidence-based investigative interviewing of children. The basic principle of this protocol is to ask hardly any questions, but to give open-ended invitations for narratives that come from the minor. It is of paramount importance for interpreters to be aware of these research findings regarding the strategic goals of questioning techniques in monolingual settings, in order to formulate questions as faithfully and accurately possible in their translation to avoid these known pitfalls.

As far as prisoners are concerned, the right to linguistic assistance seems to end at the prison walls. Research on linguistic barriers in prisons is also scarce. Martínez-Gómez is the most prominent and prolific scholar researching language barriers in prisons.[44] Her overview of interpreting in prison incorporated many countries around the world and concluded that most European countries base their strategies to meet communicative needs on in-house and *ad hoc* resources.[45] As a result, in prisons, interpreters are often fellow prisoners or bilingual staff, meaning that they are not bound by the same principles as professional interpreters (ie, ensuring the completeness and accuracy of the translation; respecting confidentiality; remaining impartial), and may thus provide a subpar 'service'. What is of concern in this chapter is to see whether, through Directive 2010/64/EU, the right to interpreting and translation in criminal proceedings is respected by the use of bilingual prisoners as translators. This kind of research has never been done before – for the simple reason that the individual (ie, not institutional) users of interpreting services are seldom questioned.

Background to the Studies/Methods

The data used in this chapter was collected as part of a series of research projects that began in 2012. An initial project on interpreting-mediated questioning of minors was carried out by Heidi Salaets and Katalin Balogh and several European partners.[46] This aimed to bring together different professionals: police officers,

42 National Institute of Child Health and Human Development Protocol on the International Evidence-Based Investigative Interviewing of Children. Available at: https://nichdprotocol.com/ (accessed 16 September 2021).

43 Michael E Lamb and others, *Tell Me What Happened: Structured Investigative Interviews of Child Victims and Witnesses* (Wiley 2008).

44 See Aída Martínez-Gómez, 'Contextual Factors as an Analytical Tool: Exploring Collaboration and Negotiation in Mental Health Interviews in Prisons Mediated by Non-professional Interpreters' (2021) 20 *Linguistica Antverpiensia, New Series – Themes in Translation Studies* 29.

45 Aída Martínez-Gómez, 'Interpreting in Prison Settings: An International Overview' (2014) 16(2) *Interpreting* 233.

46 In the two Co-Minor projects: KU Leuven, Belgium; Ministry of Defence and Safety, Netherlands; ISIT, France; Heriot-Watt University, Scotland; University of Bologna, Italy; Eszter Foundation, Hungary; Terre des Hommes, Hungary. Experts: György Virág (forensic psychologist, Hungary); Szilvia Gyurkó (expert child rights, Hungary); Eric Van der Mussele (youth lawyer, Belgium); Hans De Wiest (chief commissioner, Federal Police, Department of Behavioural Sciences); Myriam Vermeerbergen (KU Leuven, Campus Sint-Andries, Antwerp, signed language).

experts in forensic interviewing, legal actors (youth lawyers, youth magistrates and prosecutors), language and interpreting experts, child rights experts, psychologists, social workers and potentially other professionals involved in questioning foreign-language-speaking minors. The research was carried out through DG Justice (Directorate General of the European Commission) funded projects with the acronym Co-Minor-IN/QUEST I[47] and II,[48] which stands for 'Cooperation in interpreter-mediated questioning of Minors'.

The first project aimed to map the collaboration between the abovementioned stakeholders and resulted in the publication of an interdisciplinary volume.[49] The second project built on the results of the first, which showed that there was a lack of knowledge of the different stakeholders' roles and tasks during interpreter-mediated encounters with minors, leading to a lack of trust and collaboration. At the same time, stakeholders expressed both the need and the will to strengthen this collaboration in the best interests of the child. In order to fill this void in trust and collaboration, one of the deliverables of the second project was a manual on interprofessional education and a related set of training modules, which were distributed among and piloted by these stakeholders.[50] In the second project, children were involved and (language-independent) animated movies were designed to guide minors on the role of the interpreter. The third project, Children in Legal Language Settings (ChiLLS)[51] – which was still funded by the Directorate General of the European Commission – concentrated on vulnerability and resilience among minors and resulted in the construction of a website[52] that would bring together materials and knowledge from all of the projects. Vulnerable foreign-language-speaking minors were directly involved in this project; and the results of the Belgian case, which involved interviewing vulnerable minors, are presented in this chapter.

With regard to prisoners, we draw on a separate project called Translaw, funded by the Justice Programme of the European Union.[53] In this project, we asked prisoners about linguistic assistance throughout their whole journey through the criminal justice process, culminating in imprisonment. The main scope of this

---

47 Available at: https://www.arts.kuleuven.be/english/rg_interpreting_studies/research-p rojects/co_minor_in_quest (accessed 4 June 2022).

48 Available at: https://www.arts.kuleuven.be/english/rg_interpreting_studies/research-p rojects/co-minor-in-quest-ii (accessed 4 June 2022).

49 Katalin Balogh and Heidi Salaets (eds) *Children and Justice: Overcoming Language Barriers. Cooperation in Interpreter-Mediated Questioning of Minors* (Intersentia 2015). Available at: https://www.arts.kuleuven.be/tolkwetenschap/projecten/co_m inor_in_quest/children-and-justice (accessed 4 June 2022).

50 Katalin Balogh, Heidi Salaets and Dominique Van Schoor (eds) *Interpreter-Mediated Child Interviews: Tools for Interprofessional Training* (Lannoo 2018). Available at: https://www. arts.kuleuven.be/tolkwetenschap/projecten/co-minor-in-quest-ii/interpreter-mediated-child-interviews (accessed 4 June 2022).

51 Available at: https://www.arts.kuleuven.be/english/rg_interpreting_studies/research-p rojects/chills (accessed 4 June 2022).

52 Available at: https://chills-research.eu/ (accessed 4 June 2022). Aelbrecht (the third author) was involved in this project.

53 JUST-AG-2016/JUST-AG-2016–06 (official funding programme)

project was to conduct interviews with all stakeholders involved in this linguistic service path, from arrest to imprisonment – namely with legal professionals (LPs), legal interpreters (LIs) and persons accused of crime (PACs).

We asked prisoners in two Belgian (Flemish) prisons about their linguistic service path – that is, the linguistic assistance they received from arrest to imprisonment. It was beyond the scope of this research to ask for any details about their lives or the reasons for their imprisonment.

Semi-structured Interviews

The abovementioned research projects provide data which gives some insights on how effectively the right to an interpreter is implemented in practice in several European countries, specifically for minors and prisoners. This data was obtained via qualitative research methods – namely semi-structured interviews with minors (ChiLLS) and with prisoners (TransLaw). Although this research was conducted internationally, in this chapter we limit ourselves to the results from Belgium.

We decided to present the results from these two apparently very different groups in this chapter to show that foreign-language vulnerability is a concept that additionally applies to already vulnerable groups, independent of the characteristics of the vulnerable group to which they belong. We must stress, however, that the sample size analysed for this chapter was very small and that the insights are not generalisable. Such qualitative research gives us an in-depth understanding of linguistic vulnerability in naturalistic settings in the prisons and refugee centres (with unaccompanied minors) that we were allowed to visit.

Respondents: Minors

In the context of the ChiLLS research project, we asked eight foreign-language minors (aged 12 to 18) in Belgium how they experienced interpreters during their (asylum and/or criminal) proceedings. In other words, we sought information from them on what they felt they needed in order to be assisted linguistically to exercise their rights, and whether they felt these needs had been met. As is clear from Table 8.1, six of the eight minors were involved in asylum proceedings rather than criminal proceedings. We believe, however, that the findings from this context have direct relevance for the criminal justice setting and hence we draw on them in this chapter.

The minors were approached through youth judges and child support services. Due to the Covid-19 pandemic, the sample size was small and not representative – for instance, all respondents were male. The minors were interviewed after we obtained ethical clearance from the ethics committee of the University of KU Leuven and informed consent from the respondents. The minors could choose to have the interviews in the presence or absence of their legal guardian. The interviewers/researchers were accompanied by an interpreter, so that minors were free to express themselves fully in their native language. The respondents are identified by number (eg, 'M#1') instead of by name, to guarantee their anonymity. Table 8.1 gives an overview of the respondents' characteristics.

Table 8.1 Respondents in ChiLLS

	Age	Mother Tongue	Communication Language	Type of Proceeding
Minor 1	15–18	English/Crio	English	Asylum
Minor 2	12–14	Pashto	Pashto	Asylum
Minor 3	12–14	Pashto	Pashto	Asylum
Minor 4	15–18	Dari	Dari	Asylum
Minor 5	15–18	Pashto	Dari	Asylum
Minor 6	15–18	Dari	Dari	Asylum/ criminal
Minor 7	15–18	Somali	Somali	Asylum
Minor 8	15–18	Romanes/ Slovak	Slovak	Criminal

Respondents in ChiLLS (all male), including age, mother tongue, language used during the semi-structured interview and the proceedings in which they were involved.

Respondents: Prisoners

Interviews with relevant stakeholders in the TransLaw project provide important insights on the linguistic services available to prisoners throughout their criminal justice journey. In this chapter, we limit ourselves to the interviews we conducted with foreign-language-speaking prisoners, again in Belgium (n=9). We asked them about their perceptions of linguistic assistance to exercise their rights during their 'legal journey', up until they were imprisoned.[54] This was after having obtained permission from detention managerial staff (who gave us access), ethical clearance from the ethical committee of KU Leuven and informed consent from the participants/prisoners. The prisoners were interviewed by the researcher(s), accompanied by an interpreter, again to give them the opportunity to express themselves fully. Table 8.2 provides further details of the prisoners' mother tongue and the linguistic assistance they received. They are again identified by number (eg, 'P#9').

Findings

In order to compare the responses of the minors with those of the prisoners, we clustered their replies by theme. It is interesting to note that many of the same themes were evident in the responses of both the minors and prisoners concerning the use of an interpreter in their proceedings.

---

54 Throughout the project, we used the acronym 'PAC' (persons accused of crime), although we interviewed PACs who were convicted/sentenced guilty and imprisoned, since we interviewed them in prison.

Table 8.2 Mother tongue of prisoners; actual language used during the proceedings; prison location

PAC#	Mother Tongue or Preferred Language	Languages Spoken During the Procedure/Used by the Interpreter	Prison Location
1	Arabic	French/Spanish >< Dutch	Beveren-Waas
2	Berber	Dutch only	
3	Standard Arabic and French	Moroccan Arabic/ Palestinian and Syrian varieties of Arabic >< Dutch	
4	Berber	Arabic Standard >< Dutch	
5	Moroccan Arabic	Egyptian Arabic >< Dutch	
6	Russian	Russian >< Dutch	
7	Bulgarian	Bulgarian >< Dutch	
8	Arabic and French	French >< Dutch	Mechelen
9	Italian	Albanian >< Dutch	

Lack of Confidence in the Interpreter's Confidentiality

First, all minors expressed a preference to speak directly to the authorities without an interpreter (ie, in their mother tongue) because of privacy matters, as exemplified in the following quotes:

> Then you feel totally free, and you can better express some things, without someone being present, who sees and hears it all. (M#5)
>
> Now well; your asylum story ... this is a private matter, you don't tell this to everyone ... But no, I don't trust it, but I have no other choice, I have to tell it there. (M#6)

One of the prisoners expressed this lack of trust in the interpreter's role as follows:

> My only concern was to tell the truth. I didn't see the interpreter as an individual. At a certain point they [other participants in the hearing] were talking to each other. I didn't understand. I felt excluded. (P#1).

Linguistic Needs and Language Matching: Absent or 'Wrong' Interpreter

Another important insight relates to the appropriateness of the interpreter provided in terms of their ability to speak the minor or prisoner's 'mother tongue' sufficiently well. This is about much more than just a common language and the interpreter's language skills; it requires the interpreter to be familiar with the particular variant and nuances of someone's language (eg, local dialects). One minor stressed the importance of this in order for her to feel able to speak naturally or, as she put it, to talk 'deeply':

> But if I start talking really deeply, she cannot understand because she is not from my country … But this one I did in Brussels, the person was from my country; she can understand what I was saying. (M#1)

For prisoners, the situation was bleaker. All prisoners except one declared that there was no communication because of the lack of an interpreter, because the wrong interpreter was hired or because of the hostile attitude of the police:

> The police back in 2006 said that living in Belgium means I had to learn Dutch. I could speak Moroccan Arabic but no Berber. They gave me an Egyptian [Arabic] interpreter; when I told the judge, he said he was the only one available. (P#4)

Even the fundamental requirement of being able to understand and be understood – which requires that an interpreter be provided in the language that the prisoner regards as their language of expression – was violated during the service path towards the court hearing. In one case, the authorities recruited the interpreter according to nationality (Albanian), rather than the prisoner's language of expression (Italian), and refused to pay attention to the prisoner's request in a surprisingly stubborn way:

> I didn't understand. The interpreter didn't listen to my questions and needs. I needed an interpreter in Italian, not Albanian. So, I didn't have the right interpreter(s). Their intervention was completely useless … I had 6 interpreters for Albanian, none in Italian … I asked the police officer, lawyer, magistrates for an Italian interpreter. Didn't receive it. Only incomprehension. (P#9)

Professional versus Unprofessional Interpreters

The confidence that individuals had in their interpreter and their satisfaction with the service they received appear to relate to whether the interpreter was a professional – and had thus received training and accreditation[55] – or a non-professional

---

55 Professional interpreters in Belgium have had training and accreditation as legal interpreters and/or are enrolled in the National Register for Sworn Translators, Interpreters and Translators-Interpreters. Available at: https://justice.belgium.be/fr/ services_en_ligne/registre_national_et_frais_de_justice/registre_national (accessed 4 June 2022).

interpreter such as a bilingual prison guard or fellow inmate. This is apparent from one minor's experience of several different interpreters:

> [The first interpreter] was very pleasant ... I could understand the interpreter well, his Somali was good, so I had trust in him, that he was able to interpret into Dutch as well. ... Some interpreters took notes, and I found that better, because it is also better for the memory of the interpreter. Some of them only listened. (M#7)

Where non-professional interpreters were used, particularly for prisoners, their lack of professionalism was viewed as preventing the prisoners from understanding the proceedings. Their impact was perceived in a negative way and left some respondents feeling dissatisfied and distressed. One prisoner answered the question regarding the impact of the interpreter as follows:

> I didn't understand anything in my file. There was no impact at all of anything. Only that they made it more difficult. They ruined my life [starts crying]. (P#2)

One of the prisoners expressed the importance of ensuring that individuals have access to professional interpreters due to differences in their professionality and competence:

> The only thing I hope is that every individual gets a professional interpreter who does his job in giving the person the possibility to speak his own language. There is a big difference in quality, their way of working and dealing with things. (P#6)

Trustworthiness of the Interpreter

The trustworthiness of interpreters for users (both legal actors and interviewees) is both a tangible and non-tangible issue. It is tangible insofar their linguistic competences are concerned; and non-tangible but nonetheless perceptible insofar as impartiality, the attitude of the interpreter and the expression of emotions are concerned.

Linguistic Competences: Accuracy and Completeness

Interpreters constitute a very important human variable in encounters between legal actors and vulnerable groups. The experiences of both minors and prisoners with regard to the linguistic competence of interpreters were rather negative. The impact of the interpreting on the understanding of what went on was judged as being either non-existent or even negative (for seven out of nine prisoners): depending on the interpreter's competences, understanding varied from zero to good.

Insights garnered from this research included a Russian-speaking prisoner who was given a Dutch-speaking interpreter who knew only 'some Russian' (P#6). One minor who spoke Pashto also had issues with their interpreter, who spoke Dari – another official language spoken in Afghanistan – noting that:

> he [the interpreter] didn't understand some terms or words, then skipped and omitted them. (M#5)

A lack of control was another recurrent theme among both groups, because in general someone can only understand one language in the language pair and may have either limited notions of the other language, or none at all. This is an obvious reason to call an interpreter; but users apparently were not prepared to rely automatically or blindly on the interpreter due to concerns about their competence to produce an accurate and completely translate. This was evident from concerns expressed about the interpreter obviously summarising, skipping and adding comments in the translation:

> She summarised what I was saying in Russian. It was much shorter. So information was lost. (P#6)

The interpreter's ability to translate properly is important to gain the user's trust in the communication and to ensure the accuracy of the information relayed between the parties. One prisoner recounted a story where a mistranslation resulted in another individual appealing their prison sentence and ultimately ending up with additional time to serve – all as a result of an inaccurate translation:

> Once a friend of mine in court received a fixed prison sentence of 3 years and 2 years' probation. The interpreter said: a fixed prison sentence of 5 years. That is a big difference. My friend lodged an appeal. There they sentenced him to 4 years in prison, which is actually one more than what he received originally. (P#5)

Impartiality

Another important issue that both minors and prisoners raised in interviews was the impartiality of the interpreter. The interpreter should translate the interactions, rather than giving their own 'interpretation' of what has been said. This can result in negative behaviours such as interfering in the conversation, expressing unwanted opinions, showing emotion or adopting a hierarchical attitude of superiority. On the other hand, a lack of impartiality can sometimes be perceived as standing with the vulnerable party/the individual confronted with the institution. These are all different examples of impartiality failure – positive or negative, depending on the respective viewpoint; or put simply, of the interpreter not acting impartially.

One concrete example of this lack of impartiality ('showing emotion') was given by a minor who witnessed how an interpreter lost his temper:

In the middle of my interview, suddenly he [the interpreter] became angry with me, because I understand English and I understood he was talking in English and at a certain moment in time he said, "You talk a lot. You ought to wait for a moment." (M#5)

A lack of impartiality can also be experienced as a subtle behavioural issue; or can even be perceived as ethical profiling (an 'attitude of superiority'). The following testimony concerns a boy who spoke Pashto, but received a Dari interpreter:

But my interpreter was of Afghan origin, and I am not completely sure, but he saw himself ... he thought, he was different than us. He saw himself as a better person than us. He behaved in a distinct manner. (M#5)

A more positive recollection of an interpreter's impartiality came from P#1:

The interpreter was nice to me. She asked how I felt. That had nothing to do with the case. (P#1)

Concerningly, some prisoners reported that interpreters became too involved in the process or appeared to 'take sides' and assist the police or authorities in their investigations. One prisoner (#6) described some interpreters as:

Sometimes ... [acting] like a police officer. (P#6)

Another prisoner noted that the interpreter was passing judgement to the police on the veracity of his account:

Once they hired an Egyptian [Arabic speaker] who thought I did not speak a word of Dutch. He made an addition towards the police, and said: 'What he says, is not correct.' Then I have protested and told him: 'This is a conversation between myself and the police. If I don't tell the truth, it is up to the policeman to discover; it is not your task!' (P#5)

Thankfully, in this particular situation the prisoner both was able to understand Dutch sufficiently well to know that the interpreter was doing this and had the courage to mention – as was his right to do so – the incorrectness of the interpreter's work. However, it is troubling to think that there may be other instances where interpreters act in an impartial and unprofessional way that goes undetected by the user and thus risk influencing the police/other legal actors and their decision making.

Resilience: Power Differential and Assertion of Rights

We can see from the interviews that the assertion of rights and the ability of a user to speak up against, or express dissatisfaction with, an interpreter are sometimes hindered by cultural and behavioural barriers.

One minor felt that he had no power over the choice of interpreter, even to the extent that he did not raise concerns about the interpreter's competence out of politeness:

> They ask in the beginning of the interview and at the end whether you understood the interpreter well, but yeah, you can't say it at that moment, because he is looking you in the eye. You can't say anything in his presence. (M#5)

Some prisoners explained that they learned more about their rights during the procedure, such as the right to a professional and competent interpreter:

> She summarised what I was saying in Russian. It was much shorter. So information was lost. *I didn't dare to say something then, now I would.* (P#6) (emphasis added)
>
> I would like to have one interpreter for the whole case. I would like to speak with the interpreter to see whether he speaks well and understandable Berber. If I don't understand him, I must ask for a deferral/postponement and ask for an interpreter I can understand! (P#2)
>
> We are 2019, not 2012: human rights become more clear, it is not like before anymore. They introduced a new system in B. and I think it is very good. If you go to the police, then an interpreter and lawyer is present. Everything that has been said, is also registered. (P#4)

Conclusion and Recommendations

Although it is clear that the European Union has made an effort to professionalise, institutionalise and harmonise the procedural safeguards for vulnerable people in criminal proceedings through its roadmap, this chapter demonstrates through empirical findings that there is still work to be done in relation to foreign language vulnerability. This is at both the conceptual and theoretical levels, as well as in practice. The chapter argues that foreign language vulnerability is an additional layer of vulnerability that should be viewed alongside other vulnerabilities, such as young age and situational vulnerabilities (eg, imprisonment). On a conceptual level, foreign language vulnerability should be further defined and researched to raise awareness of its effects among legal practitioners.

On a practical level, this research shows that the provision of interpreters to those with foreign language vulnerability is lacking. Furthermore, interpreters may not be trained or may be unavailable (because trained interpreters are scarce); and there is evidence of other issues, including financial and organisational problems. For instance, the profession should be properly recognised as such and should consequently be adequately remunerated. Low remuneration and low status are not good incentives to undertake training; so we end up in a vicious circle, where low pay leads to inadequate training.

Insights from the interviews with minors and prisoners demonstrate that there are concerns about the ability of interpreters to accurately and completely translate the interactions in which they are instructed. This is because interpreters are not always sought or available who match the language needs of the individual user; because initial assessments of the language needs of the individual user are not properly conducted; and/or also because the interpreter may not appreciate and convey differences in meaning and expression in local dialects. This problem is intensified, it seems, when non-professional interpreters are used (eg, bilingual legal actors, prison guards or other prisoners), rather than professional third-party interpreters. Other issues highlighted include concerns about the impartiality of the interpreter; questions around their commitment to confidentiality and users' abilities to freely express themselves in the presence of a third party; and difficulties that users experience in raising issues with their interpreter. All of this serves to undermine the compliance of EU member states with the roadmap and to jeopardise the fairness of the ensuing trials and proceedings.

Going forward, we suggest two main avenues for reform. First, under the state's duty of care, it is clear that the onus rests with the authorities to ensure that their agents can guarantee that the right to an interpreter is practicable and effective. This could be done by developing a clear protocol and a system which ensures that interpreting needs are assessed whenever there are reasons to suspect that the defendant is not sufficiently proficient in the language of the proceedings. This decision should be aptly justified, including the procedure used, and should be recorded in writing. Second, an obvious prerequisite for the effective and practical application of the directive(s) is training among the legal profession about how to work effectively with an interpreter and what to expect from the service.[56] We argue that such training is necessary, but its current provision is insufficient. We suggest that inter-professional training is needed – legal professionals are not linguists or interpreters; and nor are interpreters legal professionals. The way forward lies along a multi-disciplinary research path and an inter-professional training track, which involves mutually learning about how to work with each other in a professional setting. Such inter-professional training would also help to teach all professionals involved in criminal proceedings about the professional interpreter and their role and competences, such that the institutional primary participant – the police officer, the lawyer, the judge, the prosecutor – could recognise and possibly refuse a non-professional interpreter.

Ethical education is also needed in how to deal with foreign language vulnerability. Linguistic competences, the use of language variants, accuracy and impartiality were mostly indicated as characteristics of professional interpreters; whereas a lack of accuracy, exclusive reliance on memory (without notes), partiality (in

---

56 Cornelia, Riehle and Alison Clozel, '10 years after the roadmap: procedural rights in criminal proceedings in the EU today' (2020) 20 *ERA Forum* 321; see also EU Directive 2010/64/EU, Article 6: 'Member States shall request those responsible for the training of judges, prosecutors and judicial staff involved in criminal proceedings to pay special attention to the particularities of communicating with the assistance of an interpreter so as to ensure efficient and effective communication.'

collaborating with the police) and trustworthiness were criticised in the case of non-professional interpreters. The latter was especially the case for minors, who would have preferred not to tell their private stories in the presence of a third person, indicating that they were not informed about the confidentiality that the professional interpreter must observe. This bolsters the case for the use of professional interpreters, who are accredited and who receive ongoing training in their work.

Let us conclude by returning to the example given at the beginning of this chapter. It is important for us to understand that it is not the interpreter's task to ensure that the adults involved in the car accident receive a reduced sentence, or that the wellbeing of the children who witnessed the accident is assured. However, the professional legal interpreter should ensure that everyone involved – police officers, lawyers, child support workers – can communicate effectively. Hopefully, this interaction should ensure the individual's understanding of the whole legal procedure and ability to follow everything through correct translation. Put differently, the individual should be empowered to fully exercise their right to an interpreter, and their foreign language vulnerability should thus be overcome through effective translation and an appropriate relationship between the interpreter, the individual and the police/authorities involved. If these rights are met, the right to a fair trial is more appropriately provided for, because all participants can effectively understand the proceedings and be understood themselves. This chapter highlights, through insights in the Belgian context with minors and prisoners, that while some progress has been made in this regard, there is still more work to be done to properly realise the right to an interpreter.

Part 3

Responses to Vulnerability in the Courts

9 Speech, Language and Communication Needs and the Role of the Speech and Language Therapist

Kim Turner and Claire Westwood

Introduction

Communication is the active process of exchanging information and ideas involving both understanding and expression of a shared language. Verbal language is indispensable to the enactment and enforcement of law.[1] The terminology used in courtrooms and police stations is rarely seen outside of the justice system and is difficult for even the average layman to comprehend. For individuals with specific difficulties in communication (hereinafter referred to as 'speech, language and communication needs' (SLCNs)), the language of the justice system can be impossible to decode, process or meaningfully use.[2] This can then impact on the accused's right to a fair trial under Article 6 of the European Convention of Human Rights (ECHR), as that person cannot be informed of the nature and cause of the accusation against them and prepare and effectuate their defence.[3]

This chapter outlines what SLCNs are; their prevalence; how they may manifest among the accused; and why this can make the accused vulnerable. It also details how these needs impact upon effective participation in the criminal justice system. To illustrate this phenomenon, the authors refer to research literature, legislation and clinical experience, supplemented by anecdotes from individuals with SLCNs who have first-hand experience of navigating justice processes.[4]

1 David Mellinkoff, *The Language of the Law* (Little, Brown & Co, 1963).
2 Pamela C Snow, Martine B Powell and Dixie D Sanger, 'Oral Language Competence, Young Speakers, and the Law' (2012) 43 *Language Speech and Hearing Services in Schools* 496.
3 Convention for the Protection of Human Rights and Fundamental Freedoms (European Convention on Human Rights, as amended) (ECHR) art 6.
4 With thanks to the SOLD user group who contributed their invaluable experiences via a focus group. The SOLD user group is a group of people who all have a learning disability and experience of the criminal justice system. Their network has developed a range of resources to support effective participation in legal proceedings; see https://soldnetwork.org.uk/ (accessed 15 February 2023).

DOI: 10.4324/9781003205166-13

Speech, Language and Communication Needs

Speech, language and communication are foundational for social integration, participation in society and positive life chances.[5] The World Health Organization states that communication and interpersonal skills are one of five types of globally relevant life skills.[6] They encompass the ability to understand what is being said, to interact with others and to use language to convey thoughts, feelings, wants and needs. Communication skills change across the lifespan, with recent research indicating that neural development associated with language, social skills and executive functioning continues until around 25 years of age.[7] Almost 20% of the population will experience a delay or disruption to these abilities at some point during their lifetime. SLCNs include the following:

- Developmental SLCNs: These issues originate in childhood and persist through life. They could be isolated (eg, a developmental language disorder, speech sound disorder or stammer) or secondary to other conditions (eg, a learning disability or neurodevelopmental disorders such as an autism spectrum condition (ASC) or attention deficit hyperactivity disorder (ADHD).[8] Ten per cent of children have long-term developmental SLCNs creating barriers to everyday life; these increase in areas of social deprivation, where up to 50% of children start school with delayed language skills.[9]
- Acquired SLCNs: These typically arise when developing skills become disrupted as a result of an event (eg, stroke, cancer, Parkinson's disease or dementia). The levels of acquired SLCNs depend on the individual condition. For example, up to 50% of people will experience an SLCN following a traumatic brain injury.[10]

SLCNs can have significant impacts on life outcomes, affecting areas such as:

- educational attainment (adolescents with vocabulary difficulties are less likely to achieve A* to C grades in their English language, English literature and

---

5 Judy Clegg and others, 'Developmental Language Disorders: A Follow-Up in Later Adult Life. Cognitive, Language and Psychosocial Outcomes' (2005) *Journal of Child Psychology and Psychiatry* 128

6 World Health Organization, *Partners in Life Skills Education: Conclusions from a United Nations Inter-Agency Meeting* (1999)

7 Natalia Jaworska and Glenda MacQueen, 'Adolescence as a Unique Developmental Period' (2015) 40 *Journal of Psychiatry and Neuroscience* 291

8 Dorothy VM Bishop, 'Why Is It So Hard to Reach Agreement on Terminology? The Case of Developmental Language Disorder (DLD): Terminology and the Case of DLD' (2017) *International Journal of Language and Communication Disorders.*

9 John Bercow MP, *Bercow: Ten Years On: An Independent Review of Provision for Children and Young People with Speech, Language and Communication Needs in England* (I CAN and the Royal College of Speech and Language Therapists, 2018).

10 Skye McDonald, Leanne Togher and Chris Code, *Social and Communication Disorders Following Traumatic Brain Injury* (Psychology Press 2013).

mathematics General Certificate of Secondary Education exams than their peers);[11]

- mental health (81% of children with emotional and behavioural disorders were found to have unidentified SLCNs);[12]
- employability (those with vocabulary difficulties at five years old are more than twice as likely to be unemployed aged 34.[13] In a 20-year follow-up study, those with language disorders were more likely than those without language disorders to be living below the poverty line and less likely to be in full-time employment);[14] and
- broader life prospects (the long-term impacts of SLCNs suggest that their associated costs to individuals, families and society across the lifespan are substantial. Individuals with SLCNs are less likely to be in a stable long-term relationship, and more likely to have reduced earnings and increased reliance on governmental support.)[15]

These findings demonstrate how broad ranging and devastating the impact of SLCNs can be for individuals across many areas of life. Barriers to effective participation in society can lead to individuals feeling isolated and struggling to achieve. This in turn can increase a person's likelihood of becoming involved with the criminal justice system;[16] therefore, unsurprisingly, there is increasing evidence that individuals with SLCNs are overrepresented in the criminal justice system.[17]

Prevalence of Speech, Language and Communication Needs in the Criminal Justice System

International evidence demonstrates that individuals in contact with the criminal justice system are significantly more likely to have SLCNs than those in

11 Sarah Spencer and others, 'Contribution of Spoken Language and Socio-economic Background to Adolescents' Educational Achievement at Age 16 Years' (2016) *International Journal of Language and Communication Disorders.*
12 Alexandra Hollo, Joseph H Wehby and Regina M Oliver, 'Unidentified Language Deficits in Children with Emotional and Behavioral Disorders: A Meta-Analysis' (2014) 80 *Exceptional Children* 169
13 Judy Clegg and Jane Ginsborg, *Language and Social Disadvantage: Theory into Practice* (John Wiley & Sons 2006)
14 Carla Johnson, Joseph Beitchman and Elizabeth Brownlie, 'Twenty-Year Follow-Up of Children With and Without Speech- Language Impairments: Family, Educational, Occupational, and Quality of Life Outcomes' (2010) 19 *American Journal of Speech – Language Pathology* (Online) 51
15 Paula Cronin and Rebecca Addo, 'Interactions with Youth Justice and Associated Costs for Young People with Speech, Language and Communication Needs' (2021) 56 *International Journal of Language and Communication Disorders* 797
16 Avshalom Caspi and others, 'Childhood Forecasting of a Small Segment of the Population with Large Economic Burden' (2016) 1 *Natural Human Behaviour.*
17 Stavroola AS Anderson, David J Hawes and Pamela C Snow, 'Language Impairments among Youth Offenders: A Systematic Review' (2016) 65 *Children and Youth Services Review* 195.

the wider community.[18] In the general population, SLCNs have been found to have a median prevalence of 5.9%,[19] while figures for SLCNs in those involved in the criminal justice system average 60% (ranging from 19% to over 80%).[20] Research has examined the full breadth of SLCNs – including vocabulary, narrative, sequencing, grammar, understanding and social skills – with high levels of impairment for those in the criminal justice system found across all areas.

The high prevalence of SLCNs within the criminal justice system population is not fully understood ,but may partly be explained by the overrepresentation of several sections of society in the criminal justice system who have higher levels of SLCNs than the general population. First, there is a disproportionate number of individuals with learning disabilities and/or ASCs in contact with the criminal justice system.[21] These conditions have SLCNs as core diagnostic criteria. Second, high rates of traumatic brain injury are reported among the criminal justice population;[22] as previously stated, around half of those who have had a significant traumatic brain injury will experience SLCNs.[23] Third, there is likely to be an increasing incidence of acquired communication impairments related to health conditions such as stroke or dementia[24] as the prison population ages.[25] Finally, individuals from Black, Asian and minority groups[26] who use non-standard language forms may be wrongly identified in the research as experiencing SLCNs. Research generally uses assessment tools based on 'standard' language format. The individual may have the ability to respond to the question in a 'non-standard', colloquial format, but not in a way that is acceptable to be assigned as a 'correct' response. While these individuals may not have SLCNs, their non-standard

18 Stavroola AS Anderson, David J Hawes and Pamela C Snow, 'Language Impairments among Youth Offenders: A Systematic Review' (2016) 65 *Children and Youth Services Review* 195.

19 James Law and others, 'Screening for Speech and Language Delay: A Systematic Review of the Literature' (1998) 2 *Health Technology Assessment* 1.

20 Stavroola AS Anderson, David J Hawes and Pamela C Snow, 'Language Impairments among Youth Offenders: A Systematic Review' (2016) 65 *Children and Youth Services Review* 195.

21 Stavroola AS Anderson, David J Hawes and Pamela C Snow, 'Language Impairments among Youth Offenders: A Systematic Review' (2016) 65 *Children and Youth Services Review* 195.

22 W Huw Williams and others, 'Traumatic Brain Injury in a Prison Population: Prevalence and Risk for Re-offending' (2010) 24 *Brain Injury* 1184.

23 Skye McDonald, Leanne Togher and Chris Code, *Social and Communication Disorders Following Traumatic Brain Injury* (Psychology Press 2013).

24 Martin Prince and others, 'Recent Global Trends in the Prevalence and Incidence of Dementia, and Survival with Dementia' (2016) 8 *Alzheimer's Research & Therapy* 23.

25 Council of Europe, Annual Penal Statistics SPACE I reports. Available at: https://wp.unil.ch/space/space-i/annual-reports (accessed 4 June 2022).

26 David Lammy, *The Lammy Review: An Independent Review into the Treatment of, and Outcomes for, Black, Asian and Minority Ethnic Individuals in the Criminal Justice System* (2017).

language use may still represent a barrier to effective participation in the criminal justice system.[27]

It is not sufficient to simply recognise why those with SLCNs are more likely to come into contact with the criminal justice system. We must also consider how this affects participation in the justice processes and what support is provided for persons with SLCNs.

SLCNs are both under-identified and a hidden disability:[28] often, both communication partners are unaware of the presence of a difficulty, making communication breakdown highly likely. Frequent communication breakdown could make an individual vulnerable in the criminal justice system.

Table 9.1 sets out some examples of how communication can break down.

Table 9.1 Alternative Speech and Language-Based Explanations for Common Presentations

Presentation	*Potential SLCN*	*Behind the SLCN*	*Potential Impact*
Inconsistent story	Narrative language and/or sequencing difficulties.	In trying to arrange the language elements correctly, they create 'different' stories with different meanings.	May be judged to be unreliable or lying, as seen to be trying to fill gaps in their story.
Words 'parroted back' or used out of context	Restricted vocabulary.	In trying to speak 'properly' and adapt to their surroundings, words get used out of context or without understanding.	Deemed to understand conditions when they do not.
Unrelated/unexpected reply	Receptive language impairment.	The individual may have only understood part of the question or may be guessing the answer. 'Yes' is generally deemed to be the 'correct' response when asked a question.	The accused may incorrectly implicate themselves through lack of understanding: A: 'So, you feel *culpable* of the offence?' B: 'Err, yes?'
Facial expressions incongruent	Receptive language impairment and/or pragmatic language impairment.	The individual may not have understood the interaction correctly or may not know how to respond in this unfamiliar situation.	Smiling when faced with a victim could be viewed negatively by the jury, while the individual has been taught to 'be friendly' to everyone at court.

27 Kaitlyn Alger, 'More than What Meets the Ear: Speech Transcription as a Barrier to Justice for African American Vernacular English Speakers' (2021) 13 *Georgetown Journal of Law and Modern Critical Race Perspectives* 87.

28 Dorothy VM Bishop, 'Why Is It So Hard to Reach Agreement on Terminology? The Case of Developmental Language Disorder (DLD): Terminology and the Case of DLD' (2017) *International Journal of Language and Communication Disorders*.

The impact of SLCNs upon engagement with justice processes has been explored by LaVigne and Van Rybroek,[29] who examined the effect of SLCNs on the lawyer-client relationship. They found key difficulties such as:

- processing complex sentences and following directions;
- understanding and using vocabulary;
- remembering what is said (auditory memory);
- staying on topic;
- understanding inferences including background information;
- reading written materials;
- retaining new information;
- reading social cues and recognising and articulating emotional states, motivations and thoughts of others;
- understanding and explaining what happened;
- high-order skills (eg, self-monitoring, planning and consequential thinking); and
- issues seeking clarification and recognising and controlling inappropriate behaviour

Failure to identify the SLCNs of vulnerable defendants can also lead to:

- not realising what they are involved with constitutes a crime;
- not fully understanding laws and providing false confessions; and
- issues understanding written information and filling out forms.

The authors have observed these difficulties play out in real-life situations – for example, a court reading a list of charges to a defendant who did not understand them, leading to him mixing up his innocent and guilty pleas. It is clear from the above that SLCNs can lead to serious and pervasive issues in participating effectively in the justice process. It is important, therefore, that support is swiftly implemented for these vulnerable persons to facilitate effective participation.

Support for the Vulnerable Accused in the Criminal Justice System

While a significant proportion of individuals who come into contact with the criminal justice system have SLCNs which impact on their interactions with the system, less than 25% will have received previous speech and language therapy support.[30] Overwhelmingly, these needs remain unidentified and unsupported, making the provision of support to all those who need it even more complex. Support for people with SLCNs in contact with the criminal justice system varies,

29 Michele LaVigne and Gregory Van Rybroek, *'He Got in My Face so I Shot Him': How Defendants' Language Impairments Impair Attorney-Client Relationships* (University of Wisconsin 2014)

30 Nathan Hughes and others, 'Language Impairment and Comorbid Vulnerabilities among Young People in Custody' (2017) 58 *Journal of Child Psychology and Psychiatry* 1106.

depending on their age, jurisdiction and setting. The first step towards appropriate support is the identification of SLCNs.

Identification of SLCN Prior to Contact with the Criminal Justice System

For children and young people aged up to 18, SLCNs may be identified via parents/carers, education settings or health and care professionals such as health visitors or social workers.[31] Once identified, support can be accessed via paediatric speech and language therapy (SLT) services. However, SLCNs, particularly in adolescents, can often be misattributed to behavioural and/or mental health concerns and therefore referrals to SLT services are not made.[32] This can mean that a vulnerable adolescent accused who has an SLCN can go through police interviews and court proceedings without their SLCN being identified or supported by professionals.

For adults, those with an acquired communication disorder may well receive SLT support at the time of acquisition, but may not receive continued support. Individuals may report a previous traumatic brain injury on contact with the criminal justice system; but unless the criminal justice system professional is aware that SLCNs are a common consequence, these specific needs may not be flagged. Identification and support for those with developmental SLCN is minimal among the adult population.[33] There is little research that allows us to fully understand the scope of the issue, as developmental SLCNs are often seen as solely a paediatric concern.[34] The combination of lack of services and lack of awareness of SLCNs among the general public means that the adult accused may be presumed to possess the level of communicative competence needed for participation in criminal justice proceedings[35] and therefore be unlikely to be identified as in need of support, unless they have a pre-existing diagnosis.[36]

Given the evidence that three-quarters of individuals with SLCN are undiagnosed on contact with the criminal justice system,[37] the onus is on criminal justice system professionals to identify those individuals who would benefit from support.

---

31 Royal College of Speech and Language Therapists, 'What is Speech and Language Therapy'. Available at: https://www.rcslt.org/wp-content/uploads/media/Project/RCSLT/rcslt-what-is-slt-factsheet.pdf (accessed 4 June 2022).

32 Joseph H Beitchman and others, 'Fourteen-Year Follow-up of Speech/Language-Impaired and Control Children: Psychiatric Outcome' (2001) 40 *Journal of the American Academy of Child & Adolescent Psychiatry* 75.

33 Courtenay F Norbury and Edmund Sonuga-Barke, 'Editorial: New Frontiers in the Scientific Study of Developmental Language Disorders' (2017) 58 *Journal of Child Psychology and Psychiatry* 1065.

34 Frøydis Morken, Lise Ø Jones and Wenche A Helland, 'Disorders of Language and Literacy in the Prison Population: A Scoping Review' (2021) 11 *Education Sciences* 77.

35 Glynis H Murphy and Isabel C Clare, 'Adults' Capacity to Make Legal Decisions' (2003) *Handbook of Psychology in Legal Contexts* 31.

36 See the case example of Eliot below, p11.

37 Nathan Hughes and others, 'Language Impairment and Comorbid Vulnerabilities among Young People in Custody' (2017) 58 *Journal of Child Psychology and Psychiatry* 1106.

Identification of SLCN After Contact with the Criminal Justice System

One of the main issues for identification is the limited guidance and training available for criminal justice professionals on SLCNs.[38] As SLCNs are a 'hidden' difficulty, professionals are unlikely to be able to recognise them unless they know specifically what they are looking for:[39]

- How do you identify SLCNs with limited knowledge?
- How do you then ascertain whether the level of SLCN will impact on effective participation?

Given the levels of diagnosis and public awareness, the accused may also be unaware of their own needs, so it is not a case of simply asking them if they have an SLCN or require communication support. Awareness training for staff and systematic, effective, early screening are required to support timely identification.[40]

When an SLCN is identified, the next step is to know what support is offered and how to access it. The availability and types of support vary significantly across jurisdictions and environment – for example, police interview versus courtroom.

Support at the Police Station

Increasingly, support is provided from first contact with the criminal justice system. This is important, as research has shown that even understanding a police caution can be problematic. Fenner, Gudjonsson and Clare[41] found that only 11% of suspects had fully understood a caution presented to them; however, 96% of the same suspects claimed that they had understood when asked. This shows a significant disconnect between being asked whether they have understood versus the reality of true understanding. It is not sufficient to ask an individual if they understand a police caution; their understanding should be verified.

In the United Kingdom, appropriate adults (AAs)[42] are available to vulnerable suspects during police interviews by virtue of one of the recognised vulnerabilities being an SLCN.[43] AAs should also be available to everyone under the age of 18. The aim of the AA is to safeguard the vulnerable person, but also to ensure that they can participate

---

38 Helen Howard, 'Effective Participation of Mentally Vulnerable Defendants in the Magistrates' Courts in England and Wales—The "Front Line" from a Legal Perspective' (2021) 85 *Journal of Criminal Law* 3.

39 Pamela C Snow, Martine B Powell and Dixie D Sanger, 'Oral Language Competence, Young Speakers, and the Law' (2012) 43 *Language, Speech, and Hearing Services in Schools* 496

40 Rachel Slavny-Cross and others, 'Autism and the Criminal Justice System: An Analysis of 93 Cases' (2022) 15 *Autism Research* 904.

41 Susanne Fenner, Gisli H Gudjonsson and Isabel CH Clare, 'Understanding of the Current Police Caution (England and Wales) among Suspects in Police Detention' (2002) 12 *Journal of Community & Applied Social Psychology* 83

42 See Miranda Bevan, Chapter 7 of this collection.

43 Police and Criminal Evidence Act 1984 Code C 1.7A

effectively, including in regard to communication. This could involve rephrasing questions or checking understanding. However, there is significant variation in the role of AAs even across the countries within the United Kingdom.[44] In England, Wales and Northern Ireland, AAs need not have undertaken any communication training. In Scotland, AAs must be appropriately trained for the individual they are supporting.[45] It is desirable that the supporting individual has an awareness of how to support a person with an SLCN, of the accused's specific needs and of the methods which would support effective engagement. However, there is evidence to suggest that there is limited active involvement from AAs during the interview process.[46]

Intermediaries can also support vulnerable accused with SLCNs at interview. This may be desirable where the individual has significant and complex needs. Intermediaries require specialist communication training (eg, as qualified SLTs); as previously stated, this is generally not the case for AAs who are community volunteers.[47]

Support in the Courtroom

Many jurisdictions across Europe now have a range of special measures available to support individuals with SLCNs in the courtroom.[48] In some jurisdictions, these measures have been introduced for all vulnerable participants; while in others, these take the form of specialist courts that are only available to a certain subsection of the population,[49] or only for the benefit of witnesses, or children and young people.[50] These special measures[51] include making the courtroom less formal (eg, removal of wigs and gowns and changes in seating arrangements), reducing the use of legalese and using an intermediary.[52] The focus of this section is on provision in England and Wales.

44 National Appropriate Adults Network, 'About Appropriate Adults'. Available at: http s://www.appropriateadult.org.uk/information/what-is-an-appropriate-adult (accessed 5 June 2022).

45 The Criminal Justice (Scotland) Act 2016 (Support for Vulnerable Persons) Regulations 2019.

46 Ian Cummins, '"The Other Side of Silence": The Role of the Appropriate Adult Post-Bradley' (2011) 5 *Ethics and Social Welfare* 306.

47 Brendan M O'Mahony, 'The Emerging Role of the Registered Intermediary with the Vulnerable Witness and Offender: Facilitating Communication with the Police and Members of the Judiciary' (2010) 38 *British Journal of Learning Disabilities* 232.

48 Kim Turner and Nathan Hughes, 'Supporting Young People's Cognition and Communication in the Courtroom: A Scoping Review of Current Practices' (2022) *Criminal Behaviour and Mental Health*.

49 Voula Marinos and Lisa Whittingham, 'The Role of Therapeutic Jurisprudence to Support Persons with Intellectual and Developmental Disabilities in the Courtroom: Reflections from Ontario, Canada' (2019) 63 *International Journal of Law and Psychiatry* 18

50 Laura Hoyano and Angela Rafferty, 'Rationing Defence Intermediaries under the April 2016 Criminal Practice Direction' (2017) 2 *Criminal Law Review* 93

51 See Samantha Fairclough and Holly Greenwood, Chapter 10 of this collection.

52 Robyn White and others, 'Court Accommodations for Persons with Severe Communication Disabilities: A Legal Scoping Review' (2020) *Psychology, Public Policy, and Law*.

Special measures can be utilised to make communication more accessible in the courtroom. However, there is an imbalance between the special measures afforded to vulnerable defendants and those available for vulnerable witnesses. Vulnerable witnesses have multiple options available, such as pre-recorded evidence, giving evidence from behind a screen and the removal of wigs and gowns. However, for defendants, the Youth Justice and Criminal Evidence Act 2009 permits the opportunity only to use a live link for evidence giving.[53]

As seen above, the needs of vulnerable defendants may be overlooked. While Section 104 of the Coroners and Justice Act 2009 states that intermediaries may assist with vulnerable defendants' communication, at present this legislation has not been enacted. Common law currently covers the gap in defendant legislation when considering appointing a non-registered intermediary for the accused. However, Fairclough[54] found that there is uncertainty on this legal position due to the malleability of common law and conflicting judgments that have followed. They argue that the *ad hoc* and piecemeal reform of special measures for vulnerable defendants has led to disparate and unequal provision. The general focus of intermediary usage in England and Wales has been on supporting vulnerable witnesses, which began in the United Kingdom via the registered intermediary scheme in 2004 from the Ministry of Justice.[55] There is no national protocol, but an assessment can be requested by the police, the Crown Prosecution Service, witness care units and court-based witness services.[56]

Intermediaries provide impartial assistance to legal professionals – including police officers, lawyers and courts – to ensure complete, coherent and accurate information.[57] They do this by assessing the communication needs of the vulnerable person and advising on how to implement reasonable adjustments and ensure that effective communication is achieved. A member of the SOLD user group (previously a defendant) indicated how this can be useful: 'When you ask me a question, it helps to put it in words that I can understand.'

However, even when SLCNs are recognised and supported in the courtroom, an individual's communication – or lack thereof – can still have negative implications, such as a judgment from members of the court, including a jury. One

---

53 Youth Justice and Criminal Evidence Act, Section 33A.

54 Samantha Fairclough, 'The Consequences of Unenthusiastic Criminal Justice Reform: A Special Measures Case Study' (2019) 21 *Criminology & Criminal Justice* 151.

55 Penny Cooper and David Wurtzel, 'A Day Late and a Dollar Short: In Search of an Intermediary Scheme for Vulnerable Defendants in England and Wales' (2013) *Criminal Law Review* 4. See also J Morrison and J Taggart, Chapter 11 of this collection.

56 The Advocate's Gateway, 'The Advocate's Gateway: Responding to communication needs in the justice system'. Available at: https://www.theadvocatesgateway.org/ (accessed 7 March 2022).

57 Ministry of Justice, 'Registered Intermediary Procedural Guidance Manual' (2020). Available at: https://assets.publishing.service.gov.uk/government/uploads/system/ uploads/attachment_data/file/955316/registered-intermediary-procedural-guidance-manual.pdf (accessed 30 March 2022).

example is *R v Dixon*,[58] in which the defendant was supported during their initial case by an intermediary. The Court of Appeal deemed that Dixon had been provided with the support required to facilitate effective participation and therefore adverse inferences could be drawn from the fact that he did not give evidence. Dixon was deemed to be vulnerable due to his age and diagnoses of a learning disability, stammer and ADHD. There are a multitude of reasons why he may have chosen not to give evidence: he might have been anxious about his stammer, his ability to understand questions, how he might react if he did not understand and how his communication skills could lead to an unfavourable impression. However, not giving evidence was seen as unfavourable. In some ways, it could be argued that a vulnerable defendant cannot 'win'. As stated above, an adverse inference could be drawn from not giving evidence. However, an adverse inference may also be taken from atypical communication skills[59] if they do give evidence. Research demonstrates that a 'remorseful' non-verbal demeanour favourably impacts on sentencing.[60] Those with SLCNs appear adversely impacted: if the accused has been unable to follow the proceedings, their non-verbal demeanour may read as 'confused' or, worse still, 'blank'. This may be seen as lacking remorse rather than not understanding the proceedings.[61]

Curen[62] makes the analogy that this paucity of communication support is akin to denying a defendant with physical disabilities access to a ramp in the courtroom; and concerns have been raised that this contravenes the right enshrined in Article 6 of the ECHR to effectively participate in a trial. Similarly, in England and Wales, the Equality Act 2010 requires that 'reasonable adjustments' be made for those with disabilities to address disadvantages present in comparison with a non-disabled person; yet this requirement is not consistently and equitably fulfilled.

Despite these complex and multifaceted issues, there are increasingly areas of good practice where vulnerable suspects' and defendants' SLCNs are being identified and supports are provided. The examples provided below are drawn from the UK context.

Good Practice Examples

The first area of developing good practice is in English police stations. Liaison and diversion (L&D) is available within police custody and aims to identify vulnerable

58 *Dixon v Regina* [2013] 3 All ER 242.
59 Joanne Morrison and others, 'Communication and Cross-examination in Court for Children and Adults with Intellectual Disabilities: A Systematic Review' (2019) 23 *International Journal of Evidence & Proof* 366.
60 Emily Corwin and others, 'Defendant Remorse, Need for Affect, and Juror Sentencing Decisions' (2012) 40 *Journal of the American Academy of Psychiatry and the Law* 41.
61 Emily Corwin and others, 'Defendant Remorse, Need for Affect, and Juror Sentencing Decisions' (2012) 40 *Journal of the American Academy of Psychiatry and the Law* 41.
62 Richard Curen, 'Vulnerable Adults and the Criminal Justice System in England and Wales: Some Proposals for Reform' (2005) 1 *Criminal Lawyer* 3.

people as early in the process as possible to divert them to more appropriate settings before crisis point is reached.[63] An increasing number of L&D services in England are employing SLTs who assess for SLCNs and provide written evidence based on these assessment results for the courts and probation staff. The evidence covers the reasonable adjustments required to support the accused's SLCN, such as how to adapt written materials appropriately. In research conducted by one L&D service, 77% of people in custody who were screened for SLCNs needed repetition of information; 74% had difficulties explaining thoughts, feelings and experiences; and 64% struggled to listen and pay attention.[64] This indicates the need for expansion of the SLT role within police custody.

As previously mentioned, SLCNs are a hidden disability and not well understood, so training to raise awareness and provide professionals with support strategies is essential. There are now a range of training packages and toolkits available to professionals, including:

- the Box e-learning (https://www.rcslt.org/learning/the-box-training/);
- the Advocates Gateway toolkits (https://www.theadvocatesgateway.org/toolkits-1-1-1); and
- Communication Access Training (https://communication-access.co.uk/).

Members of the SOLD user group have also compiled a list of SLCN support strategies that they recommend based on lived experience:

- Show empathy – try to understand what it's like for us.
- Take the time to understand us properly.
- Always give us a choice.
- Get trained in how to understand people with learning disabilities.
- Be passionate about your work – don't just treat it like any other job.
- Be confident about challenging other people/services when they treat us unfairly.
- Never assume you know what's in our best interest without asking us.
- Adapt your language – use simple words and be patient.

SLCNs are identified and supported in some areas where training has been provided and screening exists. However, provision for vulnerable accused is variable across Europe and across the criminal justice system.[65] Systematic, effective, early

---

63 Emma Disley and others, *Outcome Evaluation of the National Model for Liaison and Diversion* (RAND 2021).

64 Clare Holland, Patrick Hutchinson and Donna Peacock, 'The Importance of Screening for Speech, Language and Communication Needs (SLCN) in Police Custody' (2023) *The Howard Journal of Crime and Justice* 1-18.

65 Samantha Fairclough, 'The Consequences of Unenthusiastic Criminal Justice Reform: A Special Measures Case Study' (2021) 21 *Criminology & Criminal Justice* 151. Sarah Medford, Gisli H Gudjonsson and John Pearse, 'The Efficacy of the Appropriate Adult Safeguard During Police Interviewing' (2003) 8 *Legal and Criminological Psychology* 253.

assessment of vulnerability and the subsequent provision of necessary communication support are not currently widespread. Below are examples that illustrate the inequity in provision.

Case Examples of Current Practice

The cases presented below provide real-life examples of how SLCNs can impact on an individual's progression through the criminal justice system and the difference that support can make.

Ryan

Ryan was 19 years old and had been arrested over assault allegations. He had ADHD, which manifested as impulsive verbal and physical behaviour with concentration and processing difficulties (eg, struggling to understand questions and think before speaking). Ryan's solicitor noticed this and its negative impact on Ryan's engagement. She arranged for an intermediary assessment which resulted in the appointment of an intermediary. In court for the half-day trial, the intermediary was able to manage Ryan's difficulties with frequent breaks and by accompanying questions with visual prompts when giving evidence. This resulted in Ryan being able to effectively participate in the proceedings against him.

Tyra

Tyra was 17 years old when she appeared in court on driving-related charges. Tyra was a care leaver who had significant SLCNs, an aggressive attitude and antisocial behaviour. The 'unacceptable' behaviour was attributed to her behavioural difficulties and her SLCNs were unacknowledged. This meant that professionals did not recognise when she was struggling or did not understand what was being said. When Tyra misunderstood the judgment, thinking that the judge was sending her to prison immediately, she became overwhelmed, started shouting and tried to leave court. The judge interpreted this behaviour as wilful non-compliance in the court process and Tyra was taken down to the cells. The youth offending team (YOT) worker present raised concerns about Tyra's capacity to engage in proceedings. This was dismissed by the judge. Another court hearing followed where YOT staff and Tyra's solicitor raised concerns regarding Tyra's capacity. The judge agreed to a court-appointed psychiatric assessment to investigate Tara's capacity. The psychiatrist found Tyra unfit to plead or stand trial and the charges against her were dropped. If the YOT worker and solicitor had not raised concerns at that late stage regarding Tyra's capacity, she may have been found guilty of charges that she did not understand or may have acquired more charges due to her supposed inappropriate behaviour. Early identification of vulnerability would have avoided the costly court process and would have resulted in less distress for Tyra.

Eliot

Eliot was in his 50s when he was referred for an SLT assessment by the parole board due to concerns about his ability to engage with the parole meeting as a result of his perceived difficulties with both understanding others and expressing himself. There was no evidence of previous contact with SLT, although an assessment was recommended in his pre-court report. Eliot stated that he had attended a special school as a child and had learned to read and write, but felt that his skills had subsequently deteriorated. He had lived with his parents until they had died some 10 years earlier. Prior to their deaths, there had been no contact with the criminal justice system. Eliot had a history of significant alcohol consumption and several noteworthy head injuries. There were concerns that his memory and language skills were deteriorating. In prison, informal adaptations were made daily to support Eliot; he was seen as vulnerable by peers and prison officers, who assisted him with everyday tasks. From SLT assessment, Eliot demonstrated that he had a wide everyday vocabulary, but had difficulties putting words into sentences to create a coherent narrative, which often led to confusion. Eliot also frequently misunderstood questions and was unable to draw inferences. His age equivalent on formalised language assessments was 5.06. He was diagnosed with a language disorder associated with intellectual impairment. From the assessment, it was clear that Eliot would not be able to fully engage with the parole meeting without significant adaptations and support. It was shown that Eliot could benefit from visual supports to aid his memory and language skills. The assessment results were agreed by the parole board and the recommended supports were implemented. At this point, he had already been through police interviews and the court process, which are equally, if not more verbally complex. Given his support needs, it could be argued that Eliot should never have gone through this process, as he was unable to effectively participate and could have been diverted prior to litigation.

Conclusion

This chapter has outlined the high prevalence of SLCNs among vulnerable accused. The accused may be vulnerable due to unidentified SLCNs; identified but unsupported SLCNs; SLCNs exacerbated by stress; and/or adverse inferences taken from their verbal and non-verbal communication, or lack thereof.[66] SLCNs are most often unidentified and unsupported, which can lead to ineffective participation in criminal justice proceedings. Every professional working in criminal justice has a responsibility to acknowledge and understand the

---

66 Emily Corwin and others, 'Defendant Remorse, Need for Affect, and Juror Sentencing Decisions' (2012) 40 *Journal of the American Academy of Psychiatry and the Law* 41. Alliyza Lim, Robyn L Young and Neil Brewer, 'Autistic Adults May Be Erroneously Perceived as Deceptive and Lacking Credibility' (2022) 52 *Journal of Autism and Development Disorders* 490.

communication needs[67] of the people they work with, to ensure that everyone has access to a fair trial.[68] Support is increasingly available through individuals employed to support vulnerable accused in participating and measures designed to make processes more accessible.

The three cases presented serve to illustrate the range of individuals with SLCNs coming into contact with the criminal justice system. These individuals each had their needs identified at different points in the process, leading to different outcomes. It is in the best interests of the criminal justice system – from a human rights, financial and logistical perspective – to ensure the earliest identification and support for these vulnerabilities.[69] Ensuring that communication needs are identified and supported at the earliest available opportunity allows vulnerable accused to understand and engage in the process more effectively, averting significant negative impacts for all. To achieve this, a systematic and effective process for the identification of needs and standardised support measures at all levels of proceedings are required. Further research is vital to establish the most effective support measures.[70]

---

67 Police and Criminal Evidence Act 1984 (Pace) Code C, Section 3. Advocates – *R v Grant-Murray & Anor* [2017] EWCA Crim 1228, para 226.
68 Article 6(3) (a and e) of the EHCR.
69 Paula Cronin and Rebecca Addo, 'Interactions with Youth Justice and Associated Costs for Young People with Speech, Language and Communication Needs' (2021) 56 *International Journal of Language and Communication Disorders* 797.
70 Kim Turner and Nathan Hughes, 'Supporting Young People's Cognition and Communication in the Courtroom: A Scoping Review of Current Practices' (2022) *Criminal Behaviour and Mental Health*.

10 Vulnerable Defendants, Special Measures and Miscarriages of Justice in England and Wales

Samantha Fairclough and Holly Greenwood

Introduction

The Youth Justice and Criminal Evidence Act 1999 (YJCEA) introduced a special measures scheme for vulnerable and intimidated witnesses giving evidence in criminal trials.[1] These special measures provide adaptations to the traditional court process so that evidence can be given from behind a screen (outside the view of the public gallery and dock); via live link (from a room that is usually located elsewhere in the court building); or in private (with the public gallery closed for the duration of the witness's testimony). Other adaptations include the pre-recording of testimony that is played at trial in the witness's absence; the use of an intermediary (a communication specialist);[2] communication aids; and the removal of traditional court dress (wigs and gowns).

The measures were born out of growing concerns for the treatment of children as (alleged) victims of crime. The rules of evidence and the adversarial proceedings combined to make securing testimony from child victims a difficult, if not impossible task, which often allowed those accused of committing offences against this group to evade conviction.[3] Even where evidence from children was secured, there were concerns about its reliability as well as increasing worries about the detrimental impact that the process of testifying had on children.[4] These concerns also grew in relation to adult witnesses with disabilities and other intimidated witnesses. The adaptations that special measures provide were thus seen as a way of improving the evidence's quality (and perceived reliability) and the treatment of those required to provide it.

In terms of eligibility, these measures are available to all non-defendant witnesses, for the prosecution and defence, provided that they meet the criteria set

---

1 YJCEA, Sections 16–30.
2 See Joanne Morrison and John Taggart, Chapter 11 of this collection, on the role of the intermediary. See Kim Turner and Claire Westwood, Chapter 9 of this collection, on speech, language and communication needs.
3 John R Spencer, 'Child Witnesses and Cross-examination at Trial: Must it Continue?' (2011) 3 *Archbold Review* 7.
4 See Samantha Fairclough, 'The Lost Leg of the Youth Justice and Criminal Evidence Act 1999: Special Measures and Humane Treatment' (2021) 41(4) *Oxford Journal of Legal Studies* 1066.

DOI: 10.4324/9781003205166-14

out in the YJCEA. These create two categories of witnesses: vulnerable witnesses and intimidated witnesses (though they are not mutually exclusive). Vulnerable witnesses are those who are under 18 or who have a physical or mental disability/disorder, or a significant impairment of intelligence or social function.[5] Intimidated witnesses are those who are in fear or distress in connection with testifying in the proceedings[6] for reasons such as their age, social or cultural background; the nature of the offence charged; or the behaviour of the accused or their supporters towards them as a witness.[7] For witnesses who fall into one or more of these categories, it is generally[8] the case that the quality of their evidence is likely to be diminished as a result,[9] and that the use of one (or more) special measures will improve it.[10]

Notably, the defendant is excluded from the full special measures scheme.[11] In making its recommendations, the Speaking Up for Justice working group[12] omitted consideration of the accused for special measures on the basis of three (undeveloped) reasons:

- Pre-trial proceedings are already adapted for vulnerable suspects;
- Defendants are privy to fair trial rights already that other witnesses are not; and
- Special measures are designed to protect witnesses from defendants (and so would not be of benefit to the accused themselves).[13]

Each of these justifications lacks substance and validity when examined more closely.[14] We have seen previously in this collection how pre-trial adaptations, such as appropriate adults, are often insufficient safeguards when implemented and are sometimes not implemented at all due to problems in identifying a suspect's

5 YJCEA, Section 16.
6 YJCEA, Section 17(1).
7 YJCEA, Section 17(2).
8 Children and complainants of sexual offences or modern slavery offences are automatically eligible for special measures without the need to meet further eligibility criteria; see YJCEA, Section 16(1)(a) and Section 17(4).
9 YJCEA, Section 16(1)(b) and Section 17(1).
10 YJCEA, Section 19(2).
11 See YJCEA, Section 16(1) and Section 17(1).
12 This interdepartmental working group was established by Jack Straw MP, the then home secretary, to undertake a wide-ranging review of the protection for victims in rape and serious sexual offence trials as well as witnesses subject to intimidation. It was chaired by the Home Office with representation from many key stakeholders, including the Crown Prosecution Service, Victim Support, the Association of Chief Police Officers, the Department of Health and several other governmental departments.
13 Home Office, *Speaking Up for Justice: Report of the Interdepartmental Working Group on the Treatment of Vulnerable or Intimidated Witnesses in the Criminal Justice System* (Home Office 1998), para 3.28.
14 See Samantha Fairclough, 'Speaking Up for Injustice: Reconsidering the Provision of Special Measures through the Lens of Equality' [2018] *Criminal Law Review* 4, 9–16 for a full discussion and critique of each of these reasons the working group suggested.

vulnerability.[15] Even if these and other safeguards were more effective, it is not clear how this pre-trial support obviates the need for further support at the trial stage (read: it does not). With regard to fair trial rights, it is again unclear how those mentioned in the report (the provision of legal representation and the defendant's non-compellability) negate the need for special measures. A defence lawyer cannot adapt the court environment to make it more suitable for a vulnerable defendant with an anxiety disorder or attention deficit hyperactivity disorder to testify; and nor do they have the expertise to provide the bespoke communication support of an intermediary to a defendant with intellectual disabilities.[16] The argument around the non-compellability of the accused is yet more puzzling. While it is true that the defendant cannot be compelled to testify (and almost all other witnesses can), the defendant still has a right to testify should they wish to do so.[17] If, therefore, a vulnerable defendant wishes to exercise this right, it seems obvious that special measures could be useful in facilitating this and securing their best evidence in much the same way that they are for other vulnerable witnesses.

The final reason – that special measures protect witnesses from the accused – is also flimsy, betraying a very simplistic understanding of the purpose of special measures and their potential benefits. Special measures do much more than simply shield a witness from the accused: they make the courtroom less intimidating by reducing the number of people in sight/present; allow evidence to be given outside of the courtroom itself; and – most importantly – facilitate effective communication between a vulnerable individual, the advocates and the factfinder. Indeed, the expansion of special measures to vulnerable defendants, as is discussed in the following section, reveals quite how ill-informed this justification from the working group was.

Expansion of Special Measures to Defendants: The Current Legal Provision

While the full YJCEA scheme still excludes the accused from eligibility for special measures, the law has since developed to provide some comparable adaptations to this category of witness. This has largely occurred through the case law, so its evolution has been (and remains) gradual and *ad hoc*, depending on the cases

15 See Lore Mergaerts, Chapter 3 of this collection, on problems regarding identifying vulnerability.

16 This point was noted in *C v Sevenoaks Youth Court* [2009] EWHC 3088 (Admin) [17]. See also Emily Henderson, '"A Very Valuable Tool": Judges, Advocates and Intermediaries Discuss the Intermediary System in England and Wales' (2015) 19(3) *International Journal of Evidence and Proof* 154, 167.

17 This right is implicit in the ECHR (see Abenaa Owusu-Bempah, 'Understanding the Barriers to Defendant Participation in Criminal Proceedings in England and Wales' (2020) *Legal Studies* (online first)) and expressly provided in the Criminal Procedure Rules and Criminal Practice Directions of England and Wales (see Criminal Practice Direction 3D.2).

heard on appeal and the particular facts surrounding them.[18] Where Parliament has intervened to insert bespoke special measures provisions into the YJCEA for the accused, this has been unenthusiastic and 'grudging',[19] with only the bare minimum done in response to concerns from the European Court of Human Rights (ECtHR) about vulnerable defendants' protection under Article 6 of the European Convention on Human Rights (ECHR).

As a consequence of the way in which the law has developed, the provision of special measures to defendants is littered across myriad case law, statutory provisions and sources of 'soft law' (eg, the Criminal Procedure Rules and Criminal Practice Directions). The provision also remains inferior to that which is available to all other witnesses under the full YJCEA statutory scheme. The remainder of this section outlines what is now available to the accused and some of the key differences in the provision between them and non-defendant witnesses. The following section then considers this inequality in light of the Article 6 right to a fair trial.

Under the Criminal Practice Directions, the judge can authorise the removal of wigs and gowns for the duration of trials involving a vulnerable defendant and can also close the court to the public while the defendant gives evidence.[20] The power for this arose following the high-profile case of *T v United Kingdom*,[21] in which the 11-year-old defendants on trial for murder in the Crown Court appealed to the ECtHR on the basis of Articles 3, 6 and 8 of the ECHR. The ECtHR held that while their treatment was not inhuman or degrading (Article 3), they were unable to participate effectively in their trial, in violation of their Article 6 rights.

The Criminal Procedure Rules include the provision of communication aids to vulnerable defendants, such as drawings, timelines and objects.[22] The High Court decision in *R v Waltham Forest Youth Court* confirms the maintenance of the common law power to use screens for defendants, an adaptation that pre-dated the YJCEA.[23] What is not clear from this judgment, however, is who exactly is eligible and in what circumstances. The facts in question involved a 13-year-old girl on trial, with two co-accused, who was too intimidated to testify (cut-throat defence). Full eligibility criteria were not set out by the court and nor have they been since, leaving it to the judge's discretion as to when to allow screens for a vulnerable or intimidated defendant.

It is also via the common law that defendants can benefit from intermediaries should they have significant communication difficulties.[24] There has been some

---

18 The nature of this reform is discussed in detail in Samantha Fairclough, 'The Consequences of Unenthusiastic Criminal Justice Reform: A Special Measures Case Study' (2021) 21(2) *Criminology and Criminal Justice* 151.
19 Laura Hoyano, 'Reforming the Adversarial Trial for Vulnerable Witnesses and Defendants' (2015) *Criminal Law Review* 126–7.
20 See Criminal Practice Directions (October 2015, amended 2020) CrimPD 3D.2.
21 (1999) 30 EHHR 121.
22 Criminal Procedure Rules 2020, CPR 3.8(7)(b).
23 *R v Waltham Forest Youth Court* [2004] EWHC 715 (Admin) [31].
24 A statutory provision for intermediaries was enacted but is not in force. *R v Sevenoaks*

back and forth in the courts over the last 10 years with regard to how generously intermediaries should be provided to defendants. The latest Court of Appeal judgment on the matter was *R v Rashid*,[25] in which the court seemingly restricted the provision of an intermediary to a defendant, stating that for a defendant giving evidence, the appointment of an intermediary would be rare – and for the duration of the trial, extremely rare.[26] The matter is not settled. The more recent case of *TI v Bromley Youth Court*[27] saw the High Court express its view that *Rashid* had been misinterpreted, and that the Court of Appeal's statement that the appointment of intermediaries to defendants would be rare was not a tightening of the eligibility criteria. Instead, the High Court stated that this was merely a reflection of the fact that, in the context of all cases coming before the courts, the use of an intermediary by the accused would be rare as a matter of fact, but should still be available when it is needed to ensure that the defendant can effectively participate.[28] It remains to be seen how this will play out in the courts,[29] but suffice it to say that the law here is still uncertain.

The final special measure that is available to defendants is the live link, via a late insertion into the YJCEA.[30] This was enacted following the decision in *SC v UK*,[31] where the ECtHR found that the formalities of the Crown Court trial undermined the 11-year-old claimant's Article 6 right to effectively participate in the trial. There had also been some disquiet in the domestic courts surrounding the exclusion of defendants from this and other special measures, where concerns related to compatibility with the principle of equality of arms, culminating in Baroness Hale intimating that, in the right case, the court would use its inherent power to make the live link available for vulnerable/intimidated defendants.[32] The statutory live link provision for the accused, then, permits a child defendant who has a significant impairment of intelligence or social function to use a live link if their ability to participate effectively in the trial as a witness would otherwise be compromised.[33] For adult defendants, they must have a mental disorder or significant impairment of intelligence or social function that renders them unable to participate effectively in the trial as a witness.[34]

This whistlestop tour of the special measures available to defendants shows us that the landscape for vulnerable or intimidated defendants has improved.

---

25 [2017] EWCA Crim 2.
26 [2017] EWCA Crim 2 [73]; and see also Criminal Practice Directions (October 2015 edition, amended April 2016 and October 2016) CPD I General Matters, 3F: INTERMEDIARIES 3F.13.
27 [2020] EWHC 1204 (Admin).
28 [2020] EWHC 1204 (Admin) [26]; and see also *R v Dean Thomas* [2020] EWCA Crim 117.
29 And this point of law does not account for significant issues relating to sourcing and funding defendant intermediaries, as is discussed below.
30 YJCEA, Section 33A.
31 40 EHRR 10.
32 *R v Camberwell Green Youth Court* [2005] UKHL 4 [63].
33 YJCEA, Section 33A(4).
34 YJCEA, Section 33A(5).

Defendants have gone from a position of complete ineligibility to one where they can secure some comparable support to their vulnerable or intimidated non-defendant witness counterparts. However, inequalities remain both in the legal provision and in the practical availability of this support.[35] For example, there is no legal provision for live link to defendants who are intimidated or who have physical disabilities. Moreover, child defendants are not *prima facie* eligible for live link as child witnesses are. Additionally, the threshold for live link use by adult defendants is much higher, necessitating their inability to participate effectively as a witness; as opposed to the requirement for non-defendant witnesses that the quality of their evidence will likely be diminished.

For defendant intermediaries, the eligibility criteria are somewhat uncertain, but the perception has certainly been that it is more restrictive in law, and this is definitely the case in practice. The statutory scheme for witnesses is supported by the Witness Intermediary Scheme, which trains, funds and matches appropriately qualified intermediaries to vulnerable witnesses. Defendants are not privy to this scheme, leading to difficulties sourcing funding and appropriate support for vulnerable defendants.[36]

The following section considers the consequences of the current unequal and inferior provision of special measures for vulnerable and intimidated defendants' Article 6 rights to a fair trial. In particular, it focuses on their right to participate effectively in the proceedings and the principle of equality of arms. While the inferior provision of special measures arguably also has negative ramifications for the presumption of innocence, this is not discussed here due to space constraints.

Consequences of Inferior Provision for Defendants' Article 6 right to a Fair Trial

The Right to Effective Participation in Trial Proceedings

The first consequence of the inferior provision of special measures to the accused versus all other witnesses that we consider relates to the defendant's right to participate effectively in trial proceedings. This is an implied right under Article 6(1) of the ECHR, derived from the minimum rights expressed in Article 6(3).[37] These include the right to be informed promptly of the nature and cause of the accusation against them (Article 6(3)(a)); to have adequate time and facilities for the preparation of their defence (Article 6(3)(b)); to legal assistance (Article 6(3)(c));

---

35 See Samantha Fairclough, '"It doesn't happen ... and I've never thought it was necessary for it to happen": Barriers to Vulnerable Defendants Giving Evidence by Live Link in Crown Court Trials' (2017) 21(3) *International Journal of Evidence and Proof* 209; and Samantha Fairclough, 'Using Hawkins' Surround, Field and Frames Concepts to Understand the Complexities of Special Measures Decision-Making in Crown Court Trials' (2018) 45(3) *Journal of Law and Society* 457.

36 See Joanne Morrison and John Taggart, Chapter 11 of this collection.

37 *Stanford v UK* App no 16757/90 (ECtHR, 23 February 1994) at [26].

to examine witnesses (Article 6(3)(d)); and to the assistance of an interpreter (Article 6(3)(e)). The exact scope of this right is not entirely clear;[38] but as a starting point, it means that defendants have the right to be present and to hear and follow proceedings.[39] The ECtHR elaborated on this in *SC v UK*,[40] stating that effective participation:

> presupposes that the accused has a broad understanding of the nature of the trial process and what is at stake for him or her, including the significance of any penalty which may be imposed … can [with the assistance of a social worker, lawyer, interpreter or friend] understand the general thrust of what is said in court … follow what is said by the prosecution witnesses and … explain to his own lawyers his version of events, point out any statements with which he disagrees and make them aware of any facts which should be put forward in his defence.[41]

The right to effective participation is a long-established principle in England and Wales, and the ECtHR noted that it is 'implicit in the very notion of an adversarial procedure'.[42] Indeed, the Criminal Procedure Rules require the court to take 'every reasonable step to facilitate the participation of any person, including the defendant'.[43] This, according to the Criminal Practice Directions, includes 'enabling a witness or defendant to give their best evidence, and enabling a defendant to comprehend the proceedings and engage fully with his or her defence'.[44] This chapter argues, therefore, that the provision of special measures to defendants who are vulnerable or intimidated is an important part of upholding this right to effective participation.[45] This is because they can provide (some of)[46] the tools needed to help vulnerable individuals to testify to the best of their ability, through adaptations to the courtroom environment and the provision of communication support when needed. Indeed, this link with effective participation is even acknowledged in the limited provision of special measures that the accused does

---

38 Abenaa Owusu-Bempah, 'Understanding the Barriers to Defendant Participation in Criminal Proceedings in England and Wales' (2020) *Legal Studies* 3 (online first).

39 *Stanford v UK* App no 16757/90 (ECtHR, 23 February 1994).

40 *SC v UK* (2005) 40 EHHR 10.

41 *SC v UK* (2005) 40 EHHR 10, para 28.

42 *SC v UK* (2005) 40 EHHR 10, para 28.

43 Criminal Procedure Rules 2020 CrimPR 3.8(3)(b).

44 Criminal Practice Directions (October 2015, amended October 2020) CPD 3D.2.

45 Fairclough has argued this previously; see Samantha Fairclough, 'Speaking Up for Injustice: Reconsidering the Provision of Special Measures through the Lens of Equality' [2018] *Criminal Law Review* 4, 13.

46 Owusu-Bempah rightly cautions against viewing special measures as a 'catch-all' tool; see Abenaa Owusu-Bempah, 'Judging the Desirability of a Defendant's Evidence: An Unfortunate Approach to s.35(1)(b) of the Criminal Justice and Public Order Act 1994' (2011) 9 *Criminal Law Review* 690, 691. See also Samantha Fairclough, 'The Lost Leg of the Youth Justice and Criminal Evidence Act 1999: Special Measures and Humane Treatment' (2021) 41(4) *Oxford Journal of Legal Studies* 1066, 1090.

enjoy, with reference to the effective participation of the accused forming a vital part of the eligibility criteria for defendant live link.[47]

This chapter argues, however, that the current provision of special measures to the accused does not go far enough to protect this right and ensure that vulnerable defendants can participate effectively in their trials, including as witnesses in their defence. This is particularly the case given the barriers that all defendants face to participation at trial, resulting from the professionalisation and formality of the court process, the use of legal language and the way courts are designed.[48] For defendants who are particularly vulnerable – by virtue of, for instance, a mental disorder or learning difficulty – these barriers to effective and indeed meaningful participation are only exaggerated.

We argue that three things need to happen to remedy this and make an important step towards better ensuring the protection of vulnerable defendants' right to effective participation under Article 6 of the ECHR. First, we should extend the full statutory scheme (under the YJCEA) to vulnerable defendants or enact an equivalent regime. This will mean that vulnerable defendants enjoy comparable support to that which vulnerable witnesses already enjoy. Second, we should extend the use of some special measures still further for the accused. For instance, intermediaries should be readily available to defendants with communication difficulties for the duration of the trial,[49] rather than solely for the giving of evidence, as is the Court of Appeal's preference.[50] Third, we must strive to improve the quality and availability of defendant intermediaries, to avoid 'ineffective directions' whereby permission for an intermediary is granted but does not come to fruition at trial. We argue, in opposition to the approach of the courts, that it is non-sensical to appoint an intermediary to facilitate the defendant's effective participation and then to still be satisfied that the trial was fair in its absence.[51]

Equality of Arms

The second consequence of the inferior provision of special measures to the accused versus all other witnesses for consideration here is its potential to contravene the principle of equality of arms. The ECtHR has ruled that Article 6(1) of the ECHR requires that 'each party should be afforded a reasonable opportunity to present his case under conditions that do not place him at a substantial

---

47 YJCEA, Section 33A(4) and Section 33A(5).
48 Abenaa Owusu-Bempah, 'Understanding the Barriers to Defendant Participation in Criminal Proceedings in England and Wales' (2020) *Legal Studies* 2 (online first). See also Jessica Jacobson and Penny Cooper, *Participation in Courts and Tribunals: Concepts, Realities and Aspirations* (Bristol University Press 2020).
49 As argued in *R (on the application of OP) v Secretary of State for Justice* [2014] EWHC 1944 (Admin) [46]–[47].
50 *R v Rashid* [2017] EWCA Crim.
51 See *R v Cox* [2012] EWCA Crim 549 and Criminal Practice Directions (2015, amended 2020) CrimPD 3F.

disadvantage vis-à-vis his opponent'.[52] This means that 'both parties should be treated in a manner ensuring that they have a procedurally equal position to make their case'.[53]

This chapter argues that a concern for equality of arms should encompass measures that enable witnesses for both parties to give evidence effectively. Though often supplemented by documentary, physical or scientific evidence, oral witness testimony remains the central feature of many criminal trials.[54] This oral evidence can be a vital component of a prosecution or defence case, making the witnesses that give this evidence a key resource for the parties to employ. It seems essential, therefore, that vulnerable or intimidated defendants, who can be witnesses in their own defence, should be assisted to do so to the best of their ability in the way that all other witnesses are. Failure to provide special measures assistance to such defendants can leave the defence at a substantial disadvantage *vis-à-vis* the prosecution when presenting their case to the jury. This arguably falls foul of the ECtHR interpretation of the principle of equality of arms.

Miscarriages of Justice

With these points in mind, the failure of the criminal justice system to effectively identify and respond to defendant vulnerability leaves significant scope for miscarriages of justice to occur. In its narrowest form, a 'miscarriage of justice' may be understood as the wrongful conviction of a factually innocent person.[55] The current inadequacy of provisions for vulnerable defendants may risk wrongful conviction of the innocent where, for example, insufficient adjustments are made to help the defendant give their best evidence, which could lead the jury to an incorrect verdict where they wrongly reject the defendant's account.[56] However, arguably, this definition of a 'miscarriage of justice' is too restrictive. While convicting the guilty and acquitting the innocent is an important aim of the criminal justice system,[57] it is widely acknowledged that the adversarial tradition adopted in England and Wales is not necessarily the best way to go about fact finding. This is in large part due to the primacy placed on oral evidence, which is plagued with issues stemming from the lengthy delays before trials (affecting the accuracy of a witness's memory),[58] as well as the effects of the stressful courtroom

---

52 *Salov v Ukraine* App no 65518/01 (ECHR 9 September 2005) [87].

53 Stefania Negri, 'The Principle of "Equality of Arms" and the Evolving Law of International Criminal Procedure' (2005) 5 *International Criminal Law Review* 513, 513.

54 Paul Roberts and Adrian Zuckerman, *Criminal Evidence* (2nd edn, OUP 2010) 291.

55 Michael Naughton, *Rethinking Miscarriages of Justice: Beyond the Tip of the Iceberg* (Palgrave McMillan 2007) 20.

56 Samantha Fairclough, '"It doesn't happen ... and I've never thought it was necessary for it to happen": Barriers to Vulnerable Defendants Giving Evidence by Live Link in Crown Court Trials' (2017) 21(3) *International Journal of Evidence and Proof* 209–229, 212.

57 Criminal Procedural Rules 2020, Part 1.1(2)(a)

58 Louise Ellison, *The Adversarial Trial and the Vulnerable Witness* (OUP 2002) 23–27.

environment,[59] coupled with sometimes hostile cross-examination of witnesses to test their evidence and make them appear deceitful and untrustworthy.[60] Its saving grace, however, is that adversarial justice is not a 'truth at all costs' approach, but additionally pursues other important aims, such as ensuring that criminal trials are fair and that defendants' rights are respected within the process.[61] This means that verdicts arising from a criminal trial are not merely representative of factual guilt or innocence, but instead are a legal conclusion that the defendant has been found guilty (or not) in accordance with fair criminal trial procedure on the evidence admissible in court.[62]

Similarly, when a conviction is quashed (or upheld) by the Court of Appeal, this should not be equated with a conclusion on factual innocence or guilt.[63] We must therefore distinguish the above definition from a 'legal' understanding of miscarriages of justice, which only narrowly recognises their occurrence where a conviction is deemed 'unsafe' in law.[64] This reflects the legal tests adopted by the Court of Appeal in the appeal process[65] and encompasses legal and/or procedural breaches that undermine the defendant's right to a fair trial.[66] However, arguably this definition is also insufficient to capture the range of ways in which a miscarriage of justice may occur. It has been criticised for being 'legalistic' and 'retrospective' in only recognising miscarriages of justice corrected through the formal legal process after being overturned at the Court of Appeal.[67] This fails to acknowledge the potential for miscarriages of justice to occur which are not formally recognised within the legal process – perhaps because the legal procedures themselves are unfair or the laws being applied are unjust.

Due to the inadequacies of the legal regime in place to protect vulnerable defendants, we argue instead that Walker and McCartney's definition of a 'miscarriage of justice' is the most appropriate to apply in this context. They argue that in a liberal and democratic society, justice requires treating individuals with 'equal respect for their rights and the rights of others';[68] therefore, a miscarriage of

---

59 Louise Ellison, *The Adversarial Trial and the Vulnerable Witness* (OUP 2002) 12–23.

60 Paul Roberts and Adrian Zuckerman *Criminal Evidence* (2nd edn, OUP 2010) 296–7.

61 See, for example, Gary Goodpaster, 'On the Theory of American Adversary Trial' (1987) 78(1) *Journal of Criminal Law and Criminology* 118.

62 Michael Naughton, *Rethinking Miscarriages of Justice: Beyond the Tip of the Iceberg* (Palgrave McMillan 2007) 18.

63 Michael Naughton, *Rethinking Miscarriages of Justice: Beyond the Tip of the Iceberg* (Palgrave McMillan 2007), p.22

64 Stephanie Roberts and Lynne Weathered, 'Assisting the Factually Innocent: The Contradictions and Compatibility of Innocence Projects and the Criminal Cases Review Commission' (2009) 29(1) *Oxford Journal of Legal Studies* 43, 45.

65 Criminal Appeal Act 1968, Section 2.

66 Stephanie Roberts and Lynne Weathered, 'Assisting the Factually Innocent: The Contradictions and Compatibility of Innocence Projects and the Criminal Cases Review Commission.' (2009) 29(1) *Oxford Journal of Legal Studies* 43, 45.

67 Michael Naughton, 'Redefining Miscarriages of Justice: A Revived Human-Rights Approach to Unearth Subjugated Discourses of Wrongful Criminal Conviction' (2005) 45 *British Journal of Criminology* 165.

68 Clive Walker and Carole McCartney, 'Criminal Justice and Miscarriages of Justice in England and Wales' (2010) in Ronald Huff and Martin Killias (eds) *Wrongful*

justice occurs whenever defendants 'are treated by the state in breach of their rights', which may result from deficient processes or unjust laws.[69] Applying this definition allows us to conclude that a miscarriage of justice occurs whenever there is a failure to detect a potential vulnerability during the police investigation and/or trial process so that a defendant's rights are not appropriately safeguarded; and/or where a particular vulnerability is detected but insufficient safeguards or inappropriate measures are put in place to enable the defendant to fully exercise their rights during the pre-trial and/or trial process. Therefore, in light of the inferior provision of special measures that we have discussed, it is likely that miscarriages of justice are not uncommon where a defendant is vulnerable.

The potential prevalence of miscarriages of justice in this context is made worse by the barriers to challenging the conviction in the criminal appeal process. This is particularly so where the defendant has been convicted of a serious offence in the Crown Court. There is no automatic right to appeal against a conviction obtained in the Crown Court. A convicted defendant will be required to apply for leave (or permission) to appeal to the Court of Appeal.[70] Prospective appellants must show that a serious legal or procedural error has occurred during the investigation and/ or trial which undermines the 'safety' of their conviction;[71] or that they have obtained significant fresh evidence which can do the same.[72] Where a defendant has qualified for legal aid at trial, this will typically extend to cover advice on appeal from their trial representatives who may apply for leave where there are potential grounds. However, if a convicted defendant receives negative advice at this stage, it may be very difficult to source further legal assistance to help with the preparation of an appeal. Due to legal aid cuts, fewer law firms now do criminal appeal work and increasingly such individuals may be forced to rely on non-profit organisations to assist them.[73] Consequently, there is a danger that wrongly convicted defendants with viable grounds for appeal might get lost at this stage, which

Conviction: International Perspectives on Miscarriages of Justice (Temple University Press 2010) 185.

69 Clive Walker and Carole McCartney, 'Criminal Justice and Miscarriages of Justice in England and Wales' (2010) in Ronald Huff and Martin Killias (eds) *Wrongful Conviction: International Perspectives on Miscarriages of Justice* (Temple University Press 2010), 186.

70 An application for leave to appeal should be brought within 28 days of conviction or the prospective appellant should apply for an extension of time, which requires establishing good reason for the delay; see *R v James & Ors* [2018] EWCA Crim 285.

71 Section 2(1)(a) of the Criminal Appeal Act 1995 stipulates that the Court of Appeal Criminal Division shall allow an appeal against conviction if it thinks the conviction is 'unsafe'.

72 Section 23 of the Criminal Appeal Act 1968 states that in deciding whether to receive any evidence, the court must have regard to whether there is a 'reasonable explanation' for the failure to adduce evidence in prior proceedings.

73 The Westminster Commission on Miscarriages of Justice, *In the Interests of Justice: An Inquiry into the Criminal Cases Review Commission* (All Party Parliamentary Group on Miscarriages of Justice 2021). See also Roxanna Dehaghani, Rebecca Helm and Daniel Newman, Chapter 12 of this collection.

may be a particular concern where a defendant's vulnerability was missed by their trial defence team.

Where a defendant has been able to source the necessary help post-conviction, if fresh expert evidence is obtained which identifies a vulnerability that was not recognised in the trial process, this may constitute grounds for appeal. However, there are further barriers to overcome. First, the Court of Appeal must be persuaded that the fresh expert evidence should be admissible, which requires a demonstration that it is capable of belief, it may form grounds for appeal and it could not have been adduced in earlier proceedings.[74] Where the expert evidence is brought several years out of time, this may be a difficult hurdle to overcome. In *R v Jones*,[75] fresh expert evidence found that the appellant had learning difficulties that were not accounted for in the previous trial process. Although the appeal was eventually successful, two things are of note. First, leave to appeal was originally rejected by a single judge on the grounds of unreasonable delay because it had taken several years for the relevant evidence to be adduced. This decision had to be challenged to the full court before leave was granted, which raises questions over whether other meritorious cases may be prevented from proceeding at this stage. Second, in quashing the conviction, the Court of Appeal was clear to stress that it is only in 'rare' circumstances that 'new medical and psychological evidence can be successfully deployed many years after a trial' to challenge a conviction.[76] Therefore, meritorious cases may face barriers to getting fresh evidence adduced on appeal when it is brought several years out of time.

The Court of Appeal has also shown resistance to accepting fresh expert evidence on appeal on other grounds. There have been cases where the court has shown scepticism towards expert evidence where they consider it to be influenced by partisan accounts on behalf of the defendant.[77] They may be particularly reluctant to admit fresh expert evidence where they deem the defence to have been 'expert shopping' because a previous expert had come to a different conclusion.[78] This latter issue has the potential to be unfair to a defendant by overlooking the fact that experts will often disagree.[79] Furthermore, where expert evidence is adduced stipulating that certain adjustments should be (or should have been) made, this will 'not be determinative'[80] and judges are not bound to follow it.[81] Whether the trial was appropriately adjusted to meet the defendant's needs will be 'a question for the judge to resolve, who is best placed to understand what is required in order to ensure the accused is fairly tried'.[82] The Court of Appeal's

---

74 Section 23 of the Criminal Appeal Act 1968.
75 [2018] EWCA Crim 2816.
76 [2018] EWCA Crim 2816, [97].
77 *R v Janhelle Grant-Murray and others* [2017] EWCA Crim 1228.
78 See, for example, *R v Foy* [2020] EWCA Crim 270.
79 Mark Thomas, '"Expert Shopping": Appeals Adducing Fresh Evidence in Diminished Responsibility Cases' (2020) 84(3) *Journal of Criminal Law* 249.
80 *R v Dean (Thomas)* [2020] EWCA Crim 117
81 *R v Rashid* [2017] EWCA Crim 2 [71].
82 *R v Dean (Thomas)* [2020] EWCA Crim 117.

preference for its own assessment of effective participation over that of trained medical or communication experts has been criticised for 'underestimating the difficulties faced by lay people in court', while also 'overestimating the effectiveness of special measures' in analysing the fairness of the process.[83] This again demonstrates further challenges that defendants may face in utilising expert evidence, both at their original trial and in any subsequent appeal.

There are other ways in which the approach to appeals in this context suggests a tendency to underestimate the challenges faced by vulnerable defendants. First, it is insufficient to highlight that certain safeguards were absent in the trial process without directly showing how their absence impacted on the safety of the conviction. It may be possible to identify specific examples of how a defendant's particular condition impacted on the safety of the conviction, such as to explain a particular aspect of the defendant's behaviour in the courtroom[84] or to highlight the inappropriate nature of questions put to the defendant during cross-examination.[85] However, it is not always possible to identify specific examples to show how the safety of the conviction has been undermined. There is an artificiality to this which fails to recognise the diverse ways in which a miscarriage of justice could have resulted. There may be a range of unknown factors (eg, the impression upon the jury); and the lack of adequate support may have had a ripple effect which influenced the defendant's ability to meaningfully participate by giving instructions and making decisions about the conduct of their case, such as whether to give evidence.[86] This latter issue is problematic because defence decisions at trial will not typically be reviewed on appeal.

It is an important principle of the adversarial criminal trial that parties have autonomy in the selection and presentation of evidence.[87] Due to this emphasis, decisions made by the defence at trial will not typically be revisited in an appeal against conviction. However, this has the potential to be unfair when we consider the barriers to effective participation faced by defendants at trial as discussed above. Of particular concern is where a defendant's decision making may be constrained by virtue of a particular disability or disorder. One such example is *R v BC*,[88] where, on appeal, the defence decision at trial not to present expert evidence about the defendant's autism diagnosis was criticised in conjunction with the further advice against the defendant giving evidence. Trial counsel explained that aspects of the expert report about the defendant's autism diagnosis could have been 'positively damaging' to the defence case[89] and there were concerns the

---

83 Abenaa Owusu-Bempah, 'The Interpretation and Application of the Right to Effective Participation' (2018) 22(4) *International Journal of Evidence and Proof* 321, 334–335.

84 See, for example, *TS v Regina* [2008] EWCA Crim 6.

85 See, for example, *R v Jones* [2018]

86 Abenaa Owusu-Bempah, 'Understanding the Barriers to Defendant Participation in Criminal Proceedings in England and Wales' (2020) *Legal Studies* (online first)

87 Ian Dennis, *The Law of Evidence* (6th edn, Wildy 2017).

88 [2019] EWCA Crim 565.

89 [2019] EWCA Crim 565, [24].

defendant would present as 'cold, indifferent, hostile to the complainant and unemotional' in giving evidence.[90] The Court of Appeal rejected the appeal, stating it was not enough 'that some counsel may have approached the matter tactically in a different way' or 'that an error of judgment may, with hindsight, have been involved'.[91] Importantly, it emphasised that 'the appeal process is not simply a means for a disappointed defendant to have another go'.[92] While it is possible to understand the decisions made by the defence, the circumstances of this case are still troubling. This illustrates how the choices available to defendants may be constrained as a result of their own vulnerability, which brings into question whether it is fair to treat the defendant as having the autonomy to make these decisions.[93] Therefore, the reluctance to examine the safety of the conviction in light of defence decisions at trial may put an unrealistic burden both upon defendants and upon defence lawyers, who often face significant resource constraints in preparing the case for trial.[94] This, alongside the Court of Appeal's tendency to minimise the challenges faced by vulnerable defendants throughout the criminal justice process, has the potential to perpetuate miscarriages of justice.

Conclusion

Due to the inability of the criminal justice system to adequately support and mitigate against defendant vulnerability, miscarriages of justice are likely a routine occurrence. Furthermore, where a miscarriage of justice has occurred, it can be extremely difficult to correct this in the criminal appeal process. This makes it essential that we work towards ensuring better detection of potential vulnerability at the earliest possible stage in criminal proceedings, and that we have the appropriate measures to protect the defendant's right to a fair trial. Consequently, this chapter first calls for reform to provide defendants with (at least) equal access to special measures. The current inequality in the provision of special measures to defendants undermines the right to a fair trial under Article 6 of the ECHR through potential violations of the principle of equality of arms and limits to the defendant's ability to effectively participate in the proceedings. However, equal provision of special measures can only go so far in improving the current trial process for vulnerable defendants. Significant challenges remain to ensuring that vulnerable defendants can effectively participate at trial – particularly when considering whether they have the capacity, opportunity and autonomy to make important decisions about their case. The current approach to dealing with appeals around defendant vulnerability shows a failure to recognise the various challenges

---

90 [2019] EWCA Crim 565, [25].
91 [2019] EWCA Crim 565, [26].
92 [2019] EWCA Crim 565, [33].
93 Rebecca Helm, Roxanna Dehaghani and Daniel Newman, 'Guilty Plea Decisions: Moving Beyond the Autonomy Myth' (2022) 85(1) *Modern Law Review* 133.
94 See Roxanna Dehaghani and Daniel Newman, 'Criminal Legal Aid and Access to Justice: An Empirical Account of a Reduction in Resilience' (2021) *International Journal of the Legal Profession* (online first).

facing defendants throughout the process. To better safeguard the rights of vulnerable defendants, it is essential that defence lawyers be given the necessary time, resources and tools to consider where necessary adjustments are required to ensure that the defendant can participate effectively. This means not only redressing the inequality in the provision of special measures to defendants at trial, but also considering how we might ensure fairer treatment of vulnerable defendants at every stage of the criminal justice process.

11 The Role of the Intermediary in Ensuring the Effective Participation of Vulnerable Defendants

Joanne Morrison and John Taggart

Introduction

The meaningful engagement of defendants within criminal proceedings centres around the right to effective participation as guaranteed by Article 6 of the European Convention on Human Rights (ECHR). The appointment of intermediaries to assist vulnerable defendants during the trial process is intended to enable this implied right. This chapter examines the role of registered intermediaries for vulnerable defendants; how intermediaries can be used during the criminal process; and the extent to which their involvement contributes towards defendant participation. It draws on two datasets: the first includes interviews with 20 registered intermediaries in England and Wales; and the second uses focused, informal conversations to gain an insight into the experiences of registered intermediaries in Northern Ireland. The chapter highlights the often-key role of the intermediary in contributing to effective participation and calls for greater recognition of the communication expertise which intermediaries can offer to the court. It argues that 'pragmatic and flexible' intermediary appointments are vital to ensuring that the individuality of communication needs is respected.

The Intermediary Special Measure

The intermediary special measure[1] was introduced in England and Wales by the Youth Justice and Criminal Evidence Act 1999 (YJCEA) to facilitate communication between individuals with communication needs and the criminal justice system. The YJCEA outlines that the intermediary's function is to assist communication of questions put to the witness and responses from the witness – providing explanation where necessary.[2] Statutory criteria in the YJCEA specify which 'vulnerable' witnesses are eligible on account of their age or incapacity.[3] Intermediaries who work with witnesses are known as 'registered intermediaries' and

---

1 See Samantha Fairclough and Holly Greenwood, Chapter 10 of this collection.
2 Section 29(2).
3 Section 16. As per the legislation, 'capacity' in this context refers to 'mental disorder', 'impairment of intelligence and social functioning' or 'physical disability/disorder' (Section 16(2)).

DOI: 10.4324/9781003205166-15

are trained, overseen and regulated by the Ministry of Justice (MOJ). Registered intermediaries individually assess the witness's communication needs, and can advise police officers at the investigation stage and the lawyers and judges at court on how best to communicate so that the questions they ask and the answers in reply are understood.[4]

Defendants were excluded from the YJCEA's special measures regime; and although statutory provision for defendant intermediaries was introduced by Section 104 of the Coroners and Justice Act 2009, it has never been implemented. Instead, intermediaries for eligible defendants are available on an *ad hoc* basis, relying on the court's inherent jurisdiction to ensure the right to a fair trial. Judges have therefore 'stepped in to fill the gap' created by the legislation by appointing 'non-registered' intermediaries.[5] The period of communication assistance required by vulnerable individuals often differs between witnesses and defendants. Registered intermediaries facilitate communication during the period of oral testimony only. While non-registered intermediaries may be appointed to assist a defendant throughout the duration of a trial, the Criminal Practice Directions and subsequent case law state that this should be 'extremely rare'.[6] As such, there exists a presumption against the use of an intermediary for a defendant at trial.[7] Without any formalised guidance or equivalent procedural manual, the involvement of non-registered intermediaries for defendants is more varied and potentially flexible.

In Northern Ireland, a unitary system allows both witnesses and defendants to access a cohort of registered intermediaries who are recruited by the Department of Justice (DOJ). This Registered Intermediary Scheme is based on the Criminal Evidence (Northern Ireland) Order 1999, which largely mirrors Section 29 of the YJCEA. While the YJCEA specifically excludes defendants from the special measures provisions, Article 21BA of the 1999 order permits examination of the accused through an intermediary. Intermediaries in Northern Ireland are appointed on an 'evidence only' basis for defendants in court – that is, they are appointed to assist during the period of testimony. The court can, however, appoint a 'court defendant supporter', who typically also works as an appropriate adult, to provide emotional and general support to the defendant for the periods when an intermediary is not present.[8]

4 Penny Cooper and Michelle Mattison, 'Intermediaries, Vulnerable People and the Quality of Evidence: An International Comparison of Three Versions of the English Intermediary Model' (2017) 21(4) *International Journal of Evidence and Proof* 351.

5 Penny Cooper and David Wurtzel, 'A Day Late and a Dollar Short: In Search of an Intermediary Scheme for Vulnerable Defendants in England and Wales' (2013) 1 *Criminal Law Review* 1, 18.

6 Criminal Practice Directions (CPD) [2015] EWCA Crim 1567, 3F.14.

7 The Criminal Practice Directions also state that the court should be 'satisfied that a non-registered intermediary has expertise suitable to meet the defendant's communication needs' (CPD 2015, 3F.12); *R (OP) v Secretary of State for Justice* [2014] EWHC 1944 (Admin) [47].

8 Department of Justice (NI), *Northern Ireland Registered Intermediaries Schemes Pilot Project: Post-Project Review* (January 2015) 21.

Effective Participation

The eligibility criteria for witness and defendant intermediaries are distinct. In both jurisdictions, a defendant is eligible for intermediary assistance based on the right to a fair trial under Article 6 of the ECHR and, more specifically, the implied right to 'effective participation'. It is a longstanding principle in English criminal law that defendants must be able to understand and participate effectively in the criminal proceedings against them.[9] The right to effective participation not only from the guarantees contained within Article 6, but is implicit in the notion of an adversarial system of adjudication.[10] The European Court of Human Rights (ECtHR) first recognised the right to effective participation in *Stanford v UK*.[11] The court explained that a defendant enjoys not only the 'right to be present, but also to hear and follow the proceedings'.[12] In *SC v UK*, the court went further and stated that:

> '[E]ffective participation' in this context presupposes that the accused has a broad understanding of the nature of the trial process and of what is at stake for him or her, including the significance of any penalty which may be imposed. It means that he or she, if necessary with the assistance of, for example, an interpreter, lawyer, social worker or friend, should be able to understand the general thrust of what is said in court. The defendant should be able to follow what is said by the prosecution witnesses and, if represented, to explain to his own lawyers his version of events, point out any statements with which he disagrees and make them aware of any facts which should be put forward in his defence.[13]

The range and complexity of communication issues among vulnerable defendants[14] mean that the 'developed skills' of the intermediary may be required to satisfy this definition of 'effective participation'.[15] Defendants with intellectual disabilities[16] can have particular challenges with receptive and expressive communication;[17] and those with attention deficit hyperactivity disorder may be distracted easily and struggle to concentrate sufficiently to follow what is being said by others.[18] Defendants with

9 Jessica Jacobsen and Jenny Talbot, *Vulnerable Defendants in the Criminal Courts: A Rreview of Provision for Adults and Children* (Prison Reform Trust 2009) 8.

10 European Court of Human Rights, *Guide on Article 6 of the European Convention on Human Rights* (31 August 2020) 30.

11 *Stanford v UK App no 16757/90* (ECHR, 23 February 1994) at [26].

12 *Stanford v UK App no 16757/90* (ECHR, 23 February 1994) at [26].

13 *SC v UK* (2005) 40 EHRR 10 [28].

14 See, for example, Kim Turner and Claire Westwood, Chapter 9 of this collection.

15 *R (OP) v Secretary of State for Justice* [2014] EWHC 1944 (Admin) [47].

16 See Donna McNamara, Chapter 1 of this collection.

17 Joanne Morrison and others, 'Communication and Cross-examination in Court for Children and Adults with Intellectual Disabilities: A Systematic Review' (2019) 23(4) *International Journal of Evidence & Proof* 366.

18 American Psychiatric Association, *Diagnostic and Statistical Manual of Mental Disorders: DSM-5* (Fifth) (2013 American Psychiatric Publishing); Gisli Gudjonsson and

mental health disorders such as dissociative identity disorder may struggle with competing internal dialogue interfering with concentration and listening skills.[19] Autistic defendants can experience challenges with episodic memory and the use of non-literal references, and can struggle to grasp the general gist of what is being said, instead concentrating more on specific points.[20] Using the language of the ECtHR in *SC v UK*, intermediaries assess receptive communication skills, which are required to 'understand the general thrust' and to 'follow what is said'; and expressive communication skills, which are required for the defendant to 'explain to his own lawyers his version of events'. This aligns with core aspects of the best practice assessment framework whereby intermediaries are expected to assess both forms of communication needs through informal assessments and standardised tests.[21] The conclusions of this assessment are then included in a written report for the court which details the defendant's communication abilities and specific needs, together with practical suggestions on how they can best be questioned at court.[22]

The terms and duration of an intermediary appointment can influence the quality and nature of a defendant's participation in the trial process.[23] This depends significantly on whether the intermediary is appointed for the period of the defendant's oral testimony or for a longer period in the trial. For example, will the defendant also have the benefit of communication assistance in the dock when listening to the evidence of other witnesses and at other points such as during legal conferences? There is a divergence in the case law on how important such a broad understanding is to the realisation of effective participation. In *SC v UK*, the ECtHR found that the defendant need not understand 'every point of law or evidential detail' given the right to legal advice.[24] Contrastingly, in cases where the defendant is unable to hear or be present, the courts have found participation by proxy to be sufficient as long as they can instruct and adequately communicate with their lawyer.[25] As noted above, the trend in England and Wales has been towards a curtailment of intermediary assistance beyond the witness box. The

Susan Young, 'An Overlooked Vulnerability in a Defendant: Attention Deficit Hyperactivity Disorder and a Miscarriage of Justice' (2006) 11(2) *Legal and Criminological Psychology* 211.

19 Brendan O'Mahony and others, 'Investigative Interviewing, Dissociative Identity Disorder and the Role of the Registered Intermediary' (2018) 20(1) *Journal of Forensic Practice* 10.

20 Katie Maras and Dermot Bowler, 'Eyewitness Testimony in Autism Spectrum Disorder: A Review' (2014) 44 *Journal of Autism Development Disorder* 2682.

21 Penny Cooper and Michelle Mattison, 'Intermediaries, Vulnerable People and the Quality of Evidence: An International Comparison of Three Versions of the English Intermediary Model' (2017) 21(4) *International Journal of Evidence and Proof* 351, 358.

22 MOJ, Registered Intermediary Procedural Guidance (August 2019) Available at: http s://assets.publishing.service.gov.uk/government/uploads/system/uploads/attachm ent_data/file/831537/moj-registered-intermediary-procedural-guidance.pdf (accessed 4 March 2022), 16.

23 Criminal Procedure Rules (CrimPR) (October 2020) Part 18, Rule 18.27.

24 *SC v UK* (2005) 40 EHRR 10 at [29].

25 *Stanford v UK App no 16757/90* (ECHR, 23 February 1994) at [30].

amendment to the Criminal Practice Directions in April 2016 outlines that: 'Directions to appoint an intermediary for a defendant's evidence will thus be rare, but for the entire trial extremely rare ...' This was subsequently confirmed in *R v Rashid*.[26] The Court of Appeal previously rationalised this position based on the view that cross-examination represents the 'point of maximum strain' for a vulnerable accused.[27] The more recent case of *TI v Bromley Youth Court*,[28] however, signals a potential change in judicial attitude to defendant intermediary appointments, with the 'rarity' provision of the Criminal Practice Directions directly questioned.[29] In every case, the intermediary is expected to explain and justify their recommendations in their court report and this should cover the extent of their involvement with the defendant. Ultimately, however, the burden rests on the trial judge to ensure the effective participation of a vulnerable defendant, not on the intermediary.[30]

The relationship between the intermediary role and the right to effective participation warrants closer attention. While it is not argued that intermediaries unilaterally ensure the effective participation of the accused, they can play an important role through the facilitation of communication. The accused enjoys well-established rights such the right to be present at their own trial, as well as the right of confrontation; however, these rights are of limited value if the defendant cannot participate effectively.[31] How effective participation is conceptualised by intermediaries working at the coalface of the criminal justice system can aid understanding of the right's content and scope. This chapter does not attempt to address the issue of whether intermediaries should be present throughout a defendant's trial or just for the giving of evidence; rather, it reveals that intermediaries avoid rigid formulations of the level of support that vulnerable defendants require. Instead, the approach to effective participation must be individualised and responsive to individual communication needs. The examples explored below reveal how varied the communication needs of vulnerable defendants can be and, in turn, how intermediaries develop and implement communication strategies in response.

Methodological Approach

This chapter draws on two datasets – one from each author. The first dataset includes interviews with 20 registered intermediaries in England and Wales. Interviewees responded to a request sent on the author's behalf by Intermediaries for Justice, a registered charity promoting and supporting the work of intermediaries. Further requests were sent via the Registered Intermediaries Online portal, an information-sharing platform for those who work in a registered capacity operated by the National

---

26 [2017] 1 WLR 2449.
27 *R (OP) v Secretary of State for Justice* [2014] EWHC 1944 (Admin) [47], [36].
28 [2020] EWHC 3088 (Admin).
29 Laura Hoyano and Angela Rafferty QC, 'Rationing Defence Intermediaries under the April 2016 Criminal Practice Direction' (2017) *Criminal Law Review* 90.
30 *R v Grant Murray* [2017] EWHC Crim 1288 [199].
31 Abenaa Owusu-Bempah, 'Understanding the Barriers to Defendant Participation in Criminal Proceedings in England and Wales' (2020) 40(4) *Legal Studies* 609.

Crime Agency. Of the 20 intermediaries interviewed, 11 came from a speech and language therapy background, three from nursing, two from occupational therapy, two from psychology and one from teaching, and one worked with deaf people as a sign language interpreter. The interviews were conducted between January 2019 and July 2019 and lasted for an average of 90 minutes. Each interview was personally transcribed. The data was organised and coded under several initial codes which were generated inductively. A number of these codes – 'participation', 'assistance', 'monitoring', 'understanding' and 'communication' – were collated into the broader code of 'effective participation', which is the focus of the present chapter. Information from the dataset was anonymised before discussing with the second author.

The second dataset used focused, informal conversations to gain an insight into the experiences of registered intermediaries working in Northern Ireland. These were chosen to add context and enrich the existing dataset.[32] The second author was both a researcher and a research participant, collecting data from colleagues and drawing on her own experiences as well as playing a key role in the data analysis. In total, six registered intermediaries provided examples of recommendations they would make for defendants. Any information was fully anonymised before sharing with the first author.

The data is presented using the three key stages of intermediary involvement: pretrial; during defendant testimony; and during other periods throughout proceedings.

The prefix 'E&W' is used to identify intermediaries in the first dataset who were interviewed in England and Wales. The suggestions and examples from practice discussed below have come from the informal conversations of the second dataset, unless specifically referred to as 'E&W' data.

Pre-trial

When assessing effective participation, it is important to consider when a non-registered intermediary is initially appointed to assist a defendant. Cooper has highlighted the unfairness of a defendant intermediary being 'parachuted' into a case at the trial stage without a chance to assess communication difficulties at an earlier stage.[33] In England and Wales, intermediaries are very rarely asked to assess a suspect prior to police interview. However, they can be appointed pre-trial to assist with understanding of the charges and the contents of witness statements, help counsel take instructions and ensure understanding regarding decisions as to plea and whether the defendant should testify.[34] In Northern Ireland, intermediaries routinely assist at the police interview stage. A crucial difference from

---

32 Jon Swain and Zachary Spire, 'The Role of Informal Conversations in Generating Data, and the Ethical and Methodological Issues They Raise' (2020) 21(1) *Qualitative Social Research* 163.

33 Law Commission, *Unfitness to Plead Report* (Law Com No 364, 2016) para 2.59.

34 Joyce Plotnikoff and Richard Woolfson, *Intermediaries in the Criminal Justice System* (Policy Press 2015) 261. Whether an intermediary can assist at pre-trial conferences is dependent on a solicitor making an application for funding from the Legal Aid Agency; see The Advocate's Gateway, *Intermediaries: step by step* (Toolkit 16) (September 2019) 27.

practice in England and Wales, however, is that intermediaries are not involved in consultations between the defendant and their counsel. The Department of Justice (Northern Ireland) limits intermediary assistance to police interview and the period of court examination – ostensibly based on concerns for the role's neutrality.[35] In both jurisdictions, the intermediary can meet with counsel before examination to assist with preparation of questioning and any visuals that may be required.

In interview, several intermediaries in England and Wales discussed the importance of their involvement at pre-trial consultation with the defendant, solicitor and barrister. E&W-3 explained how pre-trial consultations are crucial to ensuring the defendant's prospective participation:

> [S]ometimes I've gone for conferences and it's the first time the defendant has fully understood the evidence against them and they have pleaded because they basically realise that they are not going to win and there is no point in chancing their luck because it's not going to work, but if you think about money and the time that saves in court for the sake of a conference.

E&W-17 also highlighted the importance of intermediary involvement at legal consultations:

> I might help them to plead guilty if that's what they need to do. I went to see a defendant in a pre-trial conference with his barrister. The barrister said: 'There's DNA evidence.' [The defendant] said: 'I didn't do it.' They said it five times and I said: 'They found bits of your body in her knickers.' He went: 'Yes I did it' and we had no trial. So, I am convinced that we have *such* a role to play at that stage.

Most intermediaries described similar experiences, whereby they believed their involvement was viewed as an efficient way of helping to procure a sensible guilty plea. This aspect of the intermediary role has been recognised by Plotnikoff and Woolfson as instrumental to pre-trial processes being adapted 'so far as necessary' to facilitate the defendant's effective participation.[36] It is also significant considering the terminology used by the ECtHR in *SC v UK* outlining the scope of the right. The assistance that E&W-3 and E&W-17 provided in helping to explain the strength of the prosecution case to the defendant relates to understanding of the 'nature of the process', but also of 'what is at stake' for them in terms of conviction. The intermediary role at this stage could also potentially cover explaining the significance of the sentencing options open to the court. Another intermediary,

---

35 MOJ, Registered Intermediary Procedural Guidance (August 2019) Available at: http s://assets.publishing.service.gov.uk/government/uploads/system/uploads/attachm ent_data/file/831537/moj-registered-intermediary-procedural-guidance.pdf (accessed 4 March 2022) 16, 26.

36 Joyce Plotnikoff and Richard Woolfson, *Intermediaries in the Criminal Justice System* (Policy Press 2015), 261.

E&W-19, was appointed by the judge to facilitate communication at legal consultations only. She explained that ensuring comprehension at the pre-trial stage can often be more important than assistance during the defendant's testimony:

> Well, the problem is ... usually judges will save you for evidence only. There's really no point in that because they don't understand what's already been said! But this was the other way round, this was for comprehension, and I found that more useful.

While intermediary involvement pre-trial in this manner may in some instances be preferable to assistance during testimony, this does not necessarily mean that it is sufficient. The defendant may be enabled to understand the crux of the prosecution evidence and the significance of their plea, but there will invariably be the potential for lack of understanding during the trial itself, which is unforeseeable. In many cases a vulnerable defendant will require communication assistance to understand not only the nature of their plea, but also the questions put to them during examination. As is explored further below, the individuality of communication difficulties means that intermediaries recommend tailored strategies in their court report. As E&W-16 commented in interview, intermediaries must be allowed to make 'pragmatic and flexible' recommendations to the court which are responsive to the individual needs of the vulnerable defendant.

During Defendant Testimony

During the defendant's testimony, intermediary recommendations are made with regard to three key aspects of communication: focus and attention; understanding of language; and expressive language (responding to questions). To enhance focus, silent fidget items can be used, such as a stress ball, a movable object, Play-Doh or something quite specific to the defendant (eg, a small chain or a finger following shape).[37] The role of the intermediary is important here in identifying the specific requirements of each defendant and recommending a person-centred approach. As well as enhancing focus, fidget items can be useful in helping defendants experiencing high levels of anxiety to better regulate their emotions at that specific moment. Regular breaks in questioning and the use of photographs representing key events are other examples of measures that can help to maintain

---

37 For example, one defendant had his own technique of moving his finger along each point of a square drawn on paper. This can also be used with a box-breathing technique to reduce anxiety, which involves breathing in for a count of four while moving the finger from one point to the next, holding the breath for four and breathing out for four as the finger moves to the next point; and then repeating. For further examples of the types of aids to communication, see Intermediaries for Justice, *Every Reasonable Step: A More Flexible Approach to Vulnerable Witnesses and Defendants Consolidated List of Intermediary Examples* (November 2017). Available at: https://www.intermediaries-for-justice.org/sites/default/files/consolidated-list-of-a-more-flexible-approach-november-2017.pdf (accessed 4 March 2022).

attention and focus on the area of questioning.[38] For example, E&W-20 assessed a defendant as having a very limited concentration span and recommended breaks every 20 to 30 minutes during examination. When this was not adhered to, the effect on the defendant's ability to effectively participate became obvious:

> ... the defendant became so, so fatigued very quickly and it was evidencing what I had said in the first place about the need for breaks. It was about 2.50pm and I asked for a meeting in the absence of the jury and I said the defendant is just saying yes to every question now ... it's about whether this person is awake enough to listen to the questions.

The frequency and duration of breaks will depend significantly on the nature of the defendant's communication difficulties. Implementing this strategy (as well as others contained within the intermediary's court report) also helps to satisfy the court's obligation to 'take every reasonable step' to facilitate the defendant's participation.[39] If the right to effective participation can indeed be exercised by proxy through the defendant's lawyer, the importance of breaks to facilitate communication between the two attains added significance.[40]

There can be a wide range of recommendations to assist the defendant in understanding the questions asked by advocates and the judge. These will often include a requirement for the advocate to change their style and pace, and the length and complexity of questions. These are based on what the advocate should and should not do with regard to the presentation of information and the asking of questions. Examples may include asking short questions focused on one key idea at a time; using everyday familiar language; asking questions in chronological order of events; avoiding negative-style questions ('You don't like it when that happens, do you not agree?'); avoiding time-related questions; avoiding 'why' questions; and avoiding long preambles to questions. This should normally be decided at a ground rules hearing (GRH) prior to trial. The GRH provides an opportunity for the intermediary to outline the recommendations in their court report and for the planning of any adaptations to questioning and/or the conduct of the hearing that may be necessary.[41]

To assist the defendant in responding to questions, different strategies may be employed. A written timeline can be used to aid understanding of questions, particularly regarding the sequencing of an event. This also reduces the pace of

---

38 Some of these could be referred to as 'communication aids' as provided for under Section 30 of the YJCEA and Article 18 of the Criminal Evidence (NI) Order 1999.

39 Joyce Plotnikoff and Woolfson, *Falling Short? A Snapshot of Young Witness Policy and Practice: A Report for the NSPCC, Revisiting 'Measuring up? Evaluating implementation of Government commitments to young witnesses in criminal proceedings'* (NSPCC 2019) 105.

40 Abenaa Owusu-Bempah, 'The Interpretation and Application of the Right to Effective Participation' (2018) 22(4) *International Journal of Evidence and Proof* 321, 332.

41 The CrimPR outline the court's responsibility to hold a GRH when an intermediary is involved: CPR 2020, Rules 3.8–3.9.

questioning, thereby helping with retention of information and working memory. A fast pace of questioning can be confusing and may result in the defendant missing part of the question asked, therefore impacting the accuracy of their testimony.[42] For example, one intermediary in Northern Ireland recommended the use of a timeline in testimony after seeing how the child struggled in police interview without one. She noted that the child was unable to sequence anything. He had no 'before and after': things 'just happened' and he had no concept of time. However, some defendants may struggle to recall episodic memory in a chronological order and questions may need to be tailored according to their specific mental record of events.[43]

Intermediaries may recommend that questions to be asked by the advocates are sent to them beforehand and agreed with the judge. This practice enables questions to be prepared and framed according to the communication abilities of the person, and minimises the extent to which the intermediary is likely to need to intervene during cross-examination.[44] Reviewing the questions in advance also allows the intermediary to create visuals relevant to the questions to be asked. The skills required for advocates to adapt communication to the needs of a vulnerable defendant with communication difficulties should not be underestimated. This is complex and challenging, and requires preparation. Although some advocates may view this as a restriction, agreeing questions beforehand may assist in the asking of questions that might otherwise be considered unsuitable. For instance, questions which involve 'putting the case' to a defendant who is very suggestible to leading questions can be extremely problematic; a potential question style could be: 'X said you did Y. Did you do Y?' The intermediary can work with the prosecutor to ensure that the case can be 'put' through questions that are comprehensible to the defendant and to which they are able to respond.

Unfortunately, unlike developing practice with young witnesses, questions to be asked of defendants are rarely reviewed in advance of trial.[45] Intermediaries were

42 Joanne Morrison, Jill Bradshaw and Glynis Murphy, 'Reported Communication Challenges for Adult Witnesses with Intellectual Disabilities Giving Evidence in Court' (2021) 25(4) *International Journal of Evidence & Proof* 243.

43 See Penny Cooper and others, 'One Step Forward and Two Steps Back? The "20 Principles" for Questioning Vulnerable Vitnesses and the Lack of an Evidence-Based Approach' (2018) 22(4) *International Journal of Evidence & Proof* 392.

44 In *R v Lubemba* [2014] EWCA Crim 2064 the Court of Appeal held that it would be 'an entirely reasonable step for a judge at the ground rules hearing to invite defence advocates to reduce their questions to writing in advance' [43]. The vetting of questions as a practice has now been formalised to a degree through the Criminal Practice Directions. For example, the Criminal Practice Directions explain that in all cases where the Crown Court is dealing with a child witness under Section 16 of the YJCEA, it is 'it is expected that the advocate will have prepared his or her cross-examination in writing for consideration by the court' (CPD 2015), 18E Annex para 4.

45 Joyce Plotnikoff and Woolfson, *Falling Short? A Snapshot of Young Witness Policy and Practice: A Report for the NSPCC, Revisiting 'Measuring up? Evaluating implementation of Government commitments to young witnesses in criminal proceedings'* (NSPCC 2019), 106.

clear in interview that meeting counsel beforehand to review questions ultimately leads to fewer complications during examination. E&W-14 explained:

> I say the process will be much faster, easier and slicker if we review the questions in advance but I can't really say to the barrister, 'Commit all your questions to paper' if the judge doesn't require it and the barrister doesn't want to do it … but if they at least have a chat with me before, even if it's just two minutes, we seem to go better in cross examination than those who say, 'I don't need to speak to the intermediary.'

Intermediaries in both jurisdictions explained that in the rare cases when questions are reviewed, this is often done on the morning or even immediately before examination. Consequently, there is less time for thorough preparation, which increases the likelihood of judicial/intermediary intervention at trial. The above quote from E&W-14 also reinforces the centrality of the judge's role in upholding the defendant's right to effective participation. The judicial responsibility to 'set the parameters' of questioning at the GRH will often be imperative for the intermediary to be able to perform their role and also impacts the role's contribution to effective participation.[46]

A final issue which arises during the defendant's testimony relates to their statement made to the police. A defendant with limited reading skills may be unable to refer to their statement during questioning. Research has consistently shown low literacy rates among the defendant population, which are linked to difficulties in understanding, processing and retaining information.[47] The intermediary may recommend that short chunks of information be read to the defendant, with pausing and extraction of the key points to be questioned on. Again, good practice dictates that this should be agreed at a prior GRH.[48] For those with reading skills, but with some limitations, highlighting the key points under question (underlining or highlighter pen) or using a blank page to block out other text can help the defendant to focus on the parts being read out. Using a blueprint-style layout of a room can also help the defendant to visually follow questions around positioning and locations of people within a room during an alleged event.[49]

---

46 Penny Cooper and others, 'Getting to Grips with Ground Rules Hearings – A Checklist for Judges, Advocates and Intermediaries' (2015) 6 *Criminal Law Review* 420.

47 Polly McConnell and Jenny Talbot, *Mental Health and Learning Disabilities in the Criminal Courts* (Prison Reform Trust 2013); Dr Nancy Loucks, *The Prevalence and Associated Needs of Offenders with Learning Difficulties and Learning Disabilities* (Prison Reform Trust 2007).

48 The Advocate's Gateway, *Ground Rules Hearings and the Fair Treatment of Vulnerable People in Court* (Toolkit 1) (September 2019) 7.

49 The CrimPR provide that at the GRH, the court may make directions relating to the 'use of models, plans, body maps or similar aids to help communicate a question or an answer' (Rule 3.8(7)(b)(vii)).

During Proceedings

The complexity of legal proceedings and the language used within them are barriers to participation for many participants, not least those with communication difficulties. The ability of the defendant to engage with and follow proceedings is one of the criteria against which the fairness of the trial process is evaluated.[50] As highlighted in *SC v UK*, effective participation presupposes that the defendant has a 'broad understanding of ... the trial process ... [and is] able to follow what is said by the prosecution witnesses'.[51] It is concerning, however, that the right to effective participation does not appear to require that the defendant can follow the proceedings and evidence of witnesses, as long as their lawyer can.[52] This represents something of a restriction on the right's scope; and Owusu Bempah argues that the right to hear and follow the proceedings should be a personal one which the defendant can exercise.[53]

Intermediaries make recommendations to assist the defendant in understanding the evidence of other witnesses and concentrating during proceedings. Recommendations to assist communication may be made, even if the intermediary is not permitted to be present throughout proceedings, such as use of a stress gauge with visual signs to observe that the defendant is experiencing high levels of anxiety and a break is required. Breaks after each witness has given evidence can help to ensure that the defendant does not become too overloaded with information, and allows them to focus on each witness's evidence, thereby reducing the risk of confusing it with evidence given by other witnesses.

However, for some defendants, retaining the information provided by even one witness may be too cognitively challenging – particularly if examination is lengthy or if multiple alleged events are discussed. This results in a delayed response to points raised, requiring the defendant to retain the information until they can meet with counsel. The defendant then needs to use verbal expressive communication skills to inform how and why these points differ from the defendant testimony and to instruct counsel in how to respond during cross-examination of the witness. A potential alternative is for the intermediary to be available to assist the defendant during proceedings. In England and Wales, the *ad hoc* system of defendant appointments allows for intermediary presence throughout proceedings if the judge deems it necessary.[54] The defendant can inform the intermediary of the key points to be noted and recorded during the witness testimony as they are expressed. Then, when consulting with counsel, the intermediary can assist the defendant in raising the key points, assisting with expressive language skills to be able to explain further and in more detail and to advise their counsel. This would

---

50 *R v Cox* [2012] EWCA Crim 549.
51 *SC v UK* (2005) 40 EHRR 10 at [29].
52 *Stanford v UK App no 16757/90* (ECHR, 23 February 1994) [30].
53 Abenaa Owusu-Bempah, 'The Interpretation and Application of the Right to Effective Participation' (2018) 22(4) *International Journal of Evidence and Proof* 321, 332.
54 See *R v Rashid* [2017] EWCA Crim 2 [71]; and *TI v Bromley Youth Court* [2020] EWHC 1204 (Admin).

not be a role to support the defendant, as with the court defendant supporter role available in Northern Ireland; but rather an extension of the facilitation of communication between the defendant and the court.[55] Indeed, several intermediaries interviewed in England and Wales in this research commented that the enclosure of the dock can allow for information to be verbally expressed by the defendant to the intermediary without disturbing the court.

The ability of the dock to inhibit the defendant's participation was a feature of the research interviews in England and Wales. Most intermediaries recounted stories of defendants being exhausted and confused in the enclosed space, with poor acoustics and restricted visibility.[56] The relationship between the intermediary as a communication facilitator and the defendant's effective participation comes into focus within the confines of the dock. For example, E&W-13, explained how she actively recommends the defendant's removal from the dock:

> One of my recommendations is that they don't sit in the dock. It's about the person engaging and participating in their trial, so how can it be fair if they can't properly participate? ... Also, in the dock you have those stupid leaning bars. If I need to be creating visual aids for someone about what's happening the court, who's who, what people are saying ... I can't do that on my knees!

These comments suggest that the dock not only inhibits the defendant's effective participation, but also negatively impacts on the intermediary's ability to ensure this right is effected. Where an intermediary is not appointed beyond the period of evidence, an alternative strategy could be for the solicitor to make bullet points of key factors highlighted by the witness that differ from, or may raise doubt as to, the defendant's version of events. These key points can then be used as memory triggers for the defendant during consultation. However, this again arguably amounts to participation 'by proxy', since the key points of difference are being highlighted by the solicitor, rather than the defendant personally.

Finally, stress and anxiety can further disadvantage vulnerable defendants who already encounter communication challenges and limitations. Research informs us that anxiety can have a negative impact on cognitive function.[57] Some defendants may experience high levels of trait anxiety in their day-to-day lives, perhaps due to a mental health condition or a diagnosis of autism. By the time their case reaches trial, it is likely that the trait anxiety is exacerbated by high levels of state anxiety

---

55 Law Commission, *Unfitness to Plead Report* (Law Com No 364, 2016), [2.44] and [2.51].
56 There is a developed literature critiquing the dock within the criminal court; see Lionel Rosen, 'The Dock: Should It Be Abolished?' (1966) 29(3) *Modern Law Review* 289; Linda Mulcahy, 'Putting the Defendant in Their Place: Why Do We Still Use the Dock in Criminal Proceedings? (2013) 53 *British Journal of Criminology* 1139.
57 Emily Meissel and Timothy Salthouse, 'Relations of Naturally Occurring Variations in State Anxiety and Cognitive Functioning' (2016) 98 *Personality and Individual Differences* 85.

linked to being the accused, long waiting times and having to endure a court hearing with potentially very negative consequences. The intermediary can make recommendations to help alleviate some of the state anxiety for the defendant. These may relate to the preparation prior to court and include a separate room for the defendant to go to during a break to regulate emotions and reduce high stress arousal levels. Explaining how court familiarisation visits for defendants are rarely permitted compared to witnesses, E&W-17 explained how she tackles this perceived inequality:

> I take the person to the courtroom. I walk in and I say to the clerk: 'I want to bring the defendant into the courtroom.' I want to do a practice beforehand. I don't know how useful it is to a vulnerable defendant to see the wrong court room, because every court is different ... You take them in and make sure they understand how the court room works and by the time they give evidence they've got used to the place.

Such efforts are particularly useful for defendants with sensory needs who may become overloaded by the noise, lighting or other aspects of the court environment. Outside of the courtroom, magistrates courts in particular can be a busy and chaotic environment, adding to sensory overload. Meeting with opposing counsel (and perhaps also the judge) beforehand can assist those individuals who struggle when meeting new people and adapting to new environments. For one defendant in Northern Ireland who could not understand why a security guard needed to be beside him in the dock, the intermediary recommended that the security guard remain behind the defendant, out of view. This reduced the defendant's anxiety levels and the distraction of a heightened emotional state which would have had a negative impact on his ability to communicate and follow proceedings. Such a simple recommendation can have a significant impact on the defendant's participation. In this example, it was based on the intermediary's individual assessment of the vulnerable defendant and an intimate knowledge of his emotional regulation in the court environment.

Conclusion

Understanding the scope and content of the right to effective participation is important as the communication needs of vulnerable defendants in the criminal justice system are increasingly recognised. This chapter focused on the role of the intermediary in contributing to effective participation and calls for greater recognition of the communication expertise which intermediaries can offer to the court. The individuality of communication needs will often require 'pragmatic and flexible' appointments that reflect the intermediary's assessment of the vulnerable defendant. The accounts of intermediaries explored in this chapter highlight how a 'one size fits all' policy of intermediary appointments is undesirable and should be resisted. Looking ahead, Owusu-Bempah has argued for a clearer and more comprehensive definition of the right to effective participation to be formulated with the assistance of experts and specialists such as psychiatrists, psychologists and intermediaries.[58] This chapter echoes this call and suggests that intermediaries can play a vital role in assisting judges to adapt proceedings 'so far as necessary' to facilitate the defendant's effective participation.[59]

---

58 Abenaa Owusu-Bempah, 'The Interpretation and Application of the Right to Effective Participation' (2018) 22(4) *International Journal of Evidence and Proof* 321, 335.
59 Joyce Plotnikoff and Richard Woolfson, *Intermediaries in the Criminal Justice System* (Policy Press 2015), 261.

12 The Vulnerable Accused and the Limits of Legal Aid

Roxanna Dehaghani, Rebecca K Helm and Daniel Newman

Introduction

While developments in Europe have sought to enhance and increase active assistance and representation by lawyers to address the 'particularly vulnerable position' of the accused,[1] criminal legal aid in England and Wales has seemingly gone in the opposite direction after decades of underfunding under successive UK governments. Owing to the complexity of the courts, the significant – albeit declining – resources provided to the police and prosecution, the negative (and indeed devastating) impact of a potential conviction on the accused,[2] and the principle that the ability to defend oneself should not be contingent on financial resources,[3] state-funded legal advice, assistance and representation are vital to secure access to justice. In England and Wales, this is available through criminal legal aid. Lawyers perform the vital role of ensuring access to justice for the accused in a hostile system in which the state – by design – holds the upper hand. This chapter explores the reality of how the underfunding of legal aid threatens access to justice for those who rely on criminal defence lawyers funded by the legal aid system. In doing so, it examines the structural vulnerability of the accused generally, rather than the position of those considered vulnerable in the 'traditional' sense (eg, young people and those with mental health problems, neurodiverse conditions or learning difficulties). The consequences of legal aid limitations for the 'traditional' vulnerable accused are still further concerning considering the importance of a competent and active defence lawyer in providing support such as through the application of special measures.[4]

1 *Salduz v Turkey* App no 36391/02 (ECtHR 27 November 2008). See also *Panovits v Cyprus* App no 4268/04 (ECtHR, 11 December 2008); *Shabelnik v Ukraine* App no 16404/03 (ECtHR, 19 February 2009); *Pishchalnikov v Russia* App no 7025/04 (ECtHR 24 September 2009); *Dayanan v Turkey* App no 7377/03 (13 October 2010). See also Alan Cusack, Shane Kilcommins, Gautam Gulati and Colum Dunne in Chapter 5 of this collection and Jantien Leenknecht in Chapter 2 of this collection.
2 'Suspect' and 'defendant' are used where relevant.
3 Andrew Ashworth, 'Legal Aid, Human Rights and Criminal Justice' in Richard Young and David Wall (eds) *Access to Criminal Justice* (Blackstone Press Ltd, 1996), pp 55–69.
4 For a discussion of special measures for the vulnerable accused see, for example, Samantha Fairclough, '"It doesn't happen … and I've never thought it was necessary

DOI: 10.4324/9781003205166-16

The analysis in this chapter utilises data from semi-structured interviews[5] – anonymised to prevent (jigsaw) identification – with 20 solicitors (DS) and 16 barristers[6] (BS). We begin the chapter by examining the means and merit tests to provide background on how criminal legal aid functions in England and Wales. Next, we outline the situation of fee cuts and stagnation in criminal legal aid lawyers' remuneration, before considering the impact on practice, examining the decline in provision and thereafter exploring the impact on the accused and the service that they receive. Finally, we conclude by discussing the threats to access to justice posed by the undermining of criminal legal aid.

Means and Merits

Advice and assistance at police stations are provided free of charge, regardless of the suspect's means;[7] but legal aid for criminal court proceedings – that is, in the magistrates' court and the Crown Court – is subject to means and merits testing. The accused must secure a representation order and satisfy both limbs of the legal aid test. The means test determines whether the individual can afford to pay for their own legal advice and representation; while the merits test asks whether the alleged offence is of a sufficiently serious nature and thus whether it is in the interests of justice to provide state-funded legal advice and representation. Whether the accused can access state-funded legal advice and

---

for it to happen": Barriers to Vulnerable Defendants Giving Evidence by Live Link in Crown Court Trials' (2017) 21(3) *International Journal of Evidence and Proof* 209. See also Samantha Fairclough and Holly Greenwood, Chapter 10 of this collection.

5 Interviews with these lawyers – anonymised to prevent (jigsaw) identification – lasted between 29 minutes and two hour, two minutes, and were coded using thematic analysis through NVivo12.

6 From a sub-sample of a large study, see Daniel Newman and Roxanna Dehaghani, *Experiences of Criminal Justice: Perspectives from Wales on a System in Crisis* (Bristol University Press, 2022).

7 Police station legal advice is a relatively new development in many European jurisdictions (see John Jackson, 'Responses to Salduz: Procedural Tradition, Change and the Need for Effective Defence' (2016) 79(6) *Modern Law Review* 987). However, police station legal advice in England and Wales was introduced in 1986 through the Police and Criminal Evidence Act 1984 so as to 'balance' the vast powers that the act formally awarded to the police (David Dixon, *Law in Policing: Legal Regulation and Police Practices* (Clarendon Press, 1997). Where suspected of minor offences, a suspect can be offered telephone advice alone (Rosemary Pattenden and Layla Skinns, 'Choice, Privacy and Publicly Funded Legal Advice at Police Stations' (2010) 73(3) *Modern Law Review* 349). However, the Covid-19 pandemic has seen remote attendance of lawyers permitted other than in exceptional circumstances; see Joint Interim Interview Protocol between the National Police Chiefs Council, Crown Prosecution Service, Law Society, the Criminal Law Solicitors' Association and the London Criminal Courts Solicitors' Association: Version 3 – May 2021. Available at: https://www.cps.gov.uk/sites/default/files/documents/legal_guidance/Interview-Protocol-between-NPCC-CPS-TLS-CLSA-and-LCCSA-updated-May-2021.pdf (accessed 25 August 2021).

representation, as per the means test, will depend upon their income and case type, as outlined in Table 12.1.[8]

Thus, at the magistrates' court and when committed for sentence, the accused is automatically entitled to legal aid if they are single with no dependants and receive a gross annual income of less than £12,475.[9] For the accused who earns a gross annual income of between £12,475 and £22,325, their entitlement rests on how much disposable income they have. For those with a gross annual income of £22,325 or more per year, no legal aid is available at the magistrates court or at committal for sentence. At the Crown Court, the accused may fare slightly better, but may have to make an income contribution while the case is ongoing, which is refunded with interest if the accused is found not guilty. In the magistrates court, the full costs are covered initially if the accused passes both tests; but if found guilty, the accused may be asked to contribute towards prosecution costs.[10]

Both the means and merits tests are, however, highly restrictive. The assumption that is made by the means test is that those who are earning above £12,475

Table 12.1 How the Means Test Works Depending on Case Type

Adjusted Income	Magistrates' Court	Committal for Sentence	Appeal to the Crown Court	Crown Court Trial
£12,475 or less	Funded	Funded	Funded	Funded, no income contribution
More than £12,475; less than £22,325	Depends on full means test	Depends on full means test	Possible fee; depends on full means test and outcome of appeal	Possible income contribution; depends on full means test
£22,325 or more	Not funded	Not funded	Depends on full means test and outcome of appeal	Possibly not funded or possible income contribution; depends on full means test
£37,500 or more household disposable income	Not funded	Not funded	Not funded	Not funded

8 Legal Aid Agency, 'Guidance: Criminal legal aid: means testing' (2020). Available at: https://www.gov.uk/guidance/criminal-legal-aid-means-testing (accessed 1 August 2021).
9 Family circumstances are considered: for example, calculations are made to take account of any dependent children – the older the child, the higher the weighting. See Legal Aid Agency, 'Guidance: Criminal legal aid: means testing' (2020). Available at: https://www.gov.uk/guidance/criminal-legal-aid-means-testing (accessed 1 August 2021).
10 Legal Aid Agency, 'Guidance: Criminal legal aid: means testing' (2020). Available at: https://www.gov.uk/guidance/criminal-legal-aid-means-testing (accessed 1 August 2021).

but below £22,325 should be able to make some contribution towards the cost of their case. The first, entirely practical, matter to address is that a gross income of £12,475 hardly places the accused in a financially comfortable position. Indeed, single-person households in the United Kingdom would be classed as 'low income' – or, perhaps more accurately, as living on or below the poverty line – if in receipt of a gross annual income of £19,200 or less.[11] The Minimum Income Standard project deems that a single person had to earn £20,400 annually to reach an acceptable standard of living in 2021.[12] This same single person might receive some contribution towards their legal fees, but would not be guaranteed full legal aid.

An accused must therefore be living well below the poverty line to receive state funding for their criminal case. Further, owing to the proportionately high costs involved, those earning an average annual income or more – who may be required to make large payments towards their representation or may be entirely ineligible for legal aid – may be left bankrupt when funding their own case.[13] This reality was demonstrated by the case of Sally Clark, who was accused and convicted, and then acquitted of murder. Mrs Clark was a solicitor, but legal fees prior to her acquittal forced her family to sell their house and brought them to the brink of bankruptcy.[14] Below are some illustrative examples regarding the costs of legal representation compared to rough monthly disposable income. Fee estimates are based on advertised online rates from firms.[15] Note that examples given below are rough illustrative examples, and eligibility for specific defendants will depend on personal circumstances.

- Example 1 – **a single defendant who earns £20,000 a year:** If the defendant has £3,000 a year of housing costs and £6,574 a year of other costs (including tax, national insurance, and maintenance), they have a monthly disposable income of around £645.
- This defendant would fail the full means test for representation in the magistrates' court and would not get legal aid for representation there. This representation, if pleading not guilty, would cost roughly £1,800 (£1,500 plus value added tax) for the first day of the trial and £960 for each additional day. As a result, the defendant would have to spend almost triple their monthly disposable income on one day of trial alone.

---

11 Unison, 'Get Help: Knowledge: Low Pay'. Available at: https://www.unison.org.uk/get-help/knowledge/pay/low-pay/ (accessed 25 August 2021).
12 Joseph Rowntree Foundation 'A Minimum Income Standard for the United Kingdom in 2021'. Available at: https://www.jrf.org.uk/report/minimum-income-standard-uk-2021 (accessed 25 August 2021).
13 For a rough guide to costs of criminal law solicitors time per hour, see https://www.gov.uk/guidance/solicitors-guideline-hourly-rates#guideline-hourly-rates (accessed 25 August 2021). These are legal aid rates; rates for private clients may be higher.
14 Jan Moir, 'No Redemption for Sally Clark' (*The Telegraph*, 21 March 2007).
15 Specific details from authors available on request.

- In the Crown Court, the same defendant would be eligible for legal aid but would be required to contribute towards their legal representation. This contribution would be approximately £2,905 upfront and then £581 monthly – almost five times the defendant's monthly disposable income in the first month.
- Example 2 – **a single defendant who earns £30,800 a year (the median income after taxes and benefits in the United Kingdom in the financial year ending 2020):**[16] This defendant would fail the initial assessment for legal aid in the magistrates' court and so would have to pay for their own legal representation there.
- If the defendant has £8,400 a year of housing costs and £15,790 of other costs (including tax, national insurance and maintenance), they will have a monthly disposable income of about £778. In the Crown Court, they would be eligible for legal aid but would be required to contribute towards their legal representation. This contribution would be approximately £3,500 upfront and then £700 monthly – again, almost five times the defendant's monthly disposable income in the first month.

Lawyers interviewed in our study were particularly critical of the £12,475 threshold:

> Twelve thousand and something [£12,475] is the cut off. If you go over that you won't meet the means test, you won't get legal aid … They should raise that to around about sixteen thousand or seventeen thousand, because anyone who could be on the cusp just won't get legal aid … I've seen people who have serious allegations against them, just because they work and get, not even a decent wage, they can't get funding. They have to pay for their own barrister. That's not right. (DS2)[17]
>
> If somebody doesn't qualify for legal aid, we will have to instruct them on a private basis … Most of the time we'll work out a fee, and it's not a silly fee … But you know, if you've got some single mother being done for stealing, and for whatever reason, she's not going to qualify … most of the time we'll take the hit on something like that and we'll just do the case because we're there anyway. (DS12)[18]

In addition, even if the accused qualifies on the means test, they must also satisfy the merits test. Although the merits test is satisfied in all indictable-only cases (cases triable at Crown Court only), it is not always satisfied in summary-only cases

---

16 Office for National Statistics, 'Average household income, UK: financial year ending 2020 (provisional)'. Available at: https://www.ons.gov.uk/peoplepopulationa ndcommunity/personalandhouseholdfinances/incomeandwealth/bulletins/house holddisposableincomeandinequality/financialyearending2020provisional (accessed 25 August 2021).
17 Cited in Daniel Newman and Roxanna Dehaghani, *Experiences of Criminal Justice: Perspectives from Wales on a System in Crisis* (Bristol University Press, 2022).
18 Daniel Newman and Roxanna Dehaghani, *Experiences of Criminal Justice: Perspectives from Wales on a System in Crisis* (Bristol University Press, 2022).

(cases triable at the magistrates' court only) or in either-way cases (cases that could be tried in either court). As part of the merits test, the Widgery criteria are considered – which, in essence, consider whether the accused will lose their liberty or livelihood, suffer serious damage to their reputation, or fail to understand court proceedings or be unable to present their own case.[19] In reality, at the magistrates' court, it is typically only offences with a risk of imprisonment that will result in the merits test being satisfied; non-imprisonable offences will usually automatically fail the merits test.[20]

An accused may therefore not qualify for legal aid because they earn above the thresholds or because there is no risk to livelihood or liberty. While only 5% of legal aid applications were refused in March 2015, estimates of unrepresented defendants at the magistrates' court exceeded this number, suggesting that 'a significant number of unrepresented defendants do not apply for legal aid'.[21] Prosecutors cited various reasons for this, including the accused being unable to evidence their financial situation to the Legal Aid Agency or earning too much to qualify for legal aid but not enough to pay for a lawyer privately; rejection of a legal aid application and/or non-attendance of a lawyer at court; and concerns regarding the quality of the advice and representation offered.[22] While mere access to criminal legal aid presents the first barrier for the criminal accused, there are other factors that restrict access to a lawyer. The first is that of quality of defence and, in particular, the impact of legal aid cuts and fee stagnation.

Death by Cuts and Stagnation

As noted above, research has highlighted that some defendants are opting for self-representation because of concerns about the quality of legally aided advice and representation.[23] In addition to restrictions emanating from the means and merits tests, there are significant restrictions on the fees payable to criminal legal aid lawyers for their work. While we focus predominantly on the courts in this chapter, it is worth acknowledging that fees payable at the police station are also significantly restricted – fees vary based on geographic location, but remain fixed regardless of the timing and number of visits, the amount of work undertaken, the time needed to undertake this work and the seriousness and complexity of the case. The fee is fixed regardless of when the lawyer attends the police station –

---

19 See Legal Aid Agency, 'Guidance: Work out who qualifies for criminal legal aid'. Available at: https://www.gov.uk/guidance/work-out-who-qualifies-for-criminal-legal-aid (accessed 25 August 2021).

20 Penelope Gibbs, *Justice Denied? The Experience of Unrepresented Defendants in the Criminal Courts* (Transform Justice, 2016), p 6.

21 See Legal Aid Agency, 'Guidance: Work out who qualifies for criminal legal aid'. Available at: https://www.gov.uk/guidance/work-out-who-qualifies-for-criminal-legal-aid (accessed 25 August 2021).

22 Penelope Gibbs, *Denied? The Experience of Unrepresented Defendants in the Criminal Courts* (Transform Justice, 2016), p 9.

23 Penelope Gibbs, *Denied? The Experience of Unrepresented Defendants in the Criminal Courts* (Transform Justice, 2016),

whether that be morning, noon or night, on a working day, weekend or public holiday. At the magistrates' court, payment is typically subject to a standard fee and is based on the category to which the case is considered to belong.[24] Two schemes exist at the Crown Court: the Advocates' Graduated Fee Scheme and the Litigators' Graduated Fee Scheme; the fee payable, again, depends on the type of work conducted.[25] One solicitor provided an example of how the amount of work conducted on a case did not reflect the legal aid payment resulting from that case:[26]

> We had a dangerous driving trial, a listed trial. We were able to prove that the client was innocent because his car had been in a garage on the day of the incident – his neighbour [the complainant] was crackers. Listed for a trial, prosecution pulled it on the day of the trial before a jury was sworn, we'd had maybe eight hearings, loads of conferences … A chap with no previous convictions who was very worried, and we got paid two hundred and sixty quid. (DS1)

There have been significant cuts to criminal legal aid in recent times, although these began as early as the 1990s with the government attempting to cost control.[27] The introduction of summary criminal legal aid claims through standard fees in 1993 had increased the number of legal aid claims,[28] so the government sought to limit the number of firms offering legally aided criminal defence

24 For example, guilty pleas and other uncontested or discontinued matters; trials and other contested matters (including cases that are fully prepared but do not proceed); and committals to the Crown Court subsequently discontinued (see Lucy Welsh, 'The Effects of Changes to Legal Aid on Lawyers' Professional Identity and Behaviour in Summary Criminal Cases: A Case Study' (2017) 44(4) *Journal of Law and Society* 559).

25 For example, trial, guilty pleas (where multiple hearings only the final hearing is paid); cracked trials (where the defence offers an acceptable plea or where the prosecution has offered no case to answer); appeal hearings (against conviction or sentence); and sentence hearings (proceedings arising from a committal for sentence). Fees can also be paid for review of certain types of evidence – for example, witness statements, documentary and pictorial evidence, prosecution summaries and/or transcripts of the accused's interviews, achieving best evidence interviews and streamlined forensic reports – but not for closed circuit television, video evidence or audio evidence, defence-generated evidence, pre-sentence and psychiatric reports, and applications to adduce hearsay or bad character evidence. See Legal Aid Agency, 'Crown Court Fee Guidance' (2018). Available at: https://assets.publishing.service.gov.uk/governm ent/uploads/system/uploads/attachment_data/file/745068/Crown_Court_Fee_ Guidance_-_v.1.7A_.pdf (accessed 25 August 2021).

26 Daniel Newman and Roxanna Dehaghani, *Experiences of Criminal Justice: Perspectives from Wales on a System in Crisis* (Bristol University Press, 2022).

27 Tamara Goriely, 'The Development of Criminal Legal Aid in England and Wales'. In Richard Young and David Wall (eds) *Access to Criminal Justice* (Blackstone Press Ltd, 1996) pp 26–54, 51.

28 Ed Cape and Richard Moorhead, *Demand Induced Supply? Identifying Cost Drivers in Criminal Defence Work* (Legal Services Commission, 2005).

through a franchising system – firms that wished to provide state-funded advice in criminal proceedings were required to hold a contract by the Legal Aid Board.[29] Later attempts were also made to introduce price-competitive tendering,[30] which, according to Newman, significantly devalued criminal defence work.[31] The austerity programme of the Conservative-Liberal Democrat coalition government – with its explicit focus on curtailing spending to 'balance the budget' – witnessed a fee reduction of 8.75%.[32] During the period of austerity, the Ministry of Justice suffered the most significant budget cuts of all Whitehall departments: in real terms, the budget reduction from £9.3 billion in 2010/11 to £5.6 billion by 2019/20 represented a 40% cut.

Yet lawyers have not simply seen their incomes significantly reduced; they have, in fact, been blamed for the dire situation in which the criminal justice system now finds itself. In 2020, following comments to a similar effect from Home Secretary Priti Patel, Boris Johnson claimed that the criminal justice system was 'being hamstrung by what the Home Secretary would doubtless – and rightly – call the lefty human rights lawyers, and other do-gooders'.[33] The rhetoric of 'lefty do-gooders' and 'fat cat lawyers milking the system'[34] allows the criminal legal aid budget to be decimated while also not offending the good law-abiding individuals who view access to criminal justice as no concern for them – until, of course, they require the services of a lawyer.[35] Not only have there been cuts to the criminal legal aid budget, but lawyers have not experienced an increase in their fees since 1998.[36] The cuts in 2014 were therefore particularly damaging to a profession that was already on the brink of collapse. However, considering that the cost of living has increased – in some instances steeply – since 1998, the fee is actually worth less in real terms. To use house prices in Wales as an example, the

29 Latterly the Legal Services Commission (2000–13) and the Legal Aid Agency (2013–).
30 See Lord Chancellor's Department, *Modernising Justice* (Martin Pearce Associates, 1998).
31 Daniel Newman, 'More than Money'. In Jon Robins (ed), *No Defence: Lawyers and Miscarriages of Justice*, Vol 6 (Justice Gap London, 2013) pp 40–43.
32 Owen Bowcott, 'Legal Aid Fees to be Cut by 8.75%, Confirms Ministry of Justice' (*The Guardian*, 10 June 2015). Available at: https://www.theguardian.com/law/2015/jun/10/legal-aid-fees-to-be-cut-by-875-confirms-ministry-of-justice (accessed 1 August 2021). This was intended as the first of two fee reductions, but the other 8.75% cut was not made.
33 Owen Bowcott, 'Legal Profession Hits Back at Johnson over "Lefty Lawyers" Speech' (*The Guardian*, 6 October 2020). Available at: https://www.theguardian.com/law/2020/oct/06/legal-profession-hits-back-at-boris-johnson-over-lefty-lawyers-speech (accessed 1 August 2021).
34 Steve Hynes and Jon Robins, *The Justice Gap* (Legal Action Group, 2009).
35 See Roxanna Dehaghani and Daniel Newman, 'The Dichotomy of "First Timer" and "Regular" and Its Implications for Legal Advice and Assistance' (under review).
36 Law Society, 'Criminal duty solicitors: a looming crisis'. Available at: https://www.lawsociety.org.uk/en/campaigns/criminal-justice/criminal-duty-solicitors (accessed 1 August 2021).

average house price has more than trebled since the fee increase in 1998 – from £48,294 to £162,374.[37]

The result of fee reduction and stagnation is disincentivisation, which can affect the quality of advice and representation being offered to the accused.[38] Those entering the defence profession may do so because they are deeply committed to serving the public and ensuring that access to (criminal) justice is realised. However, the reduction and stagnation in fees result in ethical determinacy, where lawyers may compromise their principles to meet the needs of the business.[39] As one solicitor pointed out, the amount of work being conducted on a case has had to be scaled back to meet business needs. The result, however, is a reduction in client care and a weakening of the accused's position:

> It's a problem because back ten years ago, if there was a road traffic collision, I'd go out and go to the road and have a look at it and take pictures. I'd go around and speak to various people about the incident ... Now with the legal aid cuts and the way things are, you don't get paid for any of that, and there's less incentive to do a good job other than pride and responsibility and they can only carry you so far, especially with a firm that wants to make money, like every firm does, otherwise we couldn't stay open. I can't go out and do the best job that I can do and justify it. I just can't. I mean, on the more serious ones you can, but on the less serious ones, which are still serious for them, you can't justify it. There's no incentive to go out and do anything above and beyond what you're expected to do and that's really, really sad. (DS2)[40]

Firms must therefore survive by undertaking volume 'sausage factory' work.[41] This may mean, however, that the accused is not receiving the advice, assistance and representation required.[42] This sentiment was echoed by the lawyers in our study, as exemplified by DS4:

37 Jared Lawthom, 'Law Society Warns Duty Solicitors Could Become Extinct' (BBC Online, 17 November 2018). Available at: https://www.bbc.co.uk/news/uk-wales-46127118 (accessed 1 August 2021).
38 Paul Fenn, Alastair Gray and Neil Rickman, 'Standard Fees for Legal Aid: An Empirical Analysis of Incentives and Contracts', *Oxford Economic Papers* (12 June 2007).
39 Cyrus Tata, 'In the Interests of Clients or Commerce? Legal Aid, Supply, Demand and "Ethical Indeterminacy" in Criminal Defence Work' (2007) 34(4) *Journal of Law and Society* 489. See also Lucy Welsh, *Access to Justice in Magistrates' Courts: A Study of Defendant Marginalisation* (Hart, 2022).
40 D.Daniel Newman and R.Roxanna Dehaghani, *Experiences of Criminal Justice: Perspectives from Wales on a System in Crisis* (Bristol University Press, 2022), np; R.); Roxanna Dehaghani and D.Daniel Newman, 'The Crisis in Legally Aided Criminal Defence in Wales: Bringing Wales into Discussions of England and Wales' (2021) 41 (2) *Legal Studies* 234.
41 Daniel Newman, *Legal Aid Lawyers and the Quest for Justice* (Hart, 2013); Hilary Sommerlad, '"I've lost the plot": An Everyday Story of Legal Aid Lawyers' (2001) 28 (3) *Journal of Law and Society* 335.
42 See, for example, Roxanna Dehaghani and Daniel Newman, '"We're vulnerable too": An (Alternative) Analysis of Vulnerability within English Criminal Legal Aid and

You probably work out how much work you need to do on a case and know that the fixed fee comes nowhere near it … to try to make a living out of this, the only way round the fixed fees is to have a lot of work. So that the volume increases, so that you're still getting lots of work in. And sometimes when that happens, because you're so busy, you can't give a certain client enough time that they really should deserve on their case. We try our best, but sometimes it doesn't happen.[43]

There were concerns that some cases cost law firms money and that firms were only able to survive owing to, in part, volume work (as noted above), but also in part due to a small number of more significant cases:

When you've got labour, time-intensive trawl of potential witnesses, solicitors are getting paid so little under the current rates they don't have the staff, they don't have the time, they don't have the resources any more to really get stuck into a case, so … it tends to be the bare minimum to make a competent job as opposed to a Rolls Royce service … Most of them make a loss on general crime and rely on a few really big cases to put them back into the black for the year. (BS9)[44]

The limitations placed on lawyers have very serious implications for the accused: they can reduce the quality of advice and representation as lawyers take on increasingly larger workloads to make their business viable. In the less serious cases (which may nevertheless be serious for the accused), the lawyer earns less money and may therefore spend less time on the case. Lawyers must also juggle multiple cases and cannot afford their clients the time and attention that is potentially required – and warranted – on the case. The accused is therefore in an increasingly vulnerable position. Yet these fee reductions and stagnations have other worrying effects: the decline in the number of lawyers available; the decline in the number of lawyers entering the profession and thus an ageing criminal defence profession; and the possibility of an absence of criminal legal aid in some areas (otherwise known as 'advice deserts').

Declining Provision and Advice Deserts

The availability of legal aid and the fees payable to practitioners are not the only obstacles that present to undermine access to justice for the accused. The criminal defence profession is an increasingly ageing profession, with the average age of duty solicitors in England and Wales being placed at 47. Taking into consideration that the

Police Custody' (2017) 7(6) *Oñati Socio-Legal Series* 1199. The notion of not having enough time was also echoed by lawyers in Newman's study pre-austerity cuts – see Daniel Newman, *Legal Aid Lawyers and the Quest for Justice* (Hart, 2013).

43 Daniel Newman and Roxanna Dehaghani, *Experiences of Criminal Justice: Perspectives from Wales on a System in Crisis* (Bristol University Press, 2022).

44 Daniel Newman and Roxanna Dehaghani, *Experiences of Criminal Justice: Perspectives from Wales on a System in Crisis* (Bristol University Press, 2022).

state pension age is 67 for those born in 1971,[45] these lawyers may well be in practice for (close to) another 20 years. However, in some areas across England and Wales, typically outside of large urban areas, nearly half of duty solicitors are over the age of 50; this rises to almost two-thirds in rural areas.[46] The Law Society has therefore warned that 'in five to 10 years' time there could be insufficient criminal defence solicitors in many regions, leaving people … unable to access their rights'.[47]

There has also been a decline in the number of criminal defence firms in England and Wales since the austerity cuts noted above. Table 12.2 illustrates the decline between 2010/11 and 2018/19.

Table 12.2 England and Wales Criminal Law Firms and Offices[48]

	2010/ 11	2011/ 12	2012/ 13	2013/ 14	2014/ 15	2015/ 16	2016/ 17	2017/ 18	2018/ 19
Firms	1861	1722	1656	1603	1517	1512	1388	1314	1271
Offices	2598	2415	2338	2282	2172	2240	1991	1998	1921

According to the Law Society, as of December 2020, there were 1,122 firms holding a criminal legal aid contract, representing a further decline of 149 firms on the figure for 2019.[49] The ageing criminal defence population accompanied by the decline in firms and offices may result in criminal defence deserts in future.[50]

The Impact of Cuts on the (Vulnerable) Accused

The reduction in fees, firms and offices, in tandem with the restrictions placed on an individual's ability to access legal aid and/or pay for their own advice and representation, raises serious concerns regarding access to justice for the accused.

45 Gov.uk, 'Check your State Pension age'. Available at: https://www.gov.uk/state-p ension-age/y/age/1971-01-01 (accessed 2 August 2021).
46 Law Society, 'Criminal duty solicitors: a looming crisis' (2018). Available at: https:// www.lawsociety.org.uk/en/campaigns/criminal-justice/criminal-duty-solicitors (accessed 1 August 2021).
47 Law Society, 'Criminal duty solicitors: a looming crisis' (2018). Available at: https:// www.lawsociety.org.uk/en/campaigns/criminal-justice/criminal-duty-solicitors (accessed 1 August 2021).
48 See Secretary of State for Justice, 'Companies: Written question – 227146' (UK Parliament 2019). Available at: https://www.parliament.uk/business/publications/written-questions-answers-statements/written-question/Commons/2019-02-28/227146/ (accessed 1 August 2021). The situation in Wales is much worse – see Daniel Newman and Roxanna Dehaghani, *Experiences of Criminal Justice: Perspectives from Wales on a System in Crisis* (Bristol University Press, 2022).
49 Law Society, 'Government support needed now for criminal legal aid firms to survive'. Available at: https://www.lawsociety.org.uk/en/contact-or-visit-us/press-office/p ress-releases/government-support-needed-now-for-criminal-legal-aid-firms-to-survive (accessed 1 August 2021).
50 See Daniel Newman, 'Attitudes to Justice in a Rural Community' (2016) 36(4) *Legal Studies* 591.

Taking the first issue – access to legal aid – it is the magistrates' court where this is felt most heavily, as at the Crown Court many of the accused 'will [typically] qualify automatically for representation' (BS2); and at the police station all individuals are entitled to free and independent legal advice. It is likely that one implication of the lack of sufficient legal aid for many defendants is to push defendants towards pleading guilty, since legal representation when pleading guilty is significantly cheaper than legal representation when contesting guilt at a full trial.[51]

On the second issue – declining fees payable to lawyers – the effect is across all sites of justice: at the police station, where lawyers are incentivised to avoid attendance; at the magistrates' court, where fees are low and often result in lawyers losing money; and at the Crown Court, where fees are higher, but arguably not enough for the work that is really required on the case.[52] The third and final issue – declining numbers of offices and firms, the ageing population of criminal duty solicitors and the emergence of defence deserts in the years to come – may make it difficult for individuals to access a lawyer at any and all stages of the criminal process. There are thus concerns at each site of justice. Yet it is typically in the magistrates' court – where offences are deemed too minor for legal aid or for attention[53] – that the defendant is arguably most marginalised, as emphasised by Welsh's recent research.[54]

The reduction in the amount of legal aid payable along with the availability of legal aid represents a serious impediment to the accused's ability to access justice. Lawyers have repeatedly expressed concerns about the unfairness and inequality of arms that emerge when the unrepresented or self-represented defendant is met with a legally qualified opponent.[55] BS3, for example, emphasised how 'horrendous' and 'wrong' it was for the prosecuting barrister to be acting 'against unrepresented defendants' in the magistrates' court – BS3 felt 'guilty, almost, for cross-examining them, and they've not been able to properly cross-examine, or put their case to the complainant'. Reflecting similar concerns, DS7 commented on how 'an unrepresented defendant could have a huge problem with a prosecutor' if that

51 See Rebecca K Helm, Roxanna Dehaghani and Daniel Newman, 'Guilty Plea Decisions: Moving Beyond the Autonomy Myth' 85(1) *Modern Law Review* 133–63; Rebecca K Helm, 'Constrained Waiver of Trial Rights? Incentives to Plead Guilty and the Right to a Fair Trial' (2019) 46(3) *Journal of Law and Society* 423.

52 Post-Covid-19, lawyers may be reluctant to move back to in-person attendance (remote attendance was largely permitted during the pandemic – see Transform Justice, National Appropriate Adult Safeguard and Fair Trials International, *Not Remotely Fair? Access to a Lawyer in the Police Station during the Covid-19 Pandemic* (2021)).

53 See Doreen McBarnet, *Conviction: Law, the State and the Construction of Justice* (Palgrave Macmillan, 1981).

54 Welsh points to myriad factors affecting the accused – namely legal aid reductions; the related low morale of lawyers; the language and layout of the court and proceedings; un- or under-explained enforced participation; and the insatiable – and entirely counterproductive – desire for efficiency; see Lucy Welsh, *Access to Justice in Magistrates' Courts: A Study of Defendant Marginalisation* (Hart, 2022).

55 The prosecution is referred to as an 'opponent' here, as the prosecution (and, earlier in the process, the police) represents the state in an adversarial system.

prosecutor were to, for example, '[recite] off a conviction for sexual assault from 1989 or something when [the accused is] there for a common assault'. While the concern of DS7 was, in part, borne out of fairness to the accused, it was also contended that 'having advice means that [the accused] understand[s] what's going to happen to them. And things run more smoothly when they understand what's happening to them, and why things are being said'. Thus, the concern was also borne out of – at least in part – questions of efficiency, as DS7 later commented:

> You're having a lot more litigants in person who are not qualifying for public funding and don't have the money to pay for their own defence, and so they have to do it themselves. That causes inefficiencies because ... you have a litigant in person who is defending themselves against some sort of assault... They don't know the criminal justice system. They don't know ... Criminal Procedure Rules. They don't know the laws of evidence.

The accused may not wish to access a lawyer because that lawyer is perceived to be – and may actually be – of poor quality.[56] The accused may be unable to access a lawyer because that lawyer does not have the time to spend on the case. The accused may access a lawyer who can take on the case, but cannot spend the time that is actually required to successfully defend the case. The accused – even if accessing a lawyer – may not qualify for legal aid and may be unable to pay privately for advice and representation; or may be passed between solicitors within the same firm.[57] In years to come, and possibly sooner rather than later, the accused may live in an area where lawyers are no longer in short supply but are instead virtually non-existent.

The accused is therefore structurally vulnerable:[58] the policies, procedures, practices and (lack of) payment have undermined the position of the accused and undermined their ability to access justice.[59] The accused is vulnerable and no longer able to fully access justice.

Conclusion

In this chapter, we have looked at the ways in which access to justice has been undermined by the underfunding of criminal legal aid. Legal aid has been variously neglected and attacked by political parties of all stripes in Westminster. This leaves behind a debased legal aid scheme that compromises and curtails lawyers.

---

56 See Penelope Gibbs, *Justice Denied? The Experience of Unrepresented Defendants in the Criminal Courts* (Transform Justice, 2016).
57 The latter is known as 'discontinuous representation' – see Mike McConville, Jacqueline Hodgson, Lee Bridges and Anita Pavlovic, *Standing Accused: The Organization and Practices of Criminal Defence Lawyers in Britain* (OUP, 2009).
58 See Roxanna Dehaghani, 'Interrogating Vulnerability: Reframing the Vulnerable Suspect in Police Custody' (2021) 30(2) *Social & Legal Studies* 251.
59 Daniel Newman, *Legal Aid Lawyers and the Quest for Justice* (Hart, 2013).

Further, as another negative impact, rather than supporting and bolstering the accused in the manner it should, legal aid often maintains – perhaps even increases – the vulnerability of the accused.

The accused is placed in an increasingly marginalised position,[60] but is also compelled to participate in the proceedings against them.[61] The accused cannot, however, avail themselves of the advice and representation that would allow them to participate in a meaningful way. While the involvement of a criminal lawyer should encourage meaningful participation of the accused, lawyers – lacking in both time and money – are unable to offer an active defence. We have thus identified that the consequence of underfunding is to leave the accused in an even more precarious position.

The criminal justice system is broken[62] and the effects of lockdown restrictions have exacerbated an already dire situation.[63] As Gibbs has highlighted, that many accused are now unrepresented signals a return to a time before the rollout of criminal legal aid.[64] Therefore, while the defence is (at least in theory) becoming more actively involved in criminal cases in many European jurisdictions following *Salduz*, the defence in England and Wales is experiencing the opposite: a decline in involvement in criminal cases.[65] The demise of criminal defence further inhibits the ability of the accused to access justice. In essence, it reduces their resilience and renders them increasingly vulnerable to miscarriages of justice.

---

60 Particularly at the magistrates court – see Lucy Welsh, *Access to Justice in Magistrates' Courts: A Study of Defendant Marginalisation* (Hart, 2022).

61 Abenaa Owusu-Bempah, *Defendant Participation in the Criminal Process* (Routledge, 2017).

62 The Secret Barrister, *The Secret Barrister: Stories of the Law and How It's Broken* (Picador, 2018).

63 Mike McConville and Luke Marsh, 'England's Criminal Justice System Was on Its Knees Long Before Coronavirus' (*The Guardian*, 6 September 2020). Available at: https://www.theguardian.com/commentisfree/2020/sep/06/england-criminal-justice-system-coronavirus-covid-19-cuts-2010 (accessed 25 August 2021).

64 Penelope Gibbs, *Justice Denied? The Experience of Unrepresented Defendants in the Criminal Courts* (Transform Justice, 2016).

65 In marked contrast with forced participation of the accused – see, for example, Abenaa Owusu-Bempah, *Defendant Participation in the Criminal Process* (Routledge, 2017). See also, for example, Lucy Welsh, *Access to Justice in Magistrates' Courts: A Study of Defendant Marginalisation* (Hart, 2022).

Conclusion

Challenges and Future Avenues to Adequately Protect the Vulnerable Accused

Lore Mergaerts, Roxanna Dehaghani, and Samantha Fairclough

Looking Back and Forth

This book has brought together a collection of contributions that explore the extent to which vulnerable suspects and defendants are protected within criminal proceedings, both in law and in practice. The chapters not only look at different stages of the proceedings and various different safeguards provided therein, but also provide an examination and commentary of such aspects of criminal proceedings across multiple jurisdictions. The book presents a rich diversity in approach, with authors drawing on original empirical data, their own experience as practitioners and more traditional academic and doctrinal materials. It brings together academics at all career stages, including postgraduate researchers and practitioners such as speech and language therapists and intermediaries with on-the-ground experience, providing an array of perspectives.

The book emerged out of concerns for the insufficient recognition of vulnerability among suspect and defendant populations in criminal justice systems across Europe and the adequacy of the criminal justice responses to such vulnerability in both law and practice. Though significant strides have been made on all these fronts, with growing recognition of vulnerability among these groups in the case law of the European Court of Human Rights (ECtHR) and EU and domestic frameworks, this book shows that they do not yet go far enough. The book provides for multi-jurisdictional perspectives, but includes a significant number of chapters from across the United Kingdom. As we have previously mentioned, this should not be surprising, as England and Wales has been lauded as leading the way with regard to the provisions in place to protect (vulnerable) suspects and defendants in criminal proceedings. Moreover, given the nature of the adversarial system – where the accused person is pitted against the state and thus takes a more active role in criminal proceedings – it could be argued that stronger protection of suspects and defendants is required to redress the adversarial imbalance. This is particularly so where the accused is vulnerable. It was, however, considered important to include other jurisdictions, because – in contrast to Anglo-American (adversarial) approaches – the suspect has a rather passive role within the civil law (inquisitorial) tradition. Moreover, to date, more mixed systems are emerging in which the characteristics of both inquisitorial and adversarial criminal proceedings are expressed.

DOI: 10.4324/9781003205166-17

The collection exposes problems within jurisdictions that adhere to both traditions and variations thereof – including systems with a longstanding tradition of protecting vulnerable suspects (at least in theory) and those which are relatively new in introducing a legislative commitment to protecting vulnerable suspects. The chapters clearly demonstrate that work still needs to be done across all explored jurisdictions (including England and Wales) to properly and consistently cater for the vulnerable accused. It is likely that this is also the case across European jurisdictions that do not feature in this collection, although the specifics of the shortfalls may differ depending on the context.

In an attempt to bring some of this work together, this concluding chapter draws out several of the core themes that cut across the different contributions in this collection. It then highlights some of the key challenges that are evident and remain in need of attention in academia, law and practice. Finally, we round off with a few signposts as to what we think needs to happen next and some future avenues for research.

Core Themes

While the developments at the European and domestic levels to address vulnerability that have been sketched throughout this collection are positive – in that they aim to recognise the potential vulnerabilities of suspects and defendants – this collection shows that they have not gone far enough. There are several points of contention that remain. These include challenges with how 'vulnerability' is defined – or left undefined, how vulnerability is identified and how vulnerability is responded to (if at all). Indeed, there is great variance in the ways that different jurisdictions address vulnerability, including how 'vulnerability' is defined and operationalised. As the European guidance is rather vague and limited, the treatment of vulnerable persons differs between EU member states with regard to the provisions in place; the extent of their implementation; the responsibilities for identifying and compensating for vulnerability; and the training provided for criminal justice practitioners such as the police, lawyers and judicial authorities.

The adequate implementation of any provisions for vulnerable suspects and defendants depends upon the interpretation of who is to be considered vulnerable. In this regard, it should be noted that defining 'vulnerability' is not straightforward. This can mean a number of things, both generally and within the criminal justice system. Suspects and defendants can be vulnerable by virtue of their young age or disability, which can be either physical, intellectual or psychosocial. For some vulnerable suspects and defendants, there may even be multiple compounding vulnerabilities (eg, a young suspect with speech, language and communication needs). The vulnerability of suspects and defendants is still mainly seen from the perspective of the individual, as a rather fixed and stable condition, instead of recognising that this vulnerability is also caused by characteristics inherent to the pre-trial investigation, the trial itself and the interactions with various individuals involved in the criminal process.

Vulnerability is not, however, a static concept. Suspects and defendants are not simply vulnerable because they possess a particular characteristic or set of characteristics, but – crucially – because they possess these characteristics within the context of the criminal justice system. It is within the criminal justice system – and the stages that make up the criminal process – that vulnerability may be created or at least exacerbated. The manifestation of vulnerability may also differ at the different stages of the process and so should be kept under constant review throughout the proceedings. The very nature of a criminal justice system where the accused is pitted against the state may already render a suspect or defendant vulnerable. The extent to which an accused becomes vulnerable is also dependent on the attitude of the criminal justice professionals with whom they interact (eg, the police and judicial authorities). For instance, pressure may be exerted on the suspect, inappropriate questions may be asked or the suspect may be exhausted. Likewise, the conduct of the defence lawyer at these moments is of importance, especially given their crucial role in helping the suspect to exercise their procedural rights.

An accused may also be vulnerable because they lack the financial capabilities to mount an effective defence. Although the need for an effective criminal defence has been bolstered (at least in law) across Europe, the right in practice can be stymied by an absence of funding. Certainly, the cuts made to the criminal justice system in a number of jurisdictions in the name of neoliberal austerity (and undoubtedly exacerbated by measures introduced to address the Covid-19 pandemic) have rendered most, if not all, accused persons vulnerable to the ills of the criminal process, and this undoubtedly has had a greater impact on those already struggling to engage with the process. As such, it is important to bear in mind that suspects and defendants can be considered vulnerable because of the very nature of the criminal justice system(s), and not only due to individual characteristics. Moreover, often vulnerabilities are hidden or not acknowledged; at times, vulnerabilities are not responded to or ameliorated; and vulnerable suspects and defendants are often required to 'perform' their vulnerability.

In this regard, the contributions in this collection demonstrate that the vulnerability of suspects and defendants is not adequately addressed within domestic legal systems and at the ECtHR and EU levels. Indeed, the criminal justice system – particularly under neoliberal austerity – may create or exacerbate pre-existing vulnerabilities, either owing to the processes and procedures or because of the lack of support available to the vulnerable accused. A first point of contention here is the notable disparity that still exists between the treatment of vulnerable complainants/witnesses and vulnerable suspects/defendants, where the latter still receive comparably inferior levels of support. In this regard, it should also be noted that a distinction exists between young suspects and defendants – who are more readily recognised as vulnerable by virtue of their age – and adult suspects and defendants, whereby the focus tends to be narrow(er). Moreover, the same safeguards tend to be applied to young and adult suspects and defendants, regardless of their needs – if indeed any safeguards are applied at all.

In addition, the measures and provisions put forward within the limited European guidance, and how these should then be implemented, are poorly or inadequately specified, difficult to enforce, and significantly open to different interpretations. As such, it is unsurprising that member states are struggling to adequately define and deal with vulnerable suspects and defendants. Much is left to their discretion and, consequently, how vulnerable persons are treated differs between member states with regard to the provisions in place; whether they are actually implemented; the responsibilities for identifying vulnerability; and the training provided for criminal justice practitioners such as the police, lawyers and judicial authorities.

It is important to acknowledge that the law in the books does not always neatly accord with the law in action: even where safeguards exist, they may not be implemented in practice. Thus, even where suspects and defendants are identified as vulnerable, they may not be provided with the support required because that support either is not available; is available only in limited circumstances and under specific conditions; or is said to be unnecessary (eg, because the accused person is not 'vulnerable enough' or because providing such support may be (seen as) counterproductive). The result is considerable variation in how vulnerable suspects and defendants are treated within law and in practice. Obviously, failure to (adequately) respond to vulnerability may have negative human rights implications – in particular, the risk of breaches of the fundamental right to a fair trial as guaranteed in Article 6 of the European Convention on Human Rights (ECHR). Ultimately, such breaches may also threaten the legitimacy of the criminal justice process. In addition, vulnerable suspects and defendants are at greater risk of providing inconsistent statements or even false confessions, which appear to be common in wrongful conviction cases and miscarriages of justice, thus hampering the truth-finding process.

Identifying and Resolving Key Challenges

The appropriate treatment and adequate implementation of special measures for vulnerable suspects and defendants both at the domestic level and in individual cases are clearly needed to avoid such detrimental consequences. To achieve this, a few key challenges need to be tackled. First, it is essential to appropriately define 'vulnerability' and to outline what this means in the particular context of criminal proceedings. The absence of clear definitions and the reluctance to provide concrete definitions are hampering the adequate treatment of vulnerable suspects and defendants in practice. To define 'vulnerability', the question of 'Vulnerability to what?' must be answered. As has been recognised earlier in this collection, vulnerability should not be restricted to the suspect's or defendant's individual characteristics, but should also be considered in light of situational factors (eg, police custody, fatigue, questioning styles, courtroom environments). Second, the early identification of vulnerability by practitioners also appears challenging. Age and manifest (mental) health issues may be relatively easy to identify; but one also needs to consider other vulnerabilities – particularly those that are compounding or contextual. The (timely) identification of such factors appears insufficient in practice, but crucially needs to be improved to take the first step towards appropriately dealing with vulnerability.

Last, it appears that a timely identification of vulnerability does not always result in the appropriate action being taken. This raises the question of how best to respond to this vulnerability and ensure that vulnerable suspects and defendants are given adequate support. In this regard, the backdrop of successive moves to undermine the position of the accused (particularly in England and Wales, but also elsewhere) should be considered; although a greater push towards better treatment of and support for the vulnerable accused across Europe at both the EU level and the ECtHR level is also notable. Unfortunately, as *Hasáliková v Slovakia*[1] demonstrates, it is imperative that legal guidance and regulation are clearer on who is vulnerable and why; and that the judicial authorities at all levels (domestic and ECtHR) understand guidance and regulation and can apply them to the facts at hand. It is of comfort that some members of the judiciary in *Hasáliková* – Judges Turković and Schembri Orland – understand what makes an accused vulnerable and how that vulnerability can interfere with the accused's right to a fair trial under Article 6 of the ECHR. Yet for special measures and safeguards to be truly effective, it is necessary for all members of the judiciary to possess and utilise the requisite knowledge and understanding of what it means to be a vulnerable accused. Until then, the vulnerable accused may go unsupported and there will be further missed opportunities to make improvements in this arena.

To address these challenges in appropriately defining, identifying and dealing with the vulnerability of suspects and defendants in criminal proceedings, it is crucial to engage with the literature on what makes a suspect or defendant vulnerable and how this vulnerability is best dealt with. Findings from academic research can lead the way in terms of how vulnerability can be better approached and catered for in suspect and defendant populations and across jurisdictions. Indeed, in *Hasáliková*, it was heartening to see that the dissenting judges had engaged with the broader literature on what makes an accused person vulnerable and had considered this in line with the facts of the case.

Moreover, there is a clear need for tools to identify vulnerability early on in criminal proceedings. Although several instruments have been developed to facilitate the identification of psychological characteristics in particular,[2] the gold standard is that these tools are used in conjunction with expert assessments of vulnerable suspects and defendants. However, a psychological examination will usually occur only when demanded by the defence lawyer, the police or a judge. A mental health expert will therefore be involved only once any awareness of vulnerability has been raised among these practitioners. Furthermore, screening for vulnerability is mostly aimed at identifying specific psychological traits and disorders, as a result of which situational and contextual factors contributing to vulnerability are not considered. In this regard, practitioners would benefit from the

---

1 *Hasáliková v Slovakia* App no 39654/15 (ECtHR 22 November 2021).
2 For instance, Toolkit 10 to support the early identification of vulnerability in witnesses and defendants, developed by the Advocate's Gateway, serves as a valuable instrument (see https://www.theadvocatesgateway.org/_files/ugd/1074f0_bc65d21318414ba8a622a99723fdb2a0.pdf).

development of 'all-inclusive' and readily applicable tools to identify vulnerability, taking into account its innate and situational nature.

In addition to such tools – and, crucially, to facilitate their effective use in practice – there is a need for greater awareness and knowledge among practitioners involved in the criminal justice process. Knowledge and expertise emerging from academic research and best practice at the domestic and global levels should be transferred through carefully developed training programmes which are widely available for all relevant practitioners. Finally, adequate resources should be provided to support vulnerable suspects and defendants, with proper remuneration for those involved in providing support.

This edited collection serves as a starting point for further action to foster the adequate and fair treatment of vulnerable suspects and defendants in criminal proceedings. The chapters in this collection include several signposts for further research, debate and discussion from a multi-jurisdictional perspective; however, there is still a need for a greater sharing of knowledge and best practice across jurisdictions. We therefore also advocate for further cross-jurisdictional research, to include jurisdictions 'neglected' in this collection. We hope to have instigated the beginnings of these conversations and we look forward to reading further research in this area.

Index